SAINT JOHN'S AT 150

Saint John's at 150

A portrait of this place called Collegeville

1856–2006

EDITED BY HILARY THIMMESH, O.S.B.

"But as we progress in this way of life and in faith,

we shall run on the path of God's commandments,

our hearts overflowing with the inexpressible delight of love."

—Rule of Benedict, Prologue

SAINT JOHN'S UNIVERSITY PRESS

COLLEGEVILLE, MINNESOTA

Saint John's University Press is a publisher of distinctive works,

illuminating the creative spirit of the communities of Saint John's and the College of Saint Benedict.

This book is dedicated to the generations of monks, sisters, teachers, students, employees, neighbors, and friends, named and unnamed in these pages, who together built a Benedictine community in this place called Collegeville.

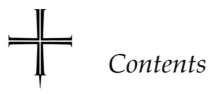

Contents

Foreword   Abbot John Klassen, O.S.B.   ix

Introduction   Outside the Pine Curtain   Annette Atkins   1

Chapter 1   A Time to Plant and a Time to Grow   Hilary Thimmesh, O.S.B.   7
                  Founding Minnesota Public Radio, by William Kling   17

Chapter 2   A Little Rule for Beginners   Columba Stewart, O.S.B.   19

Chapter 3   "A Scientific, Educational, and Ecclesiastical Institution"
                  Joseph Farry   31
                  Ojibwe Education at Saint John's and Saint Benedict's Indian Industrial School,
                  by Brenda Child   42
                  Founding the Hill Museum & Manuscript Library, by Julian G. Plante   43

Chapter 4   "Proudly Stands Our Alma Mater, Tow'ring o'er the Oak and Pine"
                  Larry Haeg   45

Chapter 5   Plowing the Fields, Scattering Good Seed upon the Earth
                  Hilary Thimmesh, O.S.B.   59

Chapter 6   Saint John's and the Liturgical Movement: A Personal View
                  R. William Franklin   71
                  Founding Collegeville Institute for Ecumenical and Cultural Research,
                  by Kilian McDonnell, O.S.B.   81

Chapter 7   Virgil Michel and the Collegeville Community: Liturgy and Social Justice
                  Bernard Evans   83

Chapter 8   Nursery of the Arts   Robin Pierzina, O.S.B.   89

Chapter 9   Going Forth to Work till Evening Falls
                  Annette Atkins, Norma Loso Koetter, Zach Lewis   101

Chapter 10   Two Benedictine Communities Seeking God Together
                  Jana and Charles Preble   111

Chapter 11   The Design and Construction of Saint John's Abbey Church
                  Victoria Young   117

Chapter 12   For Beauty as Well as Bread: Saint John's and the Land
                  Derek R. Larson   129

Afterword   Dietrich Reinhart, O.S.B.   141

Poems   "My Funeral" by Kilian McDonnell, O.S.B.   29
                  "The Mind Is the Great Poem of Winter" by Eva Hooker, C.S.C.   40
                  "Crew (St. John's)" by Carl Phillips   57

Roster of Abbots and Academic Officers   142

Acknowledgments   143

Contributors   144

Index   148

Credits   150

Foreword

Abbot John Klassen, O.S.B.

As I REFLECT ON OUR PAST, I have a profound sense of gratitude to all the students who have come to Saint John's, to the prep school, to the university, to the seminary and school of theology over many years and have gone into the world to make a positive difference; to all the parents who generation after generation have entrusted their sons and daughters to us; to our benefactors, who from our first days in Minnesota have helped us realize our dreams and in many instances have nudged us to think more creatively, more expansively. I am grateful to generations of parishioners in Benedictine parishes who have supported our pastors and handed on strong faith and ethical beliefs to their children. And most of all I am grateful to God, who has taken this good work that Benedict describes, blessed it, and made it better than anything we or our ancestors could have imagined.

An anniversary such as a sesquicentennial is an opportunity to look forward and think about the future as well as to appreciate what so many have contributed to achieve the Saint John's of today. We celebrate a community built and sustained by women and men, monks and laypersons, students and teachers, scholars and craftspersons. I am old enough to know that it is impossible to predict the future (I am reminded of the irony of the psychic who gets run over by a train). Thus, with due caution let me try to illuminate some of the challenges and changes that I believe lie ahead.

When we complete the abbey guest house in the sesquicentennial year, Saint John's will have its first facility dedicated to hospitality. The guest house will provide a meeting place for those who have a spiritual hunger. Our monastic tradition of prayer, silence, stability, contemplation, and reflection offers a quiet place of welcome and sanctuary to a society that seems stressed to the breaking point.

Saint John's has been blessed with a beautiful natural environment. In a time of rapid development around us, the rural character of our campus, lakes, and woodlands cannot be taken for granted. We must constantly renew our commitment to conservation. Furthermore, it appears that the era of inexpensive oil is coming to a close. We will contribute to the exploration of alternative energy sources in the context of sensitivity to the planet and our immediate environment.

For more than forty years Saint John's has been a center for ecumenical research and dialogue between Christian churches. I expect that in the future we will experience an increasingly multicultural and multi-faith world that will require spaces and a community for interreligious dialogue. In our own time we have seen the resurgence of violence grounded in religious intolerance. We need to equip our students and all who come to Saint John's with tools that will build bridges of understanding between us as Christians and those of other faiths and philosophies.

It is chancy to try to predict what will come, but there is certainty in our solemn obligation to be ever mindful of our duty to love our neighbors in a richly diverse international community and to value and care for the planet we are blessed to share.

Outside the Pine Curtain

Annette Atkins

THIS COLLECTION OF ESSAYS walks through some stories of the life and lives that have grown up around Saint John's Abbey in Minnesota from the 1850s to the present, highlighting the monastic communities at Saint John's and Saint Benedict's, the laypeople who have both shaped and been shaped in these communities, as well as the varied ministries inspired by the Saint John's Benedictines. None of this occurred in isolation, however, but in the context of a Minnesota, a United States, and a world undergoing its own profound changes.

When the Benedictines from Metten, Bavaria, made their way via Latrobe, Pennsylvania, to the banks of the Mississippi River in the 1850s, the United States faced monumental problems. After sixty-one years of compromises, from the U.S. Constitution to the Compromise of 1850, the North and the South made their last effort to stave off civil war. It was a devil's bargain too: California joined the Union as a free state; slavery was barred from the District of Columbia; western states were left to decide by popular vote—meaning the vote of white men—whether or not each would allow slavery; the federal government agreed to apprehend runaway slaves.

By 1856 even this compromise had crumbled. The state of Kansas was already engaged in its own homegrown civil war; South Carolina congressman Preston Brooks attacked—physically, not verbally—anti-slavery senator William Sumner on the Senate floor. James Buchanan, a man whose attitudes about slavery were not known because he'd been out of the country, was elected president; the Supreme Court declared that Dred Scott, despite his residence at Fort Snelling (then Wisconsin Territory) in the 1830s, was property and therefore not entitled to a hearing in the courts.

The Benedictines arrived in a Minnesota caught up in these slavery troubles but not yet a state of the Union for another two years. Some former slaves lived in the area and the underground railroad had depots to get current slaves into Canada. Jane Grey Swisshelm was publishing a vituperative anti-slavery newspaper in Saint Cloud. In these years in the Minnesota Territory, however, issues of black and white took second place to issues of Indian and white.

In 1850 the federal census found about seven thousand white people living here, plus an even larger number of Native Americans, as well as a population of mixed-race people. An 1836 treaty had divided the land roughly in half, designating the northeast to the Ojibwe and the southwest to the Dakota. An 1851 treaty had assigned the Dakota to two reservations along the upper Minnesota River. The Ojibwe reservations were still a bit in the future. Whites of various

Saint Paul, lower levee, 1860

◀ The sun rises over the wetlands at the entrance to Saint John's from I-94, the historic route of the Red River trail to Breckenridge. The Pine Curtain looms in the background.

denominations and ethnicities had made little headway in converting the native people or in drawing them into more "American" ways.

These various Minnesotans represented a multitude of faiths. Of course, Father Louis Hennepin had been in the Great Lakes region in the seventeenth century, but in the nineteenth century the Congregationalists, Presbyterians, and Episcopalians had been the most enthusiastic and on-site missionaries. They focused on converting the Indians and then turned to the growing numbers of white Protestants. The Catholic priests ministered mostly to the French and to their French-Indian descendants in this once very French, but by the 1850s very much more Anglo-American, place, which before 1860 became much more German as well. Between 1850 and 1860 Germans in large numbers began moving into Minnesota. Some of them were Protestant; the Bavarians, lay and monastic, who came to Stearns County, however, were Catholic.

"Minnesota" had a legal identity, but it wasn't yet an idea or a place about which anyone outside knew very much, including the first governor's wife. Theodore C. Blegen reports that when told she was going to Minnesota, she remarked: "Minnesota! Where upon earth is it? In Denmark?" (*Minnesota: A History of the State* [Minneapolis: University of Minnesota Press, 1963] 164.) The Bavarians, Benedictine and lay, knew little more. The Minnesota that these German Catholics inhabited did, actually, become a little like Denmark in those first few years, when Scandinavian immigrants poured into the state. But Stearns County became and then stayed German. Few of these immigrants had wanted to stop being German when they migrated; they wanted to be German with more opportunities and possibilities. So they spoke, thought, read, worked, prayed, and lived in as German a way as they could for the rest of the nineteenth century.

The Irish bishop John Ireland feuded with his German co-religionists about how Catholics ought to live in America. Reflecting an Irish history of religious oppression by the government, he believed that the Irish had to become American if they were going to survive. American diversity would give them access to power, opportunities, success. He welcomed it and took that path in Saint Paul and at the College of

Minnesota wasn't yet an idea or a place about which anyone outside knew very much.

Saint Thomas especially. The Benedictines, heirs to a tradition in which being Catholic meant being mainstream, protected their Germanness however they could. Their rural setting and their monastic walls and the confidence born of their fourteen-hundred-year past made them conservative by nature.

But change seeped in. Father John Katzner's efforts at improving stock, experimenting with a great variety of seeds and developing new strains, mirrored changes in agriculture all over the state. Wendelin Grimm, a German immigrant, introduced winter-hardy alfalfa to Minnesota. Other farmers experimented successfully with more weather-resistant strains of apples, with winter wheat, with new breeds of cows and chickens. The Benedictines, like their lay neighbors, experimented, developed, expanded. In this they were engaged in a supremely American activity in this period.

National and international events, too, transformed Saint John's and Stearns County, sometimes imperceptibly or gradually but dramatically: industrialization, urbanization, immigration; rural delivery of mail, the spread of the railroad, availability of store-bought things; the stringing of telegraph, then telephone wires; the invention of the tractor; the legacy of the Civil War and the 1862 Dakota war.

More and more Americans, too, were going to school. Often ethnically or religiously identified like Saint John's and Saint Thomas, nine private colleges were founded in the nineteenth century, in addition to four state "normal" schools for teachers' training and the University of Minnesota. Of course, these schools grew because none had existed before, but they grew, more significantly, because ideas were changing about education generally and about the professional education of doctors, lawyers, teachers, even of teaching monks. Curricula everywhere, including Saint John's, became less classical, more practical, more contemporary (for better or for worse).

As a result, the place that the Benedictines had come to in 1850 was not the place that they ministered to in 1900. The Yankee dominance of the state's economy and politics had been rent by the election of the Swedish-born John Lind as governor in 1900, only the second foreign-born man to hold that office in Minnesota. (The first

The Benedictines, like their lay neighbors, experimented, developed, expanded.

was Norwegian-born Knute Nelson, 1892–1895.) Lind's election signaled the growing power of immigrants in a state still mostly Protestant.

Even second- and third-generation German Americans, however, suffered through World War I when Minnesota's Commission on Public Safety decided that being German meant being suspect and probably traitorous. The commission set out to, and largely succeeded in, forcing German out of the schools. It subjected German-language newspapers to intense scrutiny, requiring independent translators to vet all stories for seditious sentiment. They didn't and couldn't keep Germans from speaking in their preferred native tongue in private, but they did a lot to keep it out of the public. Benedictine parishes and schools dropped German as the language of worship and instruction. It was a state predominantly German but sharply hostile to Germans. The Eighteenth Amendment outlawed the sale and consumption of intoxicating beverages, including the Germans' beloved beer. At the same time, Saint John's students and neighbors were called up for active service against the Germans.

Following World War I, a majority of Americans lived in urban places, but Minnesota remained predominantly rural for another thirty years. This both helped and hurt during the 1920s and 1930s, when bust followed bust. The 1930s Depression in the United States was part of a worldwide economic slump. Local conditions— drought and pestilence both in Minnesota and the Midwest—added to the pain, but the disease was neither caused nor could it be cured locally. It could only be endured. Monks, seminarians, students, neighbors, farm families—all were affected. The splendid isolation of Saint John's Abbey and University provided only slight buffering from the international economic and political nightmares of depression and war.

During and after World War II, Minnesota's economy flourished. Honeywell, IBM, 3M expanded enthusiastically. The GI bill sent thousands of returning soldiers to college in unprecedented numbers and all at once. All over the United States, colleges put up temporary housing and classrooms and packed in as many students as they could. Education was a boom industry in those postwar years, and Saint John's shared in that prosperity.

The 1950s seemed at the time and even in retrospect seem to have been a period of conservative retreat. It was, more accurately, an incubator of revolutionary ideas. Five books published in the late 1950s foretold an agenda for change that came to life in the 1960s: Betty Friedan's *Feminine Mystique*; Rachel Carson's *Silent Spring*; Michael Harrington's *The Other America*; James Baldwin's *The Fire Next Time*; Ralph Nader's *Unsafe at Any Speed*. These books called for a better America at a time when many

Born in Norway, Knute Nelson had a long life of public service in Minnesota, where he served as a member of Congress, then governor, then senator from 1895 until his death in 1923. His residence was in Alexandria. He and Abbot Alexius Edelbrock became friends. He was instrumental in procuring federal funding for the Indian Industrial Schools at Saint John's and Saint Benedict's Academy.

Americans were ready to listen. Those World War II years of rationing and saving demonstrated that each person could make a difference; even saving the foil on a gum wrapper could help to win the war. The language of the Cold War, the parlance of opportunities for all, of rights, of freedoms fed many Americans' idealism and responsibility to make the world better. John F. Kennedy, perhaps the most visible demonstration of the Catholic glory days, was elected by only a tiny majority, but he reinforced the idea that Americans could—and must—make the world better.

The five revolutions presaged and, indeed, encouraged by these books touched even the remotest parts of Stearns County and Saint John's Abbey, University, Preparatory School, Liturgical Press. So did the Vietnam War. And even more profoundly did the Second Vatican Council. The messages of all were the same: the primacy of the individual conscience, the necessity of engagement, and the call to individual action.

Traditions blew away. Habits changed. Colleges for women merged with their male counterparts or went co-ed; Lyndon Johnson declared a war on poverty; the environmental movement was born; women's and civil rights ignited hopes and resentments. The Vietnam War embroiled and scarred two nations, at least.

In some ways the Minnesota of the early twenty-first century bears a remarkable resemblance to that of the mid-nineteenth century. It's a state of enormous economic opportunity for some and remarkably limited opportunity for others; it's a state of many immigrant groups often more feared than welcomed. It's a state of food growing and processing, of people doing their jobs, living their lives, wanting to keep their children safe and get them educated.

When first in Minnesota, German monks and sisters ministered to mostly German-born and German-speaking congregations massed in a small radius in central Minnesota. They educated children of their mostly rural parishioners and deepened and disciplined their Catholicism. Now the Benedictines—still many with German names, but fewer and fewer— minister to a rapidly expanding Spanish-speaking population, as well as to Hmong and other immigrant people, in addition to the descendants of those original German parishioners.

As was the case in the 1850s, the United States faces monumental problems 150 years later. Saint John's Abbey and University are no longer such German places, and they have been drawn more and more deeply into the issues and concerns of the larger world. This is as it should be. Benedictinism requires a thoughtful, attentive response to this world as well as to the next. It might in some places, at some times, and for some people have been an escape. Not any more.

In some ways the Minnesota of the early twenty-first century bears a remarkable resemblance to that of the mid-nineteenth century.

Formation of Collegeville township in 1879 positioned Saint John's at the corner of four townships. As this 1893 map shows, Saint Louis Lake—to be named Lake Sagatagan three years later—lies in Collegeville township, but Collegeville station is in Saint Wendel township. Today baseball games take place in Avon township, but cross-country runners and skiers head out through the woods in Saint Joseph township.

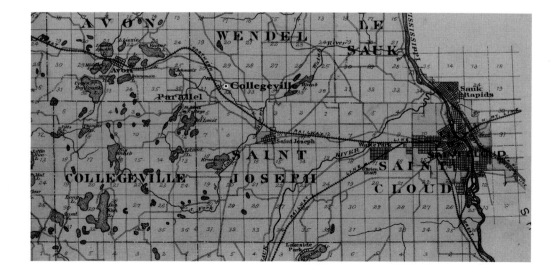

CHAPTER ONE

A Time to Plant and a Time to Grow

Hilary Thimmesh, O.S.B.

SAINT JOHN'S CELEBRATED its diamond jubilee in 1931. The midpoint in our 150-year history provides a measuring stick for what went before and what came after. In the first seventy-five years there was a decade of intensive missionary work to start with, along with founding a school and finding a permanent location. This was followed by twenty years of expansive growth, a period that came to a temporary halt with the forced resignation of the second abbot, Alexius Edelbrock, in 1889.

A destructive tornado and the election of Peter Engel as the fourth abbot in 1894 mark the beginning of a second period of steady growth. Thus when we zero in on Saint John's in 1931, we see a mature community going about its business with a high degree of self-understanding and purpose. The pioneer generation has passed away. The roughness of frontier conditions is gone. The monastic community is large and growing under the abbot who succeeded Peter Engel in 1921, Alcuin Deutsch. There are 140 priests, 41 clerics (monks studying for ordination), 21 lay brothers, 10 novices. In December, *The Record*, wrapping up its forty-fourth year as the campus newspaper, jumps the gun by half a dozen years to claim that Saint John's has surpassed its motherhouse, Saint Vincent Archabbey in Latrobe, Pennsylvania, to become the largest Benedictine monastery in North America.

The place is to a significant degree self-sustaining. Together with local workmen, the brothers run the shops and the farm. The farm includes a dairy herd, a chicken house, and, two miles away downwind, a hog farm. Much of the food consumed on the premises is produced on the premises—there is an apple cellar, a potato cellar, a root cellar, a winter cellar for the bees, a butcher shop, a smokehouse, a place where honey is extracted from the comb and candles are made. Much of the furniture comes from the woods by way of the woodworking shop. The institution provides its own utility services; the fire department is still eight years in the future. Many of the priests serve in parishes or missions; about thirty-five of them conduct the seminary, the college, and the prep school.

The twin towers look down on an architectural intruder in this 1956 photo of the new wing of the monastery reflected in the quiet waters of Lake Sagatagan. The brick boathouse on the shore originally served as the drying shed for the laundry. Marcel Breuer's new church was still on the drawing boards.

◄ Two texts stand out in the late afternoon winter sun. On the 1886 tower IOGD, the initial letters of a Latin motto, in English "Let God be glorified in all things." On the peace memorial designed by Father Cloud Meinberg, "their country." The whole text circling the granite block reads: "To the men of Saint John's who have served their country in peace and war" and on top of the block around the base of the cross, "Blessed are they who make peace for theirs is the kingdom of God."

Angelo Zankl, O.S.B., 104 years old at this writing, says that he took this west view of the buildings from across the Watab—labeled Stump Lake by the DNR—sometime prior to his ordination in 1926. Buildings in the picture from left to right and front to back are the science hall, a corner of the gymnasium, the carpenter shop and behind it Benet Hall, the powerhouse chimney, the infirmary, the powerhouse, the kitchen wing, the roof of the convent, a corner of the library building, and anchoring the whole scene, the Quadrangle and the steeples of the church.

The schools, reorganized by Abbot Alcuin as a preparatory school, a college of arts and sciences, and a seminary, are long established and respected. The seminary has 61 students; the college, 205; the prep school, 191. Thirty-six college seniors get their bachelor's degrees in June. Fred Hughes, valedictorian, will become a prominent Saint Cloud attorney and an active alumnus for nearly seventy years. Martin Schirber, O.S.B., will be ordained, earn a doctorate in economics, and be a dynamic dean of the college in the critical years 1943 to 1952. Among thirty-seven prep school graduates is Albert Eidenschink, who will take the name John in monastic life, become a professor of canon law, serve as subprior from 1947 to 1969, and then as abbot from 1971 to 1979.

Laypersons—not many but some—play a role in the schools. There are two lay professors this year, a speech instructor who will move on, and Francis Schoffman, who will teach chemistry until his retirement in 1979. George Durenberger becomes athletic director in September, a position he will hold until 1972. Joe Benda, who played under Knute Rockne at Notre Dame, starts as college coach and surprises everybody by winning four out of six football games, upsetting even Saint Olaf. This outcome is all the more satisfying because the team lost all its games the previous year under coach Bill Houle, a Saint Thomas graduate. Benda will shape the football tradition at Saint John's until his early death from Hodgkin's disease in 1950.

Women play limited but essential roles. Seventeen German Franciscan sisters do the cooking and baking. The legendary Sabina Diederichs, RN, runs a no-nonsense infirmary. These are the only women employed by Saint John's.

Virtually everyone on campus is Catholic. The monks rise at 4:30 a.m. for Prime, the Little Hours, and at least two Masses. Students are roused at 6:30 and go to Mass at 7 every day, including Sunday. Classes meet on the hour from 8 to noon Monday to Saturday and 1 to 2:45 Monday to Wednesday and Friday. Classes begin with prayer. It would be extraordinary to see a monk-teacher not dressed in his monastic habit. Breakfast, dinner, and supper are sit-down meals in the refectory that start and end with prayer led by the dean.

On May 3, the seventy-fifth anniversary of the arrival of the pioneer monks in Saint Paul, the abbot celebrates a pontifical Mass at which the subprior, Alexius Hoffmann—librarian, theology professor, chronicler par excellence —preaches on the silver, golden, and diamond jubilees of Saint John's, having been present for all of them.

The economic vitality of the place depends in large part on the labor of the monks in the schools, shops, and farm. There is careful bookkeeping but no budgetary process; the first annual audit is twelve years in the future. Tuition is $50 a semester in the college and the prep school and free in the seminary. Board and lodging are $143 a semester in this third year of the deepening Great Depression. Income from student payments is supplemented by salaries and stipends from the parishes where monks serve. In its fifth year the Liturgical Press is operating in the black. In December the alumni gift fund completes its first year with a tally of 932 subscribers for a total of $43,913.

Because Abbot Alcuin does not think that a Catholic college would be well advised to conform to secular standards, the college has not sought accreditation. He himself has a doctorate (in philosophy), as do three of the thirty-one men who constitute the college faculty—one of them in theology, two in philosophy. Otherwise there are fourteen with an MA and a handful with a BA. The average age of this group of teachers is thirty-nine; the abbot is the oldest at fifty-four. Several of them will pursue doctoral studies and become mainstays of the faculty after World War II. Father Virgil Michel is one member of the faculty who writes steadily and is known beyond the local scene, but this year he is recuperating from a breakdown brought on by overwork. Nonetheless, in him Saint John's has found a prophetic voice that will make the Collegeville postmark a symbol of leadership in the church at large.

So much for a brief look at Saint John's as it was midway in its history. Now I turn back to look at how the institution so firmly in place in 1931 took shape.

Beginning in 1856

From the founding of the community, the apostolates of education and pastoral service ran in tandem. In May 1856 Bishop Joseph Cretin ordained two of the young Benedictines who had

Alexius Hoffmann, O.S.B.

In our first century, one monk-educator and scholar stands out: Alexius Hoffmann (1863–1940). He could be given many different titles: pioneer, theologian, historian, linguist, author, musician, administrator, Christian humanist, librarian, archivist, vice president of the college (1891–1899), and subprior of the abbey (1919–1933). Alexius was an educated and cultured man who influenced much of the spirit and ethos of Saint John's Abbey and University.

Alexius was born in Saint Paul in 1863. While he was serving Mass for Abbot Alexius Edelbrock at Assumption Church, the abbot invited him to become a monk of Saint John's. Alexius began his classical studies at Saint John's in 1875, professed monastic vows in 1881, and was ordained a priest by Archbishop John Ireland in 1885.

After his ordination Father Alexius began a life of continuous teaching for some forty-eight years. He taught everything from spelling to dogmatic theology. A true Renaissance man, he was fluent in Spanish, Italian, French, and expert in Latin and German.

On October 10, 1923, in recognition of his long career as a professor of theology, he was granted a doctoral degree in sacred theology by Pope Pius XI at the request of Bishop Busch of Saint Cloud.

Father Alexius was a researcher, writer, and chronicler of much of Saint John's early history. Among the books he published was the golden jubilee book *St. John's University: A Sketch of Its History*. As a theologian, he wrote articles for the first edition of the Catholic Encyclopedia in 1907.

When he pleaded to be relieved of his duties as a college administrator in order to pursue research, Abbot Peter Engel appointed him librarian. He proceeded to build a classic college library during his seventeen-year tenure.

He died on July 7, 1940. The early history and memory of Saint John's live on in the heritage of his published work and his extensive handwritten diaries and notes preserved in the abbey archives.

Neither this photo nor the one on the next page is dated. The big house across the tracks in the summer view was constructed by the brothers and scholastics in the summer of 1879 for Henry Broker, the first Collegeville postmaster. For a time Mr. Broker, the abbot's brother-in-law, also ran a small general store on the premises. The winter view—students going home for Christmas?—may be much later if the depot with the Collegeville sign wider than the structure itself is the one built by Saint John's when the railroad picked up the original depot and moved it to Ronneby.

just arrived in Saint Paul from Pennsylvania, Bruno Riss and Cornelius Wittmann. When they got to Saint Cloud, Bruno was given charge of the Saint Joseph parish, with missions in Jacobs Prairie and Richmond. Cornelius set up a classroom in the Edelbrocks' house in Saint Cloud and taught ten pupils, boys and girls, over the winter. A year later he was the entire faculty of the newly chartered "Saint John's Seminary," when five boys began their studies under him in November 1857. At the same time he did pastoral service locally. The 1915 *History of Stearns County* was to hail him as the pioneer teacher of Stearns County.

This was the pattern of the first decade. A small group of Benedictine monks, all of them European-born and German-speaking, set about the tasks of education and ministry. A handful of students stayed with them from late autumn to late spring. One of the priests was appointed to be their professor, with some assistance from others. Benno Muckenthaler and Patrick Greil, the two lay brothers who were part of the original group of five, cared for the farm animals, built claim shacks, and formed the nucleus of a work crew that Alexius Hoffmann says included the entire personnel of the monastery to clear the land and construct the first buildings (*Saint John's University 1857–1907*, 15). All the priests were also engaged at least part-time in pastoral ministry in the Catholic settlements that were springing up in Stearns County.

INDEPENDENT STATUS AND THE FIRST ABBOT

For the first ten years Abbot Boniface Wimmer kept overall direction of the new foundation from Pennsylvania. With the election of his prior, Rupert Seidenbusch, as the first abbot of the Minnesota monastery in 1866, the new community became autonomous, and the school took on the structure of an es-

tablished institution. In 1870 the first college catalogue was published and the first degrees were conferred as authorized by legislative act the year before. Two years later a business program was introduced. Still later Abbot Alexius Edelbrock secured government funding for an industrial school for Indian boys with the support of his friend in Congress, Knute Nelson.

From 1867 to 1886 the Quadrangle took shape section by section. Abbot Alexius, like Abbot Rupert, was a builder. His 1878 inventory lists a stockpile of 450,000 bricks made on site. The church was completed in 1882, the Quadrangle in 1886. Steam heat replaced wood stoves when the powerhouse was completed in 1889, the year of Abbot Alexius's resignation under pressure from a faction within the community who gained the support of Archbishop John Ireland of Saint Paul.

Where the tracks used to be, cyclists now bike along the Lake Wobegon trail.

Abbot Bernard Locnikar, who followed Alexius, was not a builder and was devastated when the 1894 tornado took the roof off the south wing and flattened the farm buildings. Under Abbot Peter Engel (1894–1921), a scientist by training, shops and barns and a whole cluster of college buildings took shape: observatory, library, gymnasium, science hall, kitchen, infirmary.

Abbot Peter would have been described as charismatic if the term had been in use in his time. He had a sure pastoral touch to match his academic interests, and under his leadership continuance of the pastoral mission ran parallel with development of the school. It was taken for granted that many of the monks of Saint John's would serve in parishes or missions as their life work and that virtually all the ordained monks at the abbey would go out to parishes for confessions and Masses on weekends and at Christmas and Easter. In the monastic lexicon this was called "livery-horsing." The term stuck even after some monks

Abbot Alcuin Tackles Racism

Allen Tarlton was eighteen years old in 1944 and wanted to enter a seminary to begin studies for the priesthood. Because he was black, he was not welcome at various seminaries to which he applied. He learned of Saint John's through a high school counselor and wrote to Abbot Alcuin Deutsch, who took care of the racial problem with dispatch:

May 26, 1944

Mr. Allen P. Tarlton
510 John Street
Cincinnati, Ohio

Dear Mr. Tarlton,

I received your letter of the 24th instant this noon, and note with interest that you wish to become a priest of the Order of St. Benedict.

Your two problems are not so difficult: 1st, the fact that you are colored will in no wise be a hindrance to your becoming a priest and a member of the Order of St. Benedict . . .

Begging the Lord to bless and guide you, I am
        Yours sincerely,
        Alcuin Deutsch, O.S.B.
        Abbot

were able to get to their weekend assignments by train when the St. Paul and Pacific added a stop near the old farm in 1879 and named it Collegeville. The practice was still in full swing when I was ordained in 1954.

The number of parishes in Saint John's care grew steadily from pioneer days, first in Stearns County and the Twin Cities, then in the northern part of the state, in North Dakota, and in the Bronx and the Bahamas. To get ahead of my story for a moment, Colman Barry's centennial history, *Worship and Work,* lists 361 places where Benedictines had served up to 1956. In that year fifty parishes were under the care of priests from Saint John's. That was the high point. Since then the number has gradually grown smaller owing to the combined effect of a scarcity of priests and the appeal of a more contemplative or at least less clerical monasticism.

Besides parish work, the abbey repeatedly reached out to found or assist monastic houses elsewhere. There were to be eleven in all, from Saint Martin's Abbey, founded in 1895, to Saint Maur's interracial monastery in 1949. Numerous monks also served as temporary administrators of other monasteries as the need arose, a service Saint John's has continued to provide from time to time.

The involvement of Saint John's in monastic foundations reached its high point under Abbot Alcuin and testified to his largeness of outlook and the growing reputation of Collegeville in the Benedictine world. In the 1920s the Holy See called on Saint John's to play a part in conducting a Catholic university in China. After the war the abbot was generous toward European monastic communities in need. Saint John's had come through the war intact and was poised to grow. Five new priories were founded between 1946 and 1949: Saint Augustine's in Nassau, San Antonio Abad in Puerto Rico, Abadia del Tepeyac in Mexico, Saint Anselm's in Tokyo, and Saint Maur's in Kentucky.

Ironically, the energies Abbot Alcuin sought to channel to new or revitalized monastic foundations were also driving toward growth in the college, a goal he did not particularly cherish. He wanted the college to be good but small. Following the pattern established by Peter Engel, Alcuin sent 101 men away for advanced degrees during his twenty-nine years as abbot. One of them was Godfrey Diekmann, a gifted student who completed his European education in 1933 and stepped into Virgil Michel's editorship of *Orate Fratres* and a high-profile role in the national liturgical movement when Dom Virgil died in 1938.

CRITICAL TURNING POINT AT MID-CENTURY

When Alcuin Deutsch resigned because of failing health in November 1950, the community numbered nearly 300 professed monks and novices. As had happened in 1875, 1894, and 1921, the prior, Baldwin Dworschak, was elected abbot. The two decades of his tenure as abbot, 1951–1971, saw large changes at Saint John's. The schools grew, the farm died. Accepted monastic practices—separateness from secular society, liturgical prayer in Latin, devotional piety, monastic vows leading to ordination, lifetime service in parishes, the lay brotherhood as a fraternity of unlettered workmen—were questioned, abandoned, or profoundly modified. With a heady sense of freedom, the monastic community undertook a renewal that entailed rejection of much that had been intrinsic to its first century.

VATICAN II AFFECTS SAINT JOHN'S

The Second Vatican Council brought in the greatest changes. Abbot Baldwin took part in the council as president of the American-Cassinese Congregation of Benedictines. Godfrey Diekmann was involved as a liturgical expert. Theologians and others at home followed developments in Rome enthusiastically. Renewal was in the air, and in retrospect it is not surprising that the aftermath of the council was exhilarating and confusing at the same time. Changes wrought by the council rendered some carefully planned features of the splendid new church, dedicated in 1961, out of date. With the barrier of Latin removed, the brothers were incorporated into the choir, and the separate chapel for their liturgy stood empty. So did most of the thirty-four side chapels intended for daily private Masses as the essentially communal character of the Eucharist was emphasized.

The religious climate changed. The vision of all twelve hundred or fifteen hundred college students attending the 7 a.m. daily Mass, as their counterparts had done for a hundred years, somehow failed to materialize as parietal rules fell by the wayside. The monks settled for a simple form of the Divine Office in English that largely forsook the wealth of the ancient Latin tradition. Devotional exercises—Benediction with the Blessed Sacrament, the Stations of the Cross, novenas, frequent confession, the annual college retreat—became infrequent or disappeared altogether in the swirl of revolution that affected the Saint John's campus as it did many others in the late sixties.

LANDMARK PRESIDENCY OF FATHER COLMAN BARRY

Father Colman Barry became president of the university in 1964. Like Alexius Edelbrock ninety years earlier, he was a born entrepreneur. Successful para-academic enterprises that he promoted—the Hill Monastic Manuscript Library (now the Hill Museum & Manuscript Library) and Minnesota Educational Radio (to become Minnesota Public Radio)—are always mentioned,

The involvement of Saint John's in monastic foundations reached its high point under Abbot Alcuin and testified to his largeness of outlook and the growing reputation of Collegeville in the Benedictine world.

Cardinal Amleto Cicognani, Apostolic Delegate to the United States, presided at the Mass for Saint John's centennial on August 22, 1956.

A sign of the times was the renovation of quarters in the monastery to serve as a retirement center for the elderly and the infirm.

and properly so, among his achievements. He initiated the Jay Phillips Chair in Jewish Studies and supported the Institute for Ecumenical and Cultural Research founded by Father Kilian McDonnell in 1967. Not least of his achievements was a quantum leap in faculty and staff compensation. In several respects his was a landmark presidency, but the unanticipated turbulence that gripped the nation in the final years of the decade had a tendency to shorten college presidencies. It led Colman not to seek a second six-year term, although he continued in office until the summer of 1971, when Abbot Baldwin retired from office.

The decades of the 1970s, the 1980s, and the 1990s were kaleidoscopic in their variety but not seminal in the way the sixties were. The coordinate relation of Saint John's University and the College of Saint Benedict, initiated by joint curricular and calendar reform in 1967, altered and in many respects enhanced the character of both institutions in the following decades. Joseph Farry devotes particular attention to this period in the life of the colleges in chapter 3.

A program that outgrew its origins in the sociology department and acquired national significance was the campaign for natural family planning founded by Father Paul Marx. He structured the program as the Human Life Center in 1972 and broadened it to combat abortion and euthanasia as well as artificial contraception. In 1980 he went international with headquarters in Washington, D.C. By the time he retired to the abbey in 1999, he had advocated the pro-life cause in seventy countries with the personal blessing of both Pope Paul VI and Pope John Paul II.

At home a sign of the times was the 1976 renovation of quarters in the monastery to serve as a retirement center for the elderly and the infirm. The center was named Saint Raphael's Hall. It was expanded in the eighties and has rarely had fewer than twenty residents at any time since 1990. Mr. John Dockendorf has been director since 1976.

The reverse side of this coin was the disappearance of a large younger generation in the monastery. The classes of ten or twelve novices a year that were

Cardinal Basil Hume and Abbot Jerome Theisen join Abbot Primate Victor Damertz in concelebrating Mass at Saint John's in July 1980, for the 1500th anniversary of the birth of Saint Benedict. Cardinal Hume was an English Benedictine, the archbishop of Westminster and former abbot of Ampleforth Abbey in Yorkshire. Abbot Jerome was to become abbot primate in 1992.

common in the postwar period gave way to classes of three or four and then one or two. Moreover, the new novices tended to be ten or fifteen years older than their earlier counterparts. It became the usual practice to accept candidates for the novitiate only after they had managed their own affairs for a time as adults. Whether a monk would eventually seek ordination to the priesthood was treated as a separate question.

BROADENED SENSE OF BENEDICTINE VOCATION

Other ways of involving young people in the life of the monastic community developed, such as the summer Monastic Experience Program, one- or two-week live-ins for college students during the academic year, and the Benedictine Volunteer option for students ready to commit a year to teaching or working with youth at a Benedictine school or mission. The Saint John's Boys' Choir, founded by Brother Paul Richards in 1981, was incidentally a source of youthful energy on campus and enriched the monastic liturgies in which it took part.

There were some memorable ecclesiastical moments in the eighties when the United States Conference of Catholic Bishops, under the presidency of Archbishop John Roach of Saint Paul, met at Saint John's, first for a June retreat with Cardinal Basil Hume in 1982, then for three other June meetings (1985, 1986, 1988). A snapshot of Basil Hume, cardinal archbishop of Westminster and former abbot of Ampleforth Abbey, in a T-shirt as he chatted with some of the brethren in the third-floor recreation room, speaks volumes for his ease among us. A decade later Saint John's became active in assisting the church in China by bringing Chinese priests, seminarians, sisters, and laywomen to the campus to further their education and training.

In 1992 Abbot Jerome Theisen was elected head of the Benedictine Order with his office in Rome. The vacancy at Saint John's

In 1939 the carpenter shop caught fire and the community found it had no effective way of fighting a fire. The fire department was born. Frater Gervase Soukup, newly professed in 1940, grips the steering wheel of Saint John's first fire truck. Brother Steve Thell and Brother John Anderl, the latter also newly professed, ride the running board. For half a century, duty on the fire crew was one of the main jobs of the clerics, most of whom were men in their early twenties. Brother John became the fire chief and the equipment got more sophisticated. Today Jay Bohan, hired for the job, is fire chief, and the firemonks—some of whom are pictured here—are joined by other volunteers like Mike Roske, second from the left.

was unanticipated. Perhaps the most difficult matter that the acting superior, Prior Jonathan Licari, had to deal with while the community prepared to elect a new abbot was sexual abuse allegations against some members of the community. The new abbot, Timothy Kelly, found himself heavily engaged with the same matter during his eight-year term of office. His successor, John Klassen, reaped the whirlwind when sexual abuse by Catholic clergy burst on the national scene in 2002. The abbot gained respect by addressing the issue openly and giving priority to the needs of victims.

The strain on the community in this crisis was great, but we were bolstered by encouragement from many alumni and friends who recognized that this dark chapter in Saint John's history was at odds with the hospitality and care that generations of students and guests had received here. The abbot pushed ahead with plans for—what else—the guest house first announced in the January 15, 1931, issue of *The Record,* and construction of the building designed by architect Vincent James began in October 2005.

Finally, if an enduring symbol of the deepest meaning of the place called Collegeville is needed, the seven richly illuminated volumes of the first manuscript Bible in modern times will do nicely. The grandeur of this production is matched only by the sheer improbability of doing it. Generations to come will deduce something vital about Saint John's from the character of this masterwork planned by a committee of artists and theologians at Collegeville and carried out by Donald Jackson and his team of calligraphers in Wales.

The five monks who came to Saint Cloud in 1856 would probably have been at home with the community that observed its diamond jubilee in 1931 even if someone told them that the abbot had recently gone from Nassau to Miami by air. They were, after all, young adventurers in their own right. Bruno Riss would no doubt do his surveys by GPS were he to come back today.

Following Brother Andrew Coval's profession of monastic vows at Mass on September 14, 2005, the community gathers under the banner for the traditional *corona,* the circle of confreres who each greet their newly professed brother with a hug and some warm words of blessing.

Founding Minnesota Public Radio

William Kling

In the early 1960s Father Colman Barry, then a history professor, was intrigued by the college's student radio station, of which I was the manager. When I was about to graduate in 1964 and Colman was about to be appointed president, he asked me what I was planning to do. I told him I'd like to attend graduate school in either business or communications. With the support of Dr. Waldemar Wenner, Colman said, "Choose communications and we'll send you to graduate school if you'll agree to come back and begin a radio station for Saint John's."

I went off to Boston University and Stanford to study communications theory and law and hang out at WGBH in Boston and KQED in San Francisco, where some of the most advanced thinking in public broadcasting was occurring. Colman and I carried on an active correspondence about how to proceed. I wanted to broadcast on the FM band, but at the time AM had most of the audience. Colman's advisors, including Larry Haeg Sr., general manager of WCCO, and Father Vincent Yzermans, head of the National Association of Religious Broadcasters, urged him to apply for a small AM station to serve Saint Cloud. Colman went with his intuition and approved the plan for an FM station.

Colman had to persuade the monastic community to fund the project. When I returned to Saint John's in January 1966, he arranged with Abbot Baldwin Dworschak to have me address the chapter and answer questions in the abbey chapter house. I was then twenty-four years old. In the end the chapter approved funding for the station.

From that point on, my job was to get a station on the air. I read books on acoustics and designed a studio complex on the top floor of Wimmer Hall, where the museum, with its stuffed buffalo and other exhibits, had been located. Physics professor Father Casper Keogh provided an altimeter to enable me to search the campus for the highest land for the transmitter. The campus workmen, with considerable skepticism, built the studio concept as designed, including double masonry walls, isolated electrical and ventilation systems, and an oversized office for me, my reaction to spending a year in a room the size of a closet over the steaming campus kitchen.

KSJR signed on on January 22, 1967, while Colman dined at the Germain Hotel in Saint Cloud with supporters and a portable radio. Unfortunately, the station didn't manage to get on the air until about five hours after the publicized time, and then perhaps only because of the prayers of Father Fintan Bromenshenkel, head of computer science, who paced the hall waiting and wishing he could offer assistance. It brought the surrounding community a menu of classical music, lectures, jazz, poetry, and even live stereo broadcasts of Saint John's football. In many ways, lacking an NPR network of any type, these were stimulating days. The programmers had to work so hard to find quality programs that they scoured the country looking for the best and often struck gold. Sources like Ford Hall Forum in Boston and the Glide Memorial Church in San Francisco, the Center for the Study of Democratic Institutions in Santa Barbara, and other sources that reflected my graduate school geography provided a stimulating flow of programming.

The station was a programmatic success and a gem despite intermittent on-air time because of static electricity in the studio carpet and gophers gnawing through the power line to the distant transmitter, but there was little audience and little financial support. Memberships were $12 a year, and by 1970 only two thousand had been enrolled. Program underwriting was almost unheard of. Then Sarah-Maud W. (for Weyerhaeuser) Sivertsen sent a check for $5,000 to indicate her pleasure at being able to hear the Metropolitan Opera broadcasts from her lake home in rural Scandia Valley. It was a great boost for both Colman and me because it indicated what the potential might be. But she and Bob Sivertsen were rare fans.

KSJR was built as a 40,000-watt station to serve Stearns County. Soon it became clear that serving Stearns County wasn't a financially viable concept. With a gift from Dr. Wenner, the station expanded to 150,000 watts, the largest FM station in the Midwest. It still missed the key audience of the Twin Cities. Despite having a staff of fewer than seven people (including a morning classical music announcer by the name of Garrison Keillor), the station ran deeply into debt.

I suggested expanding to where the audience was—the Twin Cities. With little discretionary money left in 1968, Saint John's applied for KSJN, a 3,400-watt station in the New Brighton suburb of the Twin Cities, to expand the audience. But that station struggled with static interference whenever the wind blew, and the financial problem grew. We took advantage of FM's SCA "second channel" to add a broadcast service for the blind and gained some assistance with operating costs from the Hamm Foundation and a state agency for the visually handicapped.

While innovations like that helped, they didn't resolve the financial problem. In 1969 Father Colman, Father Gordon Tavis, Abbot Baldwin, and I decided to preserve the concept by giving the assets to a broader-based community corporation, first named Saint John's University Broadcasting, Inc., then Minnesota Educational Radio, and finally Minnesota Public Radio. Colman urged the private college presidents to join him in making MPR a private college initiative to serve all of Minnesota. We gradually transferred our principal offices and studios to Saint Paul.

Garrison Keillor

KSJR shouldn't have succeeded, but it did because neither Colman nor I understood that it shouldn't have. Normal thinking would not have trusted the instincts of a twenty-four-year-old over wiser, more successful practitioners. Few would have protected the funding and the manager as Colman did. Even fewer institutions would have given up their broadcast licenses and assets in order to help save the "mission," as Saint John's did. Those selfless acts—looking at the long-range community good, taking chances on people that may not have been defended in any rational manner, and believing it could be done—may be one of Saint John's proudest moments.

William Kling '64

CHAPTER TWO

A Little Rule for Beginners

Columba Stewart, O.S.B.

April 19, 2001. Most senior Saint John's monk, Angelo Zankl, 100. Most junior Saint John's monk, Matthew Luft, 27.

BEING A MONK OF SAINT JOHN'S ABBEY for a quarter century makes me still a relative newcomer to this way of life. I had no personal experience of monastic life in Collegeville before or immediately after the Second Vatican Council, the watershed that even after forty years dominates the monastic story of most of our monks. My personal perspective kicks in about the time things had begun to settle down.

In the monastic world Saint John's is legendary, mostly because of our size and international reach. An oft-repeated story has two men striking up a conversation on a plane and discovering that they are both priests, and Benedictines, and, lo! members of Saint John's Abbey. Even in our much smaller current numbers, we confound European monks accustomed to communities of twenty to thirty monks. Some of them have even suggested that we aren't really monks at all: our active ministry, lack of strictness, professional training, and openness to the world strike the more traditional types as more appropriate for orders like the Dominicans than for Benedictines. I once asked a famous French monk-scholar what he thought of our liturgy. "Well," he replied in his thick accent, "I notice that you begin your morning prayers with the phrase 'Lord, open my lips.' In the traditional monastic liturgy those words end the night silence and start the Office of Vigils. But here," he said, "you have neither silence nor Vigils!"

Ascetics we are not, at least not in the traditional sense of fasting, rising in the middle of the night for prayer, or practicing exceptional austerities. Our asceticism is that of the relentless cycle of the liturgy and life in community. To me it is still something just short of miraculous to go into our church at 6:55 every morning and find more than a hundred men there ready to start their day together with prayer. I've described community life to colleagues in the university as comparable to having breakfast, lunch, and dinner with the whole faculty every day for the rest of their lives. They get the point. While God may have had a sound reason for bringing each of my confreres here, sometimes that reason seems elusive to me. I am sure that they think the same about me sometimes. Never mind. The bell rings, we go to church. Evening comes, and morning follows, another day.

Our monastic observance has always been tempered by the demands of work. The monks came to Minnesota for ministry to settlers, both pastoral and educational. This emphasis on service wasn't unique to the frontier; the re-founding of monastic life in Bavaria itself was based on the notion that monasteries should have social utility. The demands of the American scene attracted monks like Boniface Wimmer, who relished the challenge, and those demands

◄ Father Jerome Tupa stops to talk with Bryan Backes and his children, Emma and Christopher, in front of Sexton Commons on his way from the student dorms, where he is a faculty resident, to the monastery.

From the journals of Thomas Merton

July 23, 1956. St. John's Abbey

I said Prime down by the lake. Quiet water, lined with thick woods, birch and pine and oak and fir trees around the monastery—and a great loon diving in the water.

July 27, 1956

Yesterday, feast of St. Anne, rowed over to Stella Maris chapel which I like. Reading Suzuki and Diadochos of Photike under the birch trees and looking at the water. And today again, after the end of this week's workshop, spent most of the afternoon in the same place.

At the end of the lake what looks like a beach is really a stretch of shallows filled with lily pads. All around the lake are swampy places full of birches that have been broken halfway up by storms.

July 29, 1956

Yesterday, spent most of the afternoon in the quiet woods behind Stella Maris reading, thinking, and realizing the inadequacy of both thinking and reading. I believe what I saw was an otter. At that end of the lake also there is a great blue heron. The lake is so beautiful it makes me feel guilty. What is there in me that makes me feel I should not have so many good things? Or, rather, not only not have them, but not even see them?

Thomas Merton, *A Search for Solitude*, ed. Lawrence S. Cunningham. HarperSanFrancisco, 1996. Used by permission.

still set the tone of our form of American Benedictine life. Rather than being one component of a carefully regulated day, as in the Rule, our work tends to be the context in which we manage our prayer, common life, rest, and recreation. A pastor in a parish or a monk in the dorm actually lives on the job. For many years I could sleep, pray, eat, and teach without having to go outdoors. Sleeping over the shop is part of who we are.

TRADITIONAL HOURS OF PRAYER

Early records describe the attempt even by solo monks out in mission stations to maintain the Bavarian monastic schedule required by the constitutions of the day, including rising at 3:30 a.m. and keeping night silence despite the demands of parishioners. At the monastery itself the very early rising of the European model soon shifted to a schedule more conducive to educational work. The traditional nocturnal Office, Vigils, came to be "anticipated" the preceding evening so that monks could stay up later. Even so, the monks rose around 4:30 a.m., about the same time as local farmers did, and had several hours of communal prayer and Masses before having breakfast and heading off to work. Within a few decades the schedule had settled into the pattern it would retain in some form or another to the present day, with liturgical Offices gathered together at day's beginning and end rather than spread more evenly throughout day and night as in Saint Benedict's model.

For most of our history we were two distinct communities. Men who entered the monastic novitiate were "choir monks." They prayed the lengthy Divine Office prescribed by the Rule of Benedict in Latin and had a protracted training of several years' duration before being ordained priests. The men who came with less formal education or were not interested in studies and ordination were called "lay brothers." During their novitiate they had periodic conferences from a monk appointed by the abbot to be the "brother master" but essentially got right down to work. These groups prayed separately, lived in different parts of the monastery, had separate places in the refectory, and gathered in different recreation rooms for conversation, reading the newspaper, and playing cards. The "fathers" wore clerical collars with their habits; the "brothers" did not. The brothers took more or less the same vows as the fathers, but theirs had a different, and lesser, canonical status. Brothers did not vote in the monastic chapter, where important business is done and abbots are elected. They were almost all craftsmen and laborers. Thomas Merton opined that the lay brothers at his Trappist monastery were probably leading the life Benedict had in mind.

With Vatican II the legal distinctions were abolished, and things started to become more integrated. The word is deliberate: "brothers' rights" echoed the larger social shifts in American culture toward greater equality, at least before the law. But as late as 1979 the brothers' mailboxes were still in the basement recreation room formerly reserved for them, while the fathers collected their mail in a recreation room just behind the abbey church on the main floor.

Shaping Monastic Identity

What has shaped our monastic identity? Our early monks had to copy out, in Latin, what were held to be the norms governing monastic life: the Rule, the Constitutions and Declarations of our congregation, and a work called the *Tyrocinium Religiosum*, a manual on monastic spirituality written by an eighteenth-century German abbot. This last, which outlined an approach to religious life similar to that of Jesuits and other modern orders, hung on until

An August picnic on chapel island in the 1890s. No sunscreen needed. The beer came from Cold Spring in barrels. Saint John's had no brewery.

Framed by the parabolic arches of the church banner, a cluster of monks carry the casket of a confrere from the Mass of resurrection to the hearse. Blanketing snow softens the lines of Benet Hall, the first college residence hall, and the Auditorium.

Vatican II, by which time many of its solemn prescriptions had become hopelessly irrelevant. A look through the books available to our community in its formative decades reveals little in the way of traditional monastic sources or spirituality. Non-liturgical prayer was described in terms taken from Counter-Reformation Catholic spirituality, and mysticism was firmly excluded as belonging only to those in contemplative (that is, truly cloistered) orders. Until Vatican II, devotional practices were those typical of the larger Catholic culture: Rosary, Stations, Adoration and Benediction of the Blessed Sacrament, litanies, and prayers appointed for special intentions. There was time appointed for "spiritual reading," normally meaning writings of a post-Reformation author rather than the Bible or patristic and monastic writings.

Some older confreres have noted that before Vatican II the terms "monk" and "monastic" were not as commonly used as they are now. We were the "Benedictine fathers and brothers" or "Benedictine religious." However we preferred to style ourselves, there was always the liturgy. An old saw reminds us, "The habit does not make the monk," but the liturgy does. From our founding we prayed the various Offices outlined by Saint Benedict, eight per day, making for the collective praying of more than the full 150 psalms each week. All this was done much more quickly than Benedict would have expected, lumped together at convenient times in a way that surely would have surprised him, but it was all there. To all this had been added daily celebrations of the Eucharist, customary since the early Middle Ages. The texts and chant of the liturgy were the primary transmitters of traditional Benedictine piety and were restored to something of their original (that is to say, medieval) integrity in the course of the nineteenth-century monastic reforms. At Saint John's the liturgy was celebrated in an increasingly solemn manner with the building of the original abbey church (now the Great Hall) in 1879–1882, its redecoration in the 1930s, and the construction of the new abbey church in 1958–1961.

European and American Benedictines led the church in rediscovering the spiritually formative shape of the liturgical year, of the traditional texts, and of the great complex of rituals in the Mass and other liturgies. The liturgical movement described by Bill Franklin in Chapter 6 had an impact here, too, not least through the publications emanating from Collegeville and, sometimes, even read here. The brothers pioneered some elements of the liturgical reform. Their communal prayer had evolved with the developing liturgical consciousness from devotional practices such as the Rosary to the praying of a "Little Office" loosely patterned on the traditional hours of prayer, and then to an English version of the traditional Benedictine Divine Office. In the 1950s an effort was made to bring the distribution of the Latin Offices more in line with liturgical principles.

CHANGE FROM LATIN TO ENGLISH

All this culminated in the first official permission to celebrate all liturgies in English, which soon led to the joining of the two separate praying communities into one. I've heard that some rebellious clerics (junior monks studying for ordination) had smuggled English Psalters into church to read surreptitiously as the psalms were chanted in Latin. That doesn't sound very easy, but the symbolism would have been potent. Soon the brothers moved from their chapel in the lower church to the larger choir of the upper church to join the clerical monks. They learned together a new way to pray the Office that would become

Monks at recreation, monks at work. Clockwise from the top, Vitus Bucher and Wendelin Luetmer at cards with Allan Bouley and Alfred Deutsch in the background; Bob Koopmann with piano student Kari Knuttila (Miss Minnesota in 2001); Aaron Raverty, editor at the Liturgical Press; Martin Schirber, Godfrey Diekmann, and Alfred Deutsch as painted by Bela Petheo.

distinctive to Saint John's: reciting the psalms slowly and reflectively, observing lengthy pauses after each psalm and reading. Centuries' worth of music and liturgical traditions were set aside for a radically simplified form of common prayer stripped to the barest essentials of hymn, a few well-chosen psalms (usually recited rather than sung), biblical readings, intercessions, and the Lord's Prayer. Gone was the chant, along with its familiar texts in antiphons (brief verses sung before and after each psalm), ancient hymns, responsories, and the like. Also gone were those vast tracts of psalmody to be gotten through as quickly as possible and the lumping together of Offices into convenient blocks of liturgy. The monks now gathered to celebrate a single liturgy with its own integrity and appropriateness for that particular time of day. The first common liturgy was moved from 4:45 a.m. to 7:00 a.m. The dozens of daily private Masses celebrated in the thirty-four small chapels of the lower church in addition to the formal "conventual Mass" gave way to one Eucharist at which ordained monks could "concelebrate."

For most of the community the changes seem to have been genuinely liberating. Some grieved the loss of chant or of Latin. The integration of the brothers and the clerical monks in the 1960s was surely the right step, but creating a single community was not always easy. I've heard some of the older brothers regret the loss of their smaller sub-community with its manifest respect for skilled work in trade and craft. But monks who did not feel called to priesthood could now pursue advanced degrees and teach in the university. Positions in community leadership were opened to the non-ordained.

When I came to Saint John's at the start of the 1980s, there was still a kind of anti-clericalism among younger monks (and some older ones), a legacy of the previous decade's struggles about liturgy, priesthood, and clerical privilege. Though it has softened, we still have some uncertainties and ambivalences about monastic priesthood. We have had many difficult conversations in the past few years about various addictions and sexual abuse. Having learned how to talk about such matters, we now find those topics to be less difficult than frank conversation about things like concelebration of the Mass or traditional Catholic devotions such as Benediction. For my generation, these issues are not nearly as highly charged as they are for some of our elders; for those in the next generation, even our wariness is incomprehensible. After forty years the marks of Vatican II and its aftershocks are still quite discernible.

Benedict Meets Freud and Associates

For twenty summers—from 1954 to 1973—Saint John's sponsored the Mental Health Institute for clergy of all faiths. Three one-week sessions each summer were funded by the Hamm Foundation, and year after year brought to the campus top psychiatrists from around the country. Men like Leo Bartemeier, Francis Braceland, Dana Farnsworth, Noel Mailloux, O.P., and Gregory Zilboorg became familiar figures on campus.

The gradual effect on the monastic community of their friendship and their conversation was informal but deep. Modern psychiatry, up to that time suspect as irreligious if not anti-religious, afforded new perspectives on separation from the world and penitential austerity. Restrictions on communication within the cloister and with the rest of the world melted away. "Vacation" entered our vocabulary, a concept that had earlier been held alien to monasticism. Going off campus for a ball game, a movie, dinner, a play, or a concert became permissible, even recommended.

It would be simplistic to attribute the large shift in monastic practice in the sixties and seventies to newfound respect for modern psychiatry alone; other factors were at play as well. Some monastic changes were simply due to the extraordinary size that the community had grown to and the practical need to let individual monks take care of their personal needs within broad guidelines. Whatever the forces for change, the result was gradually a culture more open to contemporary influences all the way from inter-faith dialogue to Monday night football.

Distinctive Monastic Spirituality

One of the greatest fruits of Vatican II for us was the renewal of our monastic identity as a distinctive gift to the church. Abbot Jerome Theisen's election in 1979 brought an experienced teacher of monastic spirituality who gave conferences on topics unfamiliar to those trained in preconciliar days. Abbot Jerome and his successor, Abbot Timothy Kelly, had both been novice masters. In their work of monastic formation as well as in their abbatial teaching they were advocates of *lectio divina,* the meditative reading of the Bible characteristic of monastic spirituality. *Lectio* was not a familiar concept to earlier generations of Saint John's monks raised on a spirituality that owed more to Jesuits or Carmelites than to Benedictines, but it has now become a staple for many of us. The recent popular success of Benedictine spirituality and the dramatic revival of our program for Oblates, lay people inspired by the Rule, have helped us gain a keener sense of what we're about and why it's important. Many monks have discovered simple forms of contemplation like "centering prayer" or the use of the Jesus Prayer. Everyone since the early 1980s has received a good dose of early monastic sources as background to study of the Rule.

My own monastic life has been deeply shaped by my work with those foundational texts, mostly from the Christian East. My contacts with Eastern Christians, especially in the Syriac and Byzantine traditions, help me to understand how much Benedict was a monk of the whole church, and his Rule a distillation of all that was best in monasticism of both East and West. We are fortunate to trace our origins to the undivided church, before Rome and Constantinople finally fell out in 1054 or the Reformation divided Western Christianity. Perhaps that is why so many people feel comfortable with Benedictine spirituality.

For all of that grand heritage, we have our very mundane realities. One of them is our community's tradition of hard work. One confrere, a very disciplined man, once described work as our principal asceticism. I think he meant this in a positive way, in that work hones our sense of ourselves before God, testing our limits and reminding us that we can't do all this alone. Fair enough. But work easily becomes our *only* asceticism. I worry about this, especially when I read about

Father Columba Stewart shows school of theology students the first printed edition of John Cassian's *Conferences,* published by the Brethren of the Common Life at Brussels in 1472.

Father Magnus Wenninger decorates the cloister with colorful polyhedrons for Christmas. He is a widely translated authority on solids formed by plane faces, and he estimates that he has fashioned 7,000 models since he got interested in the subject at Columbia Teachers College in 1961.

Brother Francis Peters worked twenty-seven years in the print shop and twenty-five years in the library, but he has never stopped working at his avocation, planting and tending borders and beds of summer flowers in the monastery garden.

Kathleen Norris—Oblate of Assumption Abbey at Richardton, North Dakota; twice resident scholar at the Ecumenical Institute; Presbyterian—draws a monastic lesson from visiting Father Omer Maus in the monastery retirement center, Saint Raphael's Hall.

It's a Sweet Life

At the end of the Monastic Institute one year, I paid a visit to one of my favorite people in the world, an elderly monk who is going blind. . . . He asked if I would come with him to call on another monk who had taken a bad fall the day before. This was a monk I'd not met, a priest who had only recently retired, in his mid-eighties, from many years of serving as a chaplain in a prison not far from the monastery. Other monks had spoken of this man with admiration, as someone who was humbly realistic about his ministry. "He knew that a lot of the prisoners came to Mass for something to do, just to get out of their cell," one young monk had told me, adding, "and that was enough for him. He just kept at it, hoping to do some good."

The nurse was leaving his room. She told us he'd been napping off and on all morning, awaiting transport to a nearby hospital for a CAT scan. He'd hit his head in the fall, and the doctors needed to know the extent of his injuries. I was nervous about disturbing a man who might be sleeping or in great pain, not wanting company. Nothing could have prepared me for what happened. Another nurse entered the room and called out, "You have a visitor. Two visitors." We heard a weak voice respond, "Ah . . . it's a sweet life." As we entered the room and he got a look at us, he said again, "It's a sweet life."

Gregory the Great tells a story in his *Dialogues* about a man who visited Saint Benedict in his hermitage, explaining that as it was Easter, he has brought a gift of food. Benedict says to him, "I know that it is Easter, for I have been granted the blessing of seeing you." Standing in the monastery nursing home, I felt that I'd just been blessed in the same earthshaking way. The monk's greeting was the epitome of Benedictine hospitality—in his Rule Benedict says simply, "All guests who present themselves are to be welcomed as Christ"—and it also brought home to me the incarnational nature of monasticism. It is not a theory or even a theology, but a way of life.

earlier monasticism (really, almost the whole history of it) with its emphasis on fasting, vigils, and other practices designed to focus attention on ultimate questions. In the North American world after Vatican II, it has all gone. Is an increasingly professionalized culture, even in ministry, really a substitute? We still joke about our German work ethic, but it looks now very much like the professional, achievement-oriented culture of American society. I'd like to see us find a way to weave the tradition more deliberately into who we are and what we do. We'll never be contemplatives or great ascetics—I couldn't stand more than a few days of strict solitude—but I would guess that our future viability will depend on presenting prospective members with a way of life more obviously different from that of our lay colleagues.

SHIFTS IN MONASTIC CULTURE

There are some signs of a shift in our monastic culture. We have more retired or semi-retired monks, which makes the monastery seem less frantic. Some of our newer members came with some experience of a career and with a desire for a more balanced life. The resistance, however, is great. What may have once been dictated by the conditions of the mission, and then by community custom, seems increasingly determined by forces beyond us: the decrease in vocations, the rise of professionalism, economic pressures. A smaller number of us seem to be doing more and more.

Although we talk a lot about work, we should also be talking about our leisure. By the time I arrived in Collegeville, monks had a fairly large degree of personal freedom. The liturgical changes of the 1960s had created more free time. Monks could now leave campus without special permission and could draw pocket money at the accounts office from a personal budget approved by the superior. Rules about personal radios or stereos and, eventually, even televisions were relaxed. Given more freedom, many have chosen to work more. Others devote time to hobbies or to watching TV or to some other form of relaxation. I don't sense that many devote a lot of their free time to prayer or spiritual reading. In common with most monasteries of our kind, we are finding that our forms of entertainment are becoming more and more like those of the culture around us. We see the same videos and TV shows, read the same books, can visit the same restaurants, stores, and Web sites. With the coming of the Internet, "separation from the world" has become even more challenging. I write this on a computer in my monastery room, with the *New York Times* just a click away. A click in another direction could find something considerably less edifying.

We've made a good start at addressing questions large and small about our monastic life. In the past thirty years we've learned a lot about the devastating effects of addiction to alcohol, prescription drugs, gambling, or the Internet. We help our

Benedictine Oblates of Saint John's Abbey

In chapter 58 of his Rule for monasteries, the chapter detailing how new members are to be received into the community, Saint Benedict states that above all other considerations, the novice master must first ascertain if the novice is truly seeking God. Oblates are men and women who "are truly seeking God," but within the framework of their daily lives outside a religious enclosure. They have affiliated themselves with a particular Benedictine community—men or women—and promised to guide their spiritual journey by the Rule of Benedict as far as their lives permit. They may be married or unmarried, Catholic or members of another Christian tradition.

Oblates do not make vows, but they do make a solemn promise to live out their commitment to the Rule. During the year of candidacy, Oblates are introduced to praying the liturgy of the hours and to the practice of *lectio divina* (spiritual reading). They study the Rule with the aid of the Oblate director and a commentary on the Rule written for Oblates. At the end of the year of candidacy, they make their final oblation or final commitment to model their journey to God on the Rule of Saint Benedict. Saint John's Oblates and candidates are invited to attend a retreat in July. Oblate days of recollection are planned for Advent and Lent. Local groups meet monthly at Saint John's and in Minneapolis, Fargo, Faribault, and Park Rapids.

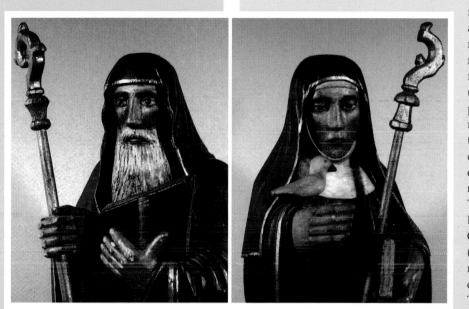

Saint Benedict and Saint Scholastica, 18-inch wood carvings by Cornelius Wittmann, O.S.B.

Several early abbots attempted to introduce the Oblate program to Saint John's, but it was the fifth abbot, Alcuin Deutsch, who in 1926 invested fifty women and men as Oblate candidates. He began the tradition of the annual Oblate retreat in July; he published the highly popular *Manual for Benedictine Oblates;* he inaugurated the *Oblate Newsletter,* still being published.

Today over 700 Oblates are affiliated with Saint John's Abbey. They live everywhere from Canada to New Mexico, from New York to California. They are located as far away as Australia, New Zealand, India, Malaysia, and the Philippines. An SJU alumnus, Ned Aarriola '81, is responsible for introducing the Oblate program to Saipan in the Mariana Islands in the South Pacific. Today the group numbers over fifty Oblates and candidates.

The first international Congress of Benedictine Oblates was scheduled for September 2005 at the Colegio di Sant' Anselmo in Rome under the local direction of Father Luigi Bertocchi, a monk of Saint John's, who is the Oblate director of Sant' Anselmo, the international headquarters of the Benedictine Order.

Service

One of Benedict's simplest imperatives is "let the brothers serve one another" (Chapter 35, first paragraph). The daily connections forged through serving food to one another, caring for the sick, reading in church or refectory form the web of community and provide much of its strength. No one in Benedict's monastery was to think himself above the obligation to serve even if some might be excused from one form of service or another because of infirmity or other duties. Saint Basil the Great had one of the richest insights into the theological value of the common life, and Benedict is his heir: life in common provides the best possible opportunity for fulfilling the commandments by serving Christ in one another (cf. Matt 25:35-40).

Benedict's teaching on service is theologically profound, for he recognized Christ in both one who serves (e.g. the abbot, Chapter 2, first paragraph; Chapter 63, second paragraph) and those who are served (the sick, Chapter 36, first paragraph; the visitor, Chapter 53). He hopes that his monks will develop altruistic reflexes, naturally placing the needs of others before their own (Chapter 72, first paragraph). Such a reflexive consideration for others requires training at every stage of monastic development. Therefore many of Benedict's "Tools for Good Works" (Chapter 4) are directed toward service of those in need. These are not ideals, but exercises for building up virtue.

Benedict also recognized that the members of the community would provide spiritual care for one another as *senpectae* or as trusted guides (Chapter 4, eighth paragraph; Chapter 27, first paragraph; Chapter 46, second paragraph); he did not reserve all pastoral work to the abbot.

Benedict concludes his famous chapter on "Good Zeal" with the hope that Christ 'may bring us all together *(pariter)* to everlasting life' (Chapter 72, first paragraph). The adverb he uses, *pariter,* can mean either "together" or "equally". A few sentences later, at the very end of the Rule, he reverts to the intimate form of address with which the Prologue began, speaking directly to the individual (Chapter 73, second paragraph). Benedict maintains his dual focus on individual vocation and communal life right to the end.

Columba Stewart, O.S.B.
(The Benedictine Handbook. Collegeville: Liturgical Press, 2003)

new members sort out who they are, spiritually, emotionally, sexually, and then help them to see how their discoveries fit into monastic life. Over the years we have typically dealt with our differences like good American males, more by coexistence than by anything more explicit or deliberate. Things were shaken up by the sexual abuse crisis, and we were forced to hear things about one another and our common past that were deeply disturbing, humbling, and embarrassing. We've learned that we live here with both perpetrators and victims of sexual abuse. We can acknowledge that in our community there are monks who are straight and monks who are gay and some who are not sure. For many of us the crisis is starting to feel like a grace, however harsh. A Trappist author once commented that he liked coming to Saint John's because he detected nary a whiff of spiritual pride. We had plenty of other kinds, and much of the non-spiritual pride we may have been carrying simply evaporated. Perhaps what is left in its place is something curiously like what Benedict called humility and regarded as the chief marker of the monk.

So what has all this made us as monks now halfway through our second century? This community is blessed with tolerance, good humor, encouragement of talent, and support for failure. We are not remotely perfect in any of those qualities, but based on what I've seen in the broader monastic world, we are very fortunate. If it has made us less than exemplary as ascetics, it has made us very human—and humane—in the common life. Pace the confrere who identified work as our principal asceticism, Saint Benedict knew what we learn soon enough, namely, that our greatest asceticism is putting up with one another and moving beyond simple forbearance to compassion and even love. I came to the monastery to seek God, but I also sought acceptance and love. Each night, when I thank God for the wonders of the day, I have to admit that I've found what I came for.

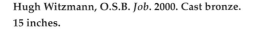

Hugh Witzmann, O.S.B. *Job.* **2000. Cast bronze.**
15 inches.

My Funeral

Brother Gregory
takes pride
in his caskets: no silks,
no satin quilting, pillowed lining,
inlaid arabesques. Only
the chastity of local pine,
sealed black,
without the sheen of polish
to soften the finality;
a new white sheet
on the bottom for a bed,
a prop for the head,
a fitted cover
to shield my ugly face,
and I am ready
to be lowered to eternity,
with the monks chanting
glad hosannas,
dropping clumps
of Stearns County,
pebbles of joy,
eight feet down
drumming on my box,
thumping on my boards,
staccato at the end.

If you return some day,
you can find my place
toward the top,
just before the hill
runs out of space,
as though I died in a December hurry
—late again—
before the ground
gave out.

It is a comfortable place
to rest, if you must
speak of comfort
—your word, not mine—
I could mention
the view of the lake
beneath the hill.
You cannot see far,
but the chapel
across the waters
commands the further
wooded shore
where dogwood
bends into the maples.

But this is thin soup,
my friend.
You cannot warm me
in my grave
with dried crusts,
after the revelers
have staggered
out the door;
nor with woods and lakes
however radiant,
though when I was with you
they claimed me,
fed my starvations.

But if you pass this way
along the lake,
by the narrow of the road
as the ground rises to a swell,
and wonder what keeps
young blood here
till they drop,
stop just before the gate,
look up the hill.
See the raw cross,
accusing and salvaging,
black against the sky.
Beneath the marshal of headstones
—our Omaha beach—
the damaged lilies of the field,
who toiled in song,
spun in penitence,
fighting with me,
for me, against me,
but gathered in praise,
dwelling in unity.

They come like
young stags
thirsting for water.

Kilian McDonnell, O.S.B.

CHAPTER THREE

"A Scientific, Educational, and Ecclesiastical Institution"

Joseph Farry

THE NOVEMBER 1857 BEGINNING was inauspicious: five students huddled together in a log cabin overlooking the Mississippi as young Father Cornelius Wittmann drilled them in the fundamentals of a classical education. Minnesota was not yet a state. The ink on the charter for "Saint John's Seminary," granted by the territorial legislature in March, was scarcely dry. Yet Father Cornelius, inspired by the Benedictine educational tradition, was determined that his students learn to conjugate Latin verbs and master German grammar.

Of this early period of the school, Father Alexius Hoffmann, abbey chronicler, was to write half a century later:

> The new institution had been chartered as a Seminary, but as that designation was not familiar to the public, the name "College" soon came into vogue. It was not a pretentious college; the buildings, staff and equipment were lacking—but all beginnings are small and the founders were confident that its future was assured (*Saint John's University, 1857–1907*, 7).

After the Benedictines had established their home on the shores of Saint Louis Lake—it would only be named Lake Sagatagan thirty years later—the college was organized in two divisions, offering courses that might today be taught in

On the church plaza Father Vincent Tegeder, historian and archivist, chats with a visitor in the afternoon sunshine with the façade of the 1882 church, now the Great Hall, for a background.

A Frontier College

Above all, Saint John's University acted as a frontier outpost for the training of candidates for the priesthood. By the turn of the century scores of priests had completed their work in the seminary department, and two of them had become bishops—Joseph Cotter of the Winona diocese and John Shanley of Jamestown, the new ecclesiastical division of the state of North Dakota.

The growth of settlement in Minnesota and the Dakotas during the 1870s and 1880s provided opportunities for trained business personnel in the growing towns. Saint John's organized a well-developed commercial course, which culminated in the granting of a special master of accounts diploma. . . . Courses of twelve lectures on commercial law by some of the outstanding lawyers in the state and four on banking formed part of the program. By 1897 a total of 522 students had enrolled in the commercial department. Merchants, entrepreneurs, and bankers in many of the expanding communities in the Upper Midwest received their training at Saint John's.

Among alumni so prepared were John and Edward Zapp (1884 and 1889) of the Zapp State Bank of Saint Cloud; John Hoeschen (1878), an early merchant at Freeport; Christopher Borgerding (1877) of the Bank of Belgrade; Francis A. Gross (1889) of the Northwestern National Bank of Minneapolis; and Herman J. Terhaar (1891) of the State Bank of New Munich.

True to the Benedictine tradition, the Minnesota monks made it possible for needy but promising boys to receive an education. The financial statement for the school year 1883–84 indicates that 43 students out of an enrollment of 203 received board, clothing, and instruction without charge.

The expansion of the school encouraged the development of a library, and by 1885 six thousand volumes were available. The formation of literary and debating societies followed naturally, and a college journal, the Saint John's University *Record*, made its first appearance toward the end of January 1888.

Vincent Tegeder, O.S.B., '33, from "Pioneer Monks," *Minnesota History* 33 (1952) 54.

◄ A group of Saint John's–Saint Ben's biology faculty members—Manuel Campos, Philip Chu in the back, Sister Jeanne Marie Lust, seated as befits the chair, Charles Rodell, and Elizabeth Wurdak—happily gather under the gaze of Albert, the college specimen of *Oreamnos americanus*.

high school, college, and divinity school. From the start their primary purpose was to prepare young men for the priesthood. Lay students could complete the classical course and earn a bachelor's degree. This degree was advertised as an excellent preparation for the professions, but not many young men from frontier towns chose to enroll.

In retrospect we can almost hear Father Wolfgang Northman, the first president, saying, "This will never do," and coming to the conclusion that to attract lay students, the school had to offer some down-to-earth vocational training. The result was that in 1872 the monks launched a one-year commercial course (and a class on telegraphy) for boys who had completed eight years of schooling. In addition, until 1919 Saint John's continued to accept boys as young as nine who needed to complete their elementary education. This multi-level institution was dignified with the title "university" by legislative enactment in 1883.

The pragmatic response of the early monks to the requirements of frontier life left a permanent imprint on the Benedictine educational enterprise at Collegeville. Balancing their Old World experience with the realities of American life, the monks learned to trust experience over theory, to value experimentation over tradition, and to focus on short-term challenges rather than long-term goals.

When Saint John's celebrated its fiftieth anniversary in 1907, Father Alexius could write that the "institution looks complacently over the work accomplished" (Hoffmann, 155). Of the 303 students enrolled, 32 were in the seminary program. The largest number of students were enrolled in the commercial department, which in 1906 had been expanded to two years in recognition that "without an ordinary fundamental education, the knowledge of bookkeeping was a pure snare and a delusion" (Hoffmann, 139). Only three students were listed as graduates of what we would today identify as the college, but under Abbot Peter Engel (1894–1921) the campus was acquiring such college facilities

The bookstore in 1898 carried books. The rest of the stock is harder to identify in this photo, although there appear to be paper and ink on the table in the foreground, and quite a nice lamp. No Johnny sweatshirts. The monastic manager is unidentified.

as a library (1901), a gymnasium (1901), an infirmary (1907), and a science building (1910).

Alexius was somewhat apologetic that "the Theological Seminary, which is small in number, is excellent in work" with only [!] 335 young men ordained priests during the first fifty years. What he did not note was that Saint John's Seminary was the first Catholic seminary in Minnesota and, until the Saint Paul Seminary was founded in 1894, the only one. The priests educated at Saint John's in that first half century served in dioceses throughout the region. As if to say that the school could count other measures of success besides ordination, Alexius pointed with pride to the three members of the 1907 Minnesota legislature who had attended Saint John's.

Completion of Benet Hall signaled an expanded commitment to collegiate education.

ABBOT ALCUIN DEUTSCH RESTRUCTURES THE SCHOOL

The early period of educational endeavor ended with the election of Abbot Alcuin Deutsch in 1921. He restructured the university as three schools: a preparatory school, a college of arts and sciences, and a seminary, each with its own dean, while he retained the abbot's role as president. Completion of Benet Hall as a dormitory for college lay students signaled an expanded commitment to collegiate education. The commercial college was discontinued, even though it was a significant source of enrollment.

Abbot Alcuin considered twentieth-century monasticism "chiefly a spiritual power, and in spiritual matters not quantity so much as quality counts" (*The Record*, May 1922). An alternative to the American secular college, Saint John's University would not be distinguished by a large enrollment but would be an ideal Catholic residential college, characterized by the moral, spiritual, and intellectual mentorship provided by the Benedictine community.

But the faculty, virtually all Benedictines, also had to take into account their students' educational preparation and ambitions. They tinkered with the

This lithograph from the 1910 college catalogue shows the academic buildings then in place: Quad, library, gymnasium. In 1910 a three-story science hall was completed next to the gymnasium. In 1937 the gym was moved 100 feet west, widened, and relieved of its Victorian battlements.

Walter Reger served as interim dean of the college when Virgil Michel died unexpectedly in 1938. He taught church history. He became known to generations of students as director of the alumni association in the decades following World War II. For years he lived on first Benet amid a clutter of books and papers, bed in one room, desk in the other, bathroom down the hall. He always had time for conversation—with students, their parents, his colleagues, alumni—the stream of people for whom he represented Saint John's at its warmest and most human. He was a valued confidant of Abbot Baldwin Dworschak and an advocate of entrepreneurship in the booming 50s and 60s. He sparked the sale of Saint John's bread commercially.

curriculum, seeking to balance the traditional classical curriculum of language and historical studies with the disciplines of Scholastic philosophy, religion, natural science, music, and fine arts. With equal energy, they offered students a full range of practical commercial and bookkeeping classes.

The Benedictine sisters in Saint Joseph had faced similar curricular and practical questions when they opened the College of Saint Benedict for women in 1913. Yet these two Benedictine communities did not engage in extensive conversation about their common challenges. Following their European traditions and existing American practice, both communities viewed the education of women and men as separate enterprises.

No account of the decade of the 1930s can overlook the impact of Father Virgil Michel, whose visionary leadership in implementing the liturgical movement brought national recognition to Saint John's. Father Virgil served as dean of the college for four years and envisioned Saint John's offering a radical alternative to the existing pragmatic American model of higher education. The Great Books curriculum advocated by Mortimer Adler and Robert Hutchins attracted him. He corresponded with Adler and was planning a pilot program involving twenty students when he died unexpectedly in November 1938.

IDEALS IN A TIME OF CHANGE

Ironically, it was the end of the Second World War and the opportunity to expand the student body that would ultimately undo Abbot Alcuin's educational vision. In August 1946 he reiterated his stand. Saint John's objective was "not merely to impart intellectual training, but also to develop character, inculcate a deep religious understanding, and build habits which are the mark of the Christian gentleman, through common participation in the liturgy of the church, common meals in the dining room, and general participation in a wide variety of campus activities" (*The Record*, August 29, 1946).

Returning veterans, however, contributed a different dynamic to campus life. Between September 1945 and September 1946 and then again in the following year, enrollment in the college doubled, with more than half the student body registered as freshmen. The curriculum was adjusted so veterans could graduate in two years. More than three hundred students lived off-campus, beyond the direct influence of their monastic mentors. The vision of Saint John's as an academic community offering an alternative lifestyle conflicted with the determination of many ex-GIs to reenter quickly into American secular life.

Growing enrollment became a catalyst for change. Reluctantly, Abbot Alcuin approved the acquisition of former military barracks for temporary student housing. By 1949 it became clear that something more permanent was needed. Saint John's sought financial help from alumni and friends as well as federal funding to build a new college dorm, Saint Mary's Hall. The era of self-sufficiency had come to an end.

During his last five years in office, the abbot had to attend to other changes in long-standing practice. Integrating the academic programs of the preparatory school and the college was increasingly difficult. In 1948 the two institutions published separate catalogs for the first time, although personnel and financial planning were not to be fully disentangled until the early 1960s. In 1949, under the prodding of the dean, Father Martin Schirber, the abbot reluctantly agreed that Saint John's should seek accreditation by—and accept the scrutiny of—the "secular" North Central Association.

Questions also arose about the abbey's continuing sponsorship of the seminary. In 1949 Abbot Alcuin and Bishop Peter Bartholome agreed that the Diocese of Saint Cloud would construct a house of studies on the Saint John's campus and assume joint responsibility for the seminary curriculum and formation program.

New Abbot and New Plans

The cornerstone of the new structure, now Emmaus Hall, was laid in 1950. Abbot Alcuin resigned late that fall. His successor, Baldwin Dworschak, and the monastic community quickly accepted the inevitability of growth and change. Within two years the abbey announced an international architectural competition to meet immediate needs and to develop a campus plan for the long term. This bold act of confidence in the future was reflected in academic changes in the college.

Enrollment expanded throughout the decade of the 1950s by an average of fifty students a year. The faculty response included developing theology courses sensitive to the concerns of laypeople. Saint John's was among the first Catholic colleges to transform traditional catechetical classes into courses focused on deepening students' appreciation of theological inquiry and reflection. The curriculum also expanded to include new academic departments and majors. Faculty members new from graduate school were bent on reforming academic practice to meet national norms. The social science faculty, for example, rejected the practice of seeking the bishop's permission to assign titles that were on the Index of Forbidden Books. (The library copies of these books continued to be shelved in a locked room—the "Hell Library"—until the Index was abolished by the Vatican in 1967.)

Because of the growing complexity of his monastic and academic responsibilities, Abbot Baldwin turned over the presidency of the university to Father Arno Gustin in 1958 and took the title of university chancellor. This change triggered a wide-ranging discussion of how to assure the monastic character of the college while establishing its autonomous administration. National consultants provided guidance on how to disentangle monastic and university governance and to create new budgetary and administrative structures. The new president formed a board of lay advisors, the associate board of trustees, as one of his first acts. While it lacked any legal responsibility, this board brought a wider perspective to managing the college. Difficult questions had to be answered: Would the senior council of the monastery continue to exercise ultimate supervisory control? Should the college operate under an independent annual budget? Would the abbot continue to approve the teaching assignments of monk-professors?

Marcel Breuer came to Saint John's in 1953 in response to Abbot Baldwin Dworschak's search for an architect to do a comprehensive plan for the growing campus. The two men became good friends, recognizing in each other similar tastes and a shared esthetic—simple materials honestly used—not far from Saint Benedict's notion of humility. They talk here against a background of buildings—the old church, the link to Benet Hall, the north windows of the Quad—that Breuer's plan would have replaced in time.

Marcel Breuer's comprehensive plan reoriented the campus to the north, where access to the interstate highway then on the drawing board would require a new entrance. In time—this was touted as a hundred-year plan—most of the old buildings would be replaced. Only the dark-colored structures in this model would remain. Focal point of the plan was the proposed church, which in this first model already exhibits the distinctive character of the completed structure.

Planners envisioned that the college would grow by fifty students a year until it reached 1,650.

When I arrived at Saint John's in the fall of 1961, the faculty and administrators were busily working together in committees and study groups reviewing the curriculum, the academic calendar, future enrollment goals, student quality, and the coordination of preparatory school and college personnel decisions. A consensus emerged from these discussions. While the college would have financial and administrative autonomy from the monastery, the members of the monastic community would continue to make up the majority of the faculty and the administration. Since the preparatory school had increased its enrollment to 390 students, the abbey laid plans for a separate prep campus, thus altering the historical integration of the tripartite university.

Planners envisioned that the college would grow by fifty students a year until it reached 1,650. Although the goal was to recruit increasingly well-qualified students, Saint John's did not aim at becoming an elite college. Qualified laypersons would be recruited for the faculty; Saint John's was among the first Catholic colleges to subscribe publicly to the AAUP's Statement on Academic Freedom. In 1963 the university secured North Central approval to offer graduate degrees in theology to build on the success of the Benedictine Institute of Sacred Theology (BIST), which originated at the College of Saint Benedict in 1958 to provide advanced theological education for religious sisters.

During Father Arno's presidency a dialogue began about establishing common educational policies with the College of Saint Benedict. A 1963 agreement permitted students to enroll in classes on the other campus when space was available. Thus began an experiment in cooperation that gradually became unique in American higher education.

When Father Colman Barry became president in 1964, there was great optimism that Saint John's would successfully make the transition from a small monastic college to a liberal arts college of national standing. Construction of a new library was underway, and planning had already begun for a science building and additional dormitories, all financed by federal grants and loans. Father Colman brought national attention to Saint John's by initiating the Hill Monastic Manuscript Library, promoting the Institute for Ecumenical and Cultural Research founded by Father Kilian McDonnell, and starting Minnesota Educational Radio, later Minnesota Public Radio, on campus.

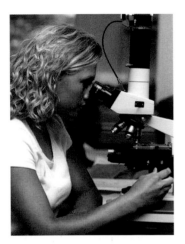

This 1967 photo shows two buildings not in Marcel Breuer's original plan, the library (1964) and the science building (1965), named for two abbots, Alcuin Library and Peter Engel Science Center.

Peter Froehle, physics and math teacher at the prep school since 1959, and Father Gordon Tavis, head of the school, the most recent of his many services in the community.

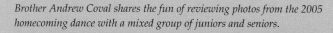

Brother Paul-Vincent Niebauer runs through notes on a summer circus camp rehearsal with performers in the tent pitched on the prep playing field.

The Prep School Today

In the late summer of 1962, when school would normally begin, prep school students were told to report a few weeks late because the new buildings on Observatory Hill were not quite finished. Father Gregory (then Cuthbert) Soukup '32 was headmaster, and he welcomed the 356 students to the new location, a four-level academic building stepping down the slope of the hill and a 55,000 square-foot dormitory, initially modeled on the austerity of Gordonstoun by architect Val Michelson, later made more comfortable and multipurpose as the number of day students grew and boarding students declined.

The 1960s were booming years for the prep school. The largest number of students enrolled for a single year in the prep school's 150-year history was 374 in 1963–64. The largest graduating class was 94 in 1969, the same year in which the distinction between priesthood and non-priesthood students was dropped.

Students from Saint Benedict's Academy had been taking classes at Saint John's Preparatory School for a number of years in the late 1960s and early 1970s. When the academy closed in the spring of 1973, it seemed logical to invite the girls to enroll at the prep school. The class of 1974 included the first female graduates.

In 1966 the exchange program with the Benedictine school in Melk, Austria, began. The longest-running high school exchange program in the U.S. will celebrate its fortieth anniversary at Melk in June 2006. It was established as one of the serendipitous results of Father Oliver Kapsner's HMML filming of monastic manuscripts in Austria; it continues today as one of the hallmarks of the prep school.

Throughout the last thirty years the prep school has strengthened and expanded its international niche, welcoming and enrolling more than fifty students from fifteen countries in 2004–2005. The percentage of international students at the prep school makes it among the most diverse student populations, by percent, of any school in America, college or high school.

In the last decade two important facilities have been added to the academic building—the Weber Center in 1997 and the Meyers Center in 2000—to provide a performance space open to the public and science classrooms and labs independent of the college facilities.

Middle school classes began in 1997 under the leadership of Father Mark Thamert '69. Local parents recruited the first twenty-one students. The middle school will observe its tenth anniversary during Saint John's 150th year.

On a final note: since 2002 the prep school has annually enrolled more than three hundred students for the first time since the 1960s.

Brother Herard Jean-Noel, a native of Haiti, points to specifics about applying the Beatitudes for Pablo from Mexico, Wei Che from Taiwan, Yan from China, Taka and Fumiko from Japan.

Brother Andrew Coval shares the fun of reviewing photos from the 2005 homecoming dance with a mixed group of juniors and seniors.

Stephen Benedict Humphrey '29, went to the University of Minnesota for an MA in English, taught briefly, served in the army during World War II, and returned to Saint John's as a college prof after the war. From 1946 to 1982 he was "Mr. Humphrey" to his students at SJU and CSB. He was a model teacher—accessible, reliably informed in the subjects he taught, precise but not fussy in what he expected of students, and an advocate of speaking in complete sentences. He was discriminating in his judgments and a connoisseur of politics and baseball. He lived in a student room on ground-floor Benet for twenty-five years, then moved to the new Bernard Hall as a faculty resident and highly valued advisor. In his later years he was occasionally seen without a tie.

Jon Hassler recalls Steve Humphrey

Besides being a superb teacher of literature, Steve Humphrey taught the Teaching Methods course I took when I attended Saint John's fifty years ago. Not that he taught us very much. I remember that we six or eight would-be high school teachers spent most of our time diagramming difficult sentences on the blackboard. And yet his style of addressing us was so engaging that I carried it away and used it during my forty-two years in the classroom. It was easy enough to imitate—simply look your students in the eye and converse with them, don't lecture.

And isn't that what we carry away from our teachers after all—their methods of engaging us, their demeanor, their disposition? I recall the tartan skirts worn by my sixth-grade teacher Miss Johnson, but nothing of the subject matter she taught. I remember the businesslike manner of Mr. Eckstein in math class, but none of the principles of solid geometry. I also remember Steve's habit of bending his head down and turning it left and right, like someone trying to rid himself of a crick in the neck. I am convinced that if any of my two thousand students will remember me, it will be for my habit of looking them in the eye and conversing with them—a habit I owe to Steve Humphrey.

Jon Hassler '55

GETTING TOGETHER WITH THE COLLEGE OF SAINT BENEDICT

With Father Colman's encouragement, the faculty undertook a thorough revision of the curriculum and calendar in cooperation with the College of Saint Benedict. The new curriculum, approved in the spring of 1967, eliminated all specific general requirements except for freshman English and a course in theology. Students were encouraged to select courses that were most relevant to their personal lives, including more courses in theology. The colleges adopted a new calendar. Saturday morning classes ended; students took only four courses each semester; January was set aside for concentrated study of one topic.

Student life underwent a metamorphosis during the 1960s. Traditional freshman orientation (and hazing) ended abruptly when the freshman class of 1963 boycotted the opening convocation conducted by the sophomore class. (The incoming class had read John Kennedy's *Profiles in Courage* before they arrived on campus!) In 1968 the role of the monks living on each dormitory floor was changed from disciplinarian to mentor and confidant, with an emphasis on encouraging students to use their new freedoms responsibly. Nor was Collegeville isolated from broader cultural changes of the 1960s—the Age of Aquarius. Students arrived on campus with an innate skepticism about all authority and institutions and with changing standards regarding alcohol consumption, drug use, and premarital sex.

FIRST LAY ADMINISTRATOR

But every age of radical transformation is followed by an era of consolidation. The decade of the 1970s was such a period. In choosing a successor for Colman Barry in 1971, the abbot and his council considered appointing a lay president. Naming Dr. Jack Lange to the new position of academic vice president in 1969 had established a precedent for appointing a layperson to a major administrative position. In appointing Father Michael Blecker president, the abbot reaffirmed monastic leadership in the university, but Michael's appointment did not halt the process of laicization of the faculty and staff. By 1979 laypeople were the majority of the faculty, and a National Advisory Council, composed of distinguished academics from across the country, probably had greater influence on academic policy than any monastic group.

Even Marcel Breuer's much-regarded one hundred-year architectural vision for Saint John's was modified. The century-old Quadrangle was not torn down but renovated. Subsequently both the auditorium and the 1910 science building were renovated, with careful attention to the rules of historic preservation. Breuer's Bauhaus concrete was just going to have to live with the homemade brick and the local architecture of Saint John's monastic past.

A tribute to three fine teachers

Thomas More: You'd be a fine teacher.
Richard Rich: And if I was, who would know it?
Thomas More: You, your pupils, your friends, God. Not a bad public.
Robert Bolt, A Man for All Seasons

Tom Creed (Psychology), Linda Mealey (Psychology), and Jim Murphy (Political Science) epitomized good teaching and died too young. Three colleagues remember them.

Tom Creed, 1977–1999, by Michael Livingston

Tom Creed was never afraid to try something new. And he had an impish sense of humor. Tom was a behaviorist by training, and for his entire time here he taught the upper-division Principles of Learning and Behavior course. Early in his career he would come to his Principles class dressed in pink tights and a cape, as Mr. Behaviorman, a superhero. While his colleagues thought this was hysterically funny, he eventually abandoned his act. Students did not seem to get as much out of it as he had hoped they would.

For many years after Mr. Behaviorman disappeared, Tom continued to hold the Rat Olympics in his Principles course. During the semester, students would train rats to run a complex maze, using the concepts they learned in the course. At the end of the semester, an Olympics was held, the winning rat (and the rat's trainers) earning fame and prizes.

Tom never ceased experimenting, always searching for better ways to teach. He later went on to be one of the first users of computer technology in the classroom and a recognized national leader in this area. This was Tom through and through: curious, irrepressible, alive.

Linda Mealey, 1985–2002, by Aubrey Immelman

Linda Mealey cared about the truth, about scientific work, and about making sure that we were precise and accurate. She passionately advocated that our study of gender issues respect biological differences between the sexes as well as the social construction of gender. Even so, she was quick to remind us, the evolutionary roots and biological basis of human behavior were not tantamount to moral justification.

Linda cared deeply about her teaching and scholarship. In her final weeks, knowing full well that the end was near, she continued discussing unfinished collaborative projects with students and colleagues. The three unifying themes in her remarkable life and work were her love of nature, her devotion to truth, and her abiding sense of ethical responsibility.

And even in the face of her own mortality, Linda remained the consummate scientist. She could step back from the disease that was claiming her life and express disappointment that the tumor was rather unremarkable, with no prospect of stimulating new scientific discovery that might lead to a cure for others.

Jim Murphy, 1976–2003, by Dave Bennetts

Great teachers come in a variety of packages. Some go so quietly about their business that they barely create a ripple, and students and colleagues often miss the greatness. Others storm through their days, leaving in their considerable wake students and colleagues who know they've witnessed something special but aren't sure yet they want to label it "greatness." Jim Murphy was of the latter variety. I remember his loud response to a student who asked if there wasn't some article he could read that would summarize the ideological origins of the American Revolution: "No, you've got to read the STUFF!!" The student was in a course I team-taught with Jim and others, and so I knew that the STUFF to which he referred included the works of Hobbes, Descartes, Locke, Blackstone—not easy reads, certainly not for first-year students. But Jim demanded and expected a lot of his "kids," and he knew they could do it. And they knew he expected them to. In reference to the assigned readings for the above-mentioned course, a considerable list, Jim announced to the class one day, "And I better not hear that any of you ever sold any one of these books." I bet most didn't.

The most significant long-term decisions made during the 1970s related to academic cooperation with the College of Saint Benedict. In 1968 a team of consultants headed by Dr. Louis Mayhew recommended the merger of Saint John's and the College of Saint Benedict. Three years later this recommendation was set aside, and a strategy of pragmatic and incremental co-institutionalization was adopted. This approach ensured that both schools would maintain their identity as single-sex colleges and their distinctive graduation requirements while seeking the maximum benefit from integrated academic programs.

GRADUAL INTEGRATION OF TWO COLLEGES

During the next thirty years the two colleges made a series of incremental but critical moves to strengthen integration. A joint registrar's office and a single catalog were established. A single director of libraries was appointed. College admissions gradually came under a single head. The business offices devised a complicated accounting formula to balance out instructional costs. Extensive debates concerned where to locate each academic department. In the natural sciences they went for consolidation: chemistry and nutrition at the new Ardolf Science Center at the College of Saint Benedict, biology and physics at Saint John's. Each college maintained separate fine arts and music facilities. Most departments elected to divide their presence between the campuses.

In 1986 the department of economics and business administration split into three departments—accounting, economics, and management—and with offices on both campuses management quickly enrolled the largest number of students in the graduating class at Saint John's. Some saw development of this department as much in harmony with the pragmatic approach evidenced more than a century earlier in the 1872 commercial course.

The appointment of Father Hilary Thimmesh as president in 1982 signaled Saint John's continued confidence in its traditional mission as a regional residential liberal arts college. Saint John's non-urban location and extensive investment in dormitories reinforced this commitment. What was different was the appointment of Sister Eva Hooker, C.S.C., from Saint Mary's College in South Bend, as academic vice president in 1983. Twenty years earlier Saint John's was truly a male-only college in terms of students, faculty, and staff. Now women were involved prominently and significantly in the classroom and in the administration and staff.

At the same time the decreasing ability of Saint John's Abbey to provide the personnel and financial support needed to sustain the university's historic mission had to

Jennifer Galovich, mathematics, was chair of the Joint Faculty Assembly in 2002–2003. Of the experience she says: "After my first JFA meeting as chair, one of my colleagues wished me well in the job of 'herding the faculty cats.' That's a pretty good description! Within a week I had to ask for an upgrade in the size of my electronic mailbox, and it seemed that the phone never stopped ringing." She adds that meeting many colleagues was one of the best parts of the job, and that she was also involved in many meetings with the provost and served as SJU faculty regent for two years. She sums up: "In retirement, I think I may join the diplomatic corps!"

be formally recognized. In 1984 new governance documents articulated a Benedictine preference in hiring. At the same time a restructured board of regents, the latter-day descendant of Arno Gustin's associate board of trustees, was given greater legal responsibility for the academic policies and financial viability of the university.

The academic life of the college was also fundamentally changed in 1988. The Saint John's faculty joined with the College of Saint Benedict faculty in creating a common core curriculum. This pivotal decision required both colleges to review and revise many of their traditional practices. During their discussions on how to supervise and manage the common curriculum, members of both faculties renewed their shared educational ideals, rooted in the Benedictine educational tradition. After some experimentation (and frustration), a system of joint faculty governance of the curriculum was put in place. Finally, existing differences in workloads, salary, and fringe benefit policies were resolved.

In 1994, following the recommendation of a faculty committee, the presidents of the two institutions appointed Dr. Clark Hendley as the first joint academic provost to oversee the merged curriculum. Thus after thirty years of discussion and debate, Saint John's and the College of Saint Benedict achieved a form of academic merger that is as unusual as it was unanticipated.

SCHOOL OF THEOLOGY FOR MEN AND WOMEN

While undergraduate education was being transformed, graduate and seminary education also took a new direction. From 1978 to the present, the school of theology (SOT), with the combined mission and resources of the school of divinity and the graduate school, has carried forward its mission of training lay and ordained ministers for the church. The offerings during the academic year have been complemented by a six-week summer term. In 1988 the Diocese of Saint Cloud returned the administration of the seminary program to Saint John's. At that time the graduate program in theological education and ministry formation became known as "Saint John's University School of Theology and Seminary." In 1999 governance of the SOT was expanded from a committee of the board of regents to a board of trustees.

The student body of the SOT typically has ranged from 90 to 100 full-time equivalent students. In 1983 the ratio of seminary students to lay men and women ministry students was 80/20; by 1993 this ratio was reversed. In recent years the number of non-residential students has increased. The format in which courses are offered has expanded to meet the needs of non-traditional students: evening and weekend classes as well as courses via the worldwide Web have become important elements in the program. The SOT has a strong reputation in the areas of liturgy and monastic studies. Numerous students have benefited from its Jerusalem program, which was initiated in 1973 by Fathers Thomas Wahl and Luke Steiner. This program was shifted to Turkey and Greece in 2000 because of heightened unrest in the Holy Land.

The Mind Is the Great Poem of Winter

Say the winter plover walks barefoot in melting
snow, stretches its slender neck then runs

And stops and lifts its head as if searching for an opening

Say the neighbor man walks with his canes and crumbling
hips constant to the absence of anyone who will call

His name or fold his weighted red wool shirt after he sleeps

Say I, like an oystercatcher, slip my bill into the bivalve
and sever the abductor muscle before

The shell can close

Then, feed on barnacles
and snails

Title: Wallace Stevens

Eva Hooker, C.S.C.

Maintaining steady enrollment was among Brother Dietrich Reinhart's first concerns when he became president in 1991. Decline in the number of Minnesota high school graduates caused a temporary dip in enrollment. At the same time college-bound students demanded more campus amenities. A cluster of new houses in Flynntown and on the north side of the Tundra—one of those student labels, like "The Reef" for the refectory, that stick to a feature of the campus without institutional encouragement—now provide apartment-style living for juniors and seniors. The student center, Sexton Commons, and improved athletic and fitness facilities are other attractions for prospective students. There are new academic buildings: the art center and the environmental wing of the science center. Yet some ask whether this "new" Saint John's will continue to exemplify what legendary professor Steve Humphrey described as Benedictine virtues: "moderation, tolerance, and a sense of membership in a kind of common civilizing enterprise" (*The Record,* May 14, 1982).

Today, with a decreasing number of monks associated with the college, it is perhaps more accurate to describe Saint John's University as Benedictine-sponsored rather than as a Benedictine institution. However, the college continues to attract a majority of its students from Catholic families living in Minnesota. Many of these families, descendants of nineteenth-century immigrants, have achieved success in income level and social status. To avoid the danger of too great homogeneity, today's challenge is to attract students from less affluent backgrounds and less privileged social classes. In addition, students are encouraged to enroll in one of sixteen semester-long study abroad programs sponsored by Saint John's and the College of Saint Benedict. On campus, students continue to benefit from the mentorship provided by dedicated Benedictine and lay faculty residents, professors, and university staff; they are sustained in their personal growth by a vibrant student community.

The 150-year history of this educational institution is not the inevitable unfolding of a Benedictine educational blueprint. Rather, it is the story of individuals, some prominent and some forgotten, who approached the uncertainties they confronted with a spirit of innovation, risk-taking, and experimentation. Some of their decisions were mistakes; some were good enough for their day; and some provided wise guidance for those who followed. In the words of Father Alexius Hoffmann one hundred years ago:

> [Saint John's] has endeavored to meet the wants of the youth of this new region by affording them an opportunity of acquiring an education for secular pursuits as well as for the ministry. True to the intentions of its founders and the character of the men in whose hands its destinies rested, it has aimed to be a Catholic school in spirit and deed (155).

Ojibwe Education at Saint John's and Saint Benedict's Indian Industrial Schools

American Indian education has a unique history in the United States. Beginning in the late nineteenth century, policymakers, reformers, missionaries interested in the "Indian problem" promoted boarding-school education for the purpose of separating Indian children from their Native backgrounds and families. Boarding-school advocates argued that the institutions were designed for "cultural assimilation" and "progress," but the boarding-school policy coincided with an era of intense interest in lands that tribal people owned in the United States. During the fifty-year period that boarding schools were the primary means of educating Indians, millions of acres of tribal lands passed out of Indian ownership, and the total tribal land base declined by some 85 percent.

Boarding school history cannot be understood apart from the land policies that dominated federal policy toward American Indian tribes from 1887, the year of the passage of the General Allotment Act, until 1934, when the allotment of Indian reservations ended. The purpose of a segregated system of Indian education in off-reservation boarding schools was to indoctrinate Indian children with American values in a setting where they would speak the English language, begin to practice Christianity, and learn a vocation that would enable them to be productive but second-class citizens in the mainstream of American society. Boarding-school graduates would have no need for a tribal homeland.

Saint John's Indian Industrial School began receiving boarding students from the White Earth Reservation in 1885, the heyday of the allotment era in Minnesota. Congressman Knute Nelson of Minnesota was instrumental in bringing Indian students to Saint John's, which contracted with the government for financial support. Nelson also sponsored Minnesota's version of the allotment act and called for the end of communal, tribal landholding on Minnesota Indian reservations. The legislation for "the relief and civilization of the Chippewa Indians in Minnesota" was passed in 1889 and is referred to as the "Nelson Act."

In the aftermath of allotment, residents of the White Earth Reservation lost over 90 percent of their landholdings, thousands of acres of which were fraudulently taken. The early literature from Saint John's Indian Industrial School reported that White Earth Ojibwe students were "in the hands of efficient teachers and practical craftsmen, whose endeavor it is to carry out the best intentions of the government in the work of civilizing its wards and making them self-sustaining and worthy citizens of a great country."

Nineteenth-century Ojibwe boys aged ten to seventeen came to Saint John's Indian Industrial School from reservations at White Earth, Leech Lake, Fond du Lac, and Grand Portage. Ojibwe girls enrolled at Saint Benedict's Academy Industrial School. Alexius Edelbrock, abbot and president of Saint John's University, argued for an increase in the paltry sum the government paid per annum for each Indian pupil at Saint John's and Saint Benedict's in a strongly worded letter to Washington in 1888. He wrote, "The Indians are wards of our Government. The Government has taken their lands and has obligations towards them." Edelbrock's letter suggests that the Indian Industrial schools were plagued with problems similar to other Indian boarding schools. Schools were poorly funded, and as a consequence diet, health, and the quality of education itself were persistent problems for Indian families during the boarding-school era. At Saint John's, students were expected to stay at school for three years before returning home. Students resisted such impossible expectations by running away. American Indian students and their families responded in complex and creative ways to the boarding-school agenda.

Brenda Child

Five boys from the Indian Industrial School pose with Frater Dominic Hoffmann in 1885. A later photo shows fifty-three boys in school uniform—knee pants, long black stockings, buttoned jacket, round cloth hat, the older boys with vests and ties.

Julian G. Plante

Founding the Hill Museum & Manuscript Library

The origins of the Hill Museum & Manuscript Library can be traced back to 1957, when Father Colman Barry, O.S.B., had an audience with Pope Pius XII arranged by Father Virgil O'Neill, then prefect of students at Sant' Anselmo, the Benedictine college in Rome. In this semi-private audience the Pope conversed briefly with each of the dozen or so persons present. When Colman's turn came, he took the opportunity to request papal permission to consult documents in the secret archives of the Vatican in connection with his current research.

Pius XII's response was affirmative; then he put a request to Colman. The Pope had been nuncio to Germany before World War II and was conscious of the physical and cultural devastation wrought by the war, particularly in cities like Dresden. Referring to his permission for the Jesuits of Saint Louis University to microfilm the manuscripts of the Vatican Library, the Pope said in effect:

> We have set the pace. Now it is time for you to continue the work we have started. You are a Benedictine with a long history of learning and preservation of the written word. You are American [implying the means to carry out the project]. Now it is time for you to go into the hills and valleys of Europe and elsewhere to preserve the manuscript treasures of civilization before it's too late.

In 1964 Father Colman was appointed president of Saint John's University. One of his first projects was to develop the Monastic Manuscript Microfilm Library, to be renamed the Hill Monastic Manuscript Library in 1973 (changed to the Hill Museum & Manuscript Library in 2004). With the support of Abbot Baldwin Dworschak, O.S.B., he worked with other confreres to plan an approach to the monasteries of Europe—at first only Benedictine houses. He recruited Father Oliver Kapsner, O.S.B., a former Saint John's librarian whose German was excellent, to serve as field director for the project.

Father Oliver did yeoman work in selecting the collections to be filmed and arranging with University Microfilms of Ann Arbor, Michigan, and its president, Eugene B. Power, to render technical services. He also kept in touch with donors whom Colman recruited, the first being the Louis W. and Maud Hill Family Foundation, later the Northwest Area Foundation. Jerome Hill, an artist and filmmaker living in New York and Cassis, France, and grandson of railroad baron James J. Hill, was one of the earliest supporters of the effort, having been persuaded of its merits by Mr. A. A. Heckman, president of the Hill Family Foundation. The plan was to begin in Austria, since Saint John's Abbey had contributed generously to postwar reconstruction of monasteries there.

I became involved in the project when Colman approached me about being director. I was teaching Latin and Greek in the department of classical languages and Hebrew at the City University of New York. I was not only surprised and honored by his offer, but as a young, inexperienced classical and medieval philologian, I felt inadequate, even frightened, by the prospect of leading a fledgling cultural institution from infancy to maturity. Nonetheless, I accepted the position in 1965 and served as founding director of HMML until 1992.

In retrospect, I know that we achieved much in those early years. After working nine years in Austria, we microfilmed in Spain, Malta, Ethiopia, Germany, Portugal, South Africa, and elsewhere. I am grateful for the opportunity to have made a contribution, however modest, to establishing international recognition of HMML in the scholarly world.

Julian G. Plante '61

Colman Barry professed monastic vows in 1942, was ordained priest in 1946, gained a doctoral degree in American church history from Catholic University in 1952, and wrote the centennial history of Saint John's, Worship and Work, *for publication in 1956. He served as president of Saint John's University from 1964 to 1971.*

CHAPTER 4

"Proudly Stands Our Alma Mater, Tow'ring o'er the Oak and Pine"

Larry Haeg

EVERY JOHNNY, slumped over homework in his dorm room in first Tommy or third Patrick, drumming pencil rhythm to some iPod tune, owes a debt of sorts today to those first humble five—those young German kids: Henry Emmel and Anthony Edelbrock of Saint Cloud, Joseph Duerr of Saint Joseph, Henry Klostermann of Richmond, Andrew Stahlberger of Lake George. With winter moving in, their parents had sent them in November 1857 to live, study, and worship at the newly chartered Saint John's Seminary. (We can safely assume that there was no student dining plan, although, who knows, maybe they built their own lofts.) They found that it was nothing more than a "poor and miserable house" that sat above the Mississippi on wind-swept prairie belonging to the Winnebago Indians two miles south of a clutch of shanties and mud streets known as Saint Cloud, Minnesota Territory.

It was such a dreary existence for these five and the monk who taught them that even in elderly reminiscence Edelbrock (who later became Abbot Alexius, the inspiration for IOGD—"In Omnibus Glorificetur Deus," "May God be glorified in all things"—on the northwest tower of the Quadrangle) found it hard to summon the glow of nostalgia. The food was "poor and scanty," tallow candle the only light. They rose in the dark in a chilled stupor at 5 a.m. by the heat of an iron box stove, said prayers, celebrated the Eucharist.

"The Chimneys of Collegeville" this photo might be called. Sometime between completion of the Quad in 1886 and demolition of the stone house with the belfry in 1893, a photographer—probably Peter Engel—took this unusual picture of the monastery and school from the southwest. To the right are the original structures: the frame house (1863), moved to this site from the Old Priory in the Indianbush, and the stone house (1866). The two-story south wing (1868) with curtains in the windows housed the Ojibwe boys in the Industrial School. They were led to safety only minutes before the attic and part of the second floor blew away in the 1894 tornado, which also cleared the roof of chimneys and wrecked the farm buildings. The Quad housed most of the students and monks. Prep school and college students slept in dorms under the mansard roof. Seminarians had individual rooms on the floor beneath them. Monks lived in the original main building with cupola (1871) and the original north wing (1874) leading to the church.

Breakfast of coffee and bread at 7 a.m. There were few books. "The Professor lectured, we had to write."

The "Professor" was the newly ordained Cornelius Wittmann, O.S.B., 29, of Oberengbach, Bavaria, "zealous and amiable," one of five monks who had ventured west from Pennsylvania a year earlier to minister to German immigrants, the Dakota, Chippewa, and Winnebago in the Minnesota Territory. He may have wondered at least once if it had been the right career move. Here was a rudimentary transfer of the liberal arts from the European *gymnasium* system: history, English, Latin, Greek, astronomy, rhetoric, and math. A "dinner" at 11 a.m. of soup, potatoes, meat, bread, and water. They huddled again at 1 p.m. for "class," then a snack of dry bread and fresh water at 3, study at 4, supper at 6, study at 7:30, night prayers and silence at 8:30. And yet, even in this lonely, frost-bitten existence there was the reassuring rhythm, simplicity, silence, and discipline of the Rule of Saint Benedict, which had its hypnotic effect. "One day the same as the other," wrote Alexius years later, "every hour had its affixed duty, everything moved regularly as clockwork . . . such regularity and punctuality inspired us with love and awe."

A PERMANENT HOME

For eight uncertain years they had no permanent home. Then in 1864 they loaded their meager belongings in carts and horse-drawn wagons and drove with squeaking axles down a rutted road four miles northwest of Saint Joseph to the forest Indianbush, and finally in 1866 built a stone house on high ground above the north shore of a glistening lake surrounded by pine and maple trees. By 1870 there were more than 80 students; by 1875, 130 with a faculty of 22.

It was not really a university, simply an elementary school (spelling, reading, penmanship, arithmetic, and religion), a classical course (a high school or junior college), and a theological course. From the beginning it was to be for clergy and laity together, each with their separate schedules but living together as one community. To meet the frontier demand for bookkeepers and accountants, the monks created a "commercial department." This hybrid college-seminary became a nineteenth-century seedbed not only for Benedictine priests and brothers but also for young merchants and bankers across the Upper Midwest, including young entrepreneurs such as William Hamm (brewing) and Frank Schlick (department stores).

Smallpox and diphtheria posed a constant epidemic threat. Benedictine discipline was swift and inflexible; there was a formidable dean of discipline. "Any display of degenerate passion," declared Father Wolfgang Northman, "is promptly corrected." Smoking was prohibited. Students could not leave the grounds or go "out of bounds" without permission.

Outdoor sports were born. How could they not have been? Monks and students, cabin-fevered and isolated for months, rejoiced in the outdoors. They cleared maples for a baseball diamond, the outfield studded with stumps near

The Sag is heaven for skaters when it freezes mirror smooth on a November night with no snowfall to mar the glassy surface. Across the lake the first Stella Maris chapel lifts its white steeple against the dark winter woods. This dates the picture before 1903, when the first chapel burned to the ground.

It looks as if the stock in Rupp's candy wagon was successfully depleted by this stop in front of the church on a gray spring day in 1909. Mr. Rupp had opened a shop on the west side of the lake just beyond the cemetery in 1901. No list of his line of merchandise survives, but he was filling a market niche left vacant when Mr. Broker discontinued the general store at Collegeville station. The horse-drawn station wagon may be loaded for a run down to the station or for picture-taking. The nearer porch is the entrance to the school, the further porch to the monastery.

"the college gate." In scows, bathing trunks, at night to spear fish, skating across a fresh, snow-swept sheet of green ice, they took joyously to the lake— jewel of the landscape and part of the abbey's original name: Saint Louis by the Lake. In 1896 they lovingly named it Sagatagan, Chippewa for "tinder wood." Students marked their calendars by its seasonal rhythm; first ice-out date, first swim of the season, "our lines in the water we pass, and rowed right along to the tune of light song, as we hauled in the pickerel and bass." They hiked around it in all seasons—"Round the Beat" they called it; "there's no walk that will compare, with that humble path we wear." For six generations it has inspired more student poetry than perhaps any other part of the campus. "Exquisite opaline," one student in the 1920s called it.

Landmarks rose from sweat and sacrifice that students of the next century took for granted. A red glare lit up the night sky from the kiln on campus where clay was fired into bricks for the bold, twin-spired church (1882) and the noble Quadrangle (1886). Then came the gymnasium (1901) with Menomonee brick from Saint Cloud and its Medieval Revival tower and polished hardwood floor, sawed, cut, laid, and varnished by the monks from maples in the woods.

The student newspaper, *The Record,* was born in 1888. A year later, on the evening of October 10, someone flipped a switch at the new powerhouse. A collective gasp and hurrah! from students and monks. Incandescent bulbs illuminated the sanctuary of the church, and the study halls in the Quad "were now brilliantly lit up by dazzling clusters of lamps." Electric lights, of course, were a

Excerpt from **College Life,** *by Alexius Hoffmann, 1898*

Man is not an isolated being, he is part of a great community; he must have regard for his fellowmen, as they, in turn, are obliged to respect him.

Many books have been written on the proper behavior of gentlemen. Young people, as a rule, abhor "moralizing"—or lengthy discourses upon their duties. Particularly is this true of students, who court freedom from restraint as far as it may be conceded.

Nevertheless, they are anxious to learn what is right in the different phases of life: how they should conduct themselves at college and abroad.

The student who has at heart the correct formation of his external conduct will begin to lay the foundation during the years spent at college. There he may devote himself exclusively to the task of making a man of himself, spiritually, intellectually, socially.

The precepts of religion will impart the requisites for citizenship in the visible kingdom of God on earth; it is our task to speak of the requirements of college life.

mixed blessing for students: evening study hall stretched to infinity, unrestricted by the dim glow of oil lamps. In 1894 the monks on their knees carefully planted and cultivated rows of pine seeds from Bavaria, which a half century later rose into part of the legendary "pine curtain."

THE FIELD OF PLAY

In 1900 Father Louis Traufler collected a grand total of $50 from the students and created an intramural league for football, basketball, and baseball. The first football team, including the soon-to-be-expelled Ignatius O'Shaughnessy at tackle (nine years later, as an oil wildcatter, he struck it rich in Oklahoma and proceeded over the next half century to shower millions of dollars on the College of Saint Thomas and Notre Dame University), practiced

Harry Comeau came from New London, Connecticut, in 1905 to teach physical culture, which included coaching football. He poses here on the steps of the gymnasium with the football team and Father Pius Meinz, athletics moderator. Comeau is the natty dresser in the top row with his hands in his pockets. The team has eleven nose guards, enough to go around on a given play. One member is dressed for fencing, another skill in Mr. Comeau's portfolio. The college played Saint Cloud on October 21, the sole game of the season, and won 6–0 when a disputed call in the second half led Saint Cloud to quit the game, which the referee, a Saint John's man, then declared forfeited.

Saint John's first horseless station wagon was this 1914 Buick Model 4 Flair Side truck, made to order by the innovative company. New in Buick this year were steering on the left side and the electric starter. The front seat passenger's jaunty boot suggests a casual attitude toward twentieth-century progress in the automotive line.

on a gravel mall in front of the Quadrangle. A year later the "extramural" or "representative" team boarded the train to Saint Paul to play Saint Thomas at Lexington Park. The "hayseeds" from Saint John's could not afford helmets and wore canvas jackets. Final score: Saint John's 15, Saint Thomas 6. The cranberry marsh in a natural bowl was cleared and graded for a football field in 1908, but the sport was abolished for "promoting unfriendliness towards other schools." It didn't resume on campus until 1920, when the "Fighting Johnnies" in cardinal and blue joined the new Minnesota Intercollegiate Athletic Conference.

Autumn after autumn, in carriages drawn by two horses from Jim Hill's Great Northern station at Collegeville or by hired surrey from Saint Joseph four and a half miles away, the sons of farmers and merchants came to Saint John's from the hamlets and "the Cities." Polish, French, Italian. The Irish— Galvin, Ryan, Connor, McDonald, Rooney, Marrin, Connolly, Hogan, Cronin, Moynihan, McKickle, Delaney, Gallagher, Gleason, Conway, Mulrooney and Sweeney. The Germans— Reuter, Weber, Leisen, Scherer, Stein, Zenner, Schoenbechler, Botz, Grode, Klein, Froehle, Krebsbach, Schoenecker, Linnemann, Schultz, Buscher, Kapsner, Kremer, Osendorf, Dittberner, Himsl, Mischke, Dahlheimer, Winzenburg, Schneider. One of them, Aloysius J. Schwinghammer, '87, came with his father and a team of oxen (barter for tuition), thus giving rise to the joke: "What are you studying for?" "Two pigs and a cow."

The students assumed that monks were born monks. Later they were astonished to learn that these gray men had come to Saint John's once upon a time as wide-eyed freshmen just like them. The old saying was that they entered the monastery the first day they came to prep school. As Sister Joan Chittister, O.S.B., wisely observed many decades later, "The flow of the student body was lost in the stability of the monks."

Students Came and Stayed as Monks

Henry Deutsch came to America from Hungary at age three, then to Saint John's Prep School in the fall of 1890 as a thirteen-year-old from Saint Paul. He became Alcuin, the fifth abbot and one of the most influential Benedictines in Saint John's history.

George Michel, the second of fifteen children of a homemaker and the owner of a general store in Saint Paul, enrolled at Saint John's Prep School in 1903. He was the sort you could find reading a book while waiting for his classmate to arrive to play tennis. He was editor of *The Record* for three years, later entered the monastery and became Father Virgil, was founder of the Liturgical Press, professor and dean of the college, soulmate of Dorothy Day and promoter of the *Catholic Worker,* had the transformative genius to connect the concept of social justice with the social nature of the liturgy.

My Folks, Isabelle and George

Most Saint John's alumni of the twentieth century knew my folks, Isabelle and George Durenberger. Some came to consider the pair their away-from-home parents. Near the middle of that century George was one of just three married men on the faculty and living on campus. Dad met Mom at Saint Ben's and married her a year after her graduation from the College of Saint Teresa in Winona. They raised three boys and two girls in Flynntown, the "campus town" that was named for his predecessor as athletic director, a job Dad took on at age twenty-three and retired from at sixty-five.

Both Mom and Dad valued athletics, and especially in this unique Collegeville community. He was an All American in football and basketball and the first kid to go to college from his small southern hometown of LeSueur, Minnesota. As a coach he won MIAC football championships. He was devoted to maintaining athletic fields, tracks, courts, and outdoor rinks. With alumni volunteers, he created and for many years directed one of the nation's biggest high school invitational track meets until he couldn't do it any more.

Our home had an open door for any Johnny alumnus after any campus game. Many monks also found it a place of warmth, congeniality, and wide-ranging conversation. Mom and Dad, Isabelle and George, developed and handed over to Father Walter Reger a Saint John's Alumni Association. The association's early alumni mailings were processed in their home by family volunteers. Isabelle and George were Scout leaders and leaders of the Saint Cloud Diocesan National Council of Catholic Men and Women. Dad saved lives practicing what he taught in his Red Cross life-saving courses.

Mom helped start the May Bowle, the popular annual spring gala to benefit the three Saint Cloud-area colleges. Once she saved the Quadrangle from burning down by extinguishing a fire started by one of Father Walter's cigars. In the early days of Minnesota Public Radio, she spent hours reading books for the network's Books for the Blind channel. Dad provided leadership to help build and expand the Minnesota Intercollegiate Athletic Conference. He was in high demand as an "after" speaker—after breakfast, after lunch, or after dinner. With enormous enthusiasm, he preached lifelong learning, and especially lifelong recreational skills to fend off emotional and physical illness and achieve long life, which he enjoyed. And Isabelle, my mom, still does.

Dave Durenberger '55

William Tucker became Dunstan, the Dante scholar, baseball coach, and academic dean.

Henry Reger came to the prep school from Minneapolis in 1908 at age fourteen and became the beloved, cigar-chomping Father Walter, dean of men, history professor, prefect, violinist in the orchestra, head of alumni relations, and promoter of Johnny Bread ("the loaf that became a legend").

Gerhard Zankl came in 1913 as a twelve-year-old from Almena, Wisconsin, when board, lodging, books, laundry, and tuition all came to $250. He became Father Angelo, created the school's emblem, choosing Saint Paul's "Induamur arma lucis" ("Let us put on the armor of light") as its motto (this was war—we were being armed with light for combat against the forces of evil). At this writing he remains a miraculous living link to 1857. As a young cleric in 1921, he wheeled to Mass in the chapel Father Cornelius Wittmann, deaf and almost totally blind, last survivor of the original five monks who came to the territory from Pennsylvania in 1856.

Conrad Diekmann came to the prep school from Roscoe in 1917 at age thirteen and became the Shakespearean stalwart of the English faculty. Two years later came his kid brother, eleven-year-old Leo, who took the name Godfrey and became heir to Virgil Michel and a *peritus* at the Second Vatican Council. William Tucker, delayed by pleurisy and tuberculosis, came from Tintah in Traverse County in 1920 and at twenty-eight became Dunstan, the Dante scholar, baseball coach, and academic dean. Fourteen-year-old Wilfrid Dworschak came the same year to the prep school from Arcadia, Wisconsin, took the name Baldwin, served as abbot for more than twenty years, and was the guiding spirit behind the new abbey church and the hundred-year building plan.

Boys and young men from small towns across the Upper Midwest entered through the pine curtain for the first time as prep or college students and stayed. Many took vows and faithfully taught students for the better part of the next half century, including (it would take pages to name them all) Aloysius Wegleitner (Fabian) from Saint Paul in 1923; George Tegeder (Vincent) from Minneapolis in 1925; Edward Schirber (Martin) from Mobridge, South Dakota, and Walter Thuente (Adelard) from Festina, Iowa, both in 1926; Henry Deutsch (Alfred) from Rice Street in Saint Paul in 1927; the Soukup brothers, Gregory (Cuthbert) and Joseph (Gervase), from Saint Paul in 1930 and 1937 respectively; James Barry (Colman) from Lake City in 1938; Arnold Weber from Saint Martin in 1940; Don Talafous (Camillus) from Duluth in 1943; John Collins (Corwin) in 1944 from the Bronx; Donald Durken (Daniel) from Janesville, Minnesota, and Donald (Hilary) Thimmesh from Osakis, both in 1945; Andrew McCall (Aidan) from Washington, D.C.; Richard Culhane (Alberic) from Mitchell, South Dakota, in 1948; Don LeMay (Lanfranc) from Cloquet in 1944. Students were encouraged to read and appreciate the Rule of Saint Benedict, but this "variety of characters" (Benedict's words) were the Rule come to life.

Two college seniors—regrettably unnamed but note their class rings—are the picture of tidiness in a ground floor Benet Hall room in 1932. The room is eight feet wide. A metal locker, sink, and medicine cabinet are behind the photographer. Rugs, rocker, floor lamp, cushions, wall hangings make the room comfortable. Smoking is permitted. Lights out at 11, even for seniors.

When football resumed in 1920, it seemed scripted intentionally for the dramatic arrival of sixteen-year-old John Vincent McNally from New Richmond, Wisconsin. Dashing Black Irish, poet and actor and athlete all in one, expelled from Notre Dame, he became Saint John's first four-sport letter winner, captain of the basketball team, winner of nine of thirteen spring track events. This was the birth of Johnny football as we know it today. "If they're breakin' through each time, makin' tackles behind the line, get tough! Get sore!

Don't take more! Hit 'em low!" McNally dropped out of Saint John's to play professional football as "Johnny Blood" with the Green Bay Packers, became a charter member of the Pro Football Hall of Fame, and returned to the campus after World War II to earn his degree and coach Saint John's football for four mediocre years before the extraordinary Gagliardi Era, now a remarkable half century plus and counting.

MR. FLYNN OF FLYNNTOWN

During McNally's student days, however, intramurals were where the action was. "Moderator of Athletics" Edward J. Flynn believed athletics "must be conducted in enthusiastic moderation . . . to bring the greatest good to the greatest number" for lifelong use. In the early 1920s one-third of the student body played intensely competitive intramural baseball on teams named the Super Sizes, the Pall Malls, the Zips, the Butts, and the Phantoms. The old gym became the domain of Flynn's successor, George Durenberger, who came as a college freshman from Le Sueur in 1924. He played center on the football team, was first to be named all-MIAC for three years, and was both football and basketball captain. For the next forty-four years "Big George" presided over the growth of sports on campus and off: as professor, head coach of the football, basketball, and baseball teams, athletic director, even creating a physical fitness regimen for the 87th Airborne Detachment during World War II.

The Johnnies all lived together, the "small boys" and the "older boys," in dorms on the top floor of the Quadrangle. They all played together; preps even joined college students on intramural teams. They all ate together, prep boys and college men, in the refectory, family style, with students as table waiters. They all hit the books together in the Quad's study halls, seated in long rows of large flip-top desks—Saint Gregory Hall for the commercial students, Saint Bede Hall for the pre-divinity students, Saint Anselm Hall for the priesthood students. The first building on campus for exclusive use of the students was not built until 1921—Saint Bennet Hall (as it was first spelled), five stories of Spanish and Romanesque architecture with study halls, classrooms, dorms, and even bowling alleys, handball courts, and lounges on the ground floor.

The students smoked and drank—even then. They could smuggle homebrew from nearby farms. The gymnasium had a smokers' room, "the only place within the building," said *The Record* in 1901 with a touch of modernity, "in which the older students, who have obtained due permission, may enjoy a quiet smoke." Father Alfred Deutsch, who wrote a gentle, vivid collection of *roman à clef* short stories about abbey life sixty years later, confessed that he learned to smoke as a fourteen-year-old student behind the gym with Rusty Hogan and others. "The owner would smoke some and then pass it on. The second guy would get what we called 'butts.'" He also learned to play poker in the tower of the gym.

It was Alfred's uncle, Alcuin, compensating for his short stature with a "stern countenance and a cold eye," who governed student life with a firm hand as both abbot and president from 1921 to 1950 ("to develop character, inculcate a deep religious understanding and build habits which are the mark of a Christian gentleman"). He was a stubborn advocate of the small "model college" and effectively capped enrollment at 425. How could you run a college

In the middle of the last century bowling leagues thrived with mixed teams of students and faculty. Hundreds of alumni surely remember the ten-pin competition and recall with appreciation the mystery student workers who reset the pins by hand. Pictured here is a humanities team consisting of history professor Joe Heininger, history major Bernie Kinnick '58, and English professor Father Alfred Deutsch. Kinnick went on to earn his doctorate in history and become a professor of history at the University of Northern Colorado in Greeley.

larger than the monastery and still maintain the Benedictine ideal? He wanted nothing to do with those secular accrediting agencies. There he is, gazing out paternalistically from his portrait on the opening pages of the 1921–22 *Sagatagan*, with an ominous warning for students: choose self-denial over self-indulgence. "You shrink from that; it is too hard. Don't be frightened . . . if you walk the way of self-indulgence onto the transgression of the law, the wages of your sin will be short-lived pleasure, long and comfortless suffering, darkness unto death." If "darkness unto death" didn't get a student's attention, what would?

GI Invasion

Another World War came and ended, the GIs came home, and time and events conspired to pass Alcuin by, administratively at least. The question no longer was how to keep enrollment down but where to put them all. Students slept on the dirt-floor basement of the old gym, in the gym loft. There were desks in the handball courts. Five pre-fab army barracks materialized on what is now the Saint Mary's parking lot. Enrollment: 434 in 1945, 793 in 1946, 935 in 1947. Mary Hall was built on the site of handball courts, north of the auditorium; Saint Thomas Hall was built where a flour mill and chicken coop once stood.

Then began the era of illustrious laymen on the faculty, including (again, it would take pages to do justice to all of them): Emerson Hynes (sociology), Joe Heininger and Ross Horning (history), Herbert Burke (English), Ed Henry and Joe Farry (political science), Jack Lange (mathematics), Bill Cofell and Sylvester Theisen (sociology), and Jim Smith and John Gagliardi (physical education). For all his accomplishments (becoming the "winningest" college football coach of all time), what mattered then as now was Gagliardi's ability to focus players on what matters (execution), to think for themselves (no playbooks, quarterbacks calling many of the plays), not to confuse what was just a game with life.

Then began the era of illustrious laymen on the faculty.

The auditorium was packed for the variety show on the Friday night before Homecoming in 1955. Laughing in the middle of the crowd sits Joe O'Connell, artist from Chicago, who was to become Collegeville's resident interpreter of the human comedy in sculpture, prints, photographs, and the gift of good talk among friends.

He holds a penny to the sun for his players; football is just the penny, the sun is life, don't confuse the two.

Perhaps the students' most beloved lay faculty member was a soft-spoken, diminutive man who was called simply Mr. Humphrey. He transferred from Saint Thomas in 1927, graduated in 1929, and after graduate school returned to teach English and live on the first floor of Benet Hall, becoming part of Saint John's for fifty-five years. Never married, Steve Humphrey was as close to being Benedictine as you could get without living in the monastery. "He had an uncanny instinct," Father Emeric Lawrence wrote, "for detecting the kind of future vocation a young man was fitted for . . . to discern their potential."

Rigorous discipline lingered through the 1950s: common meals in the dining room; obligatory Sunday Mass and three-day annual *silent* retreats; Saturday classes until noon; only seniors could have cars on campus; freshmen wore green beanies for six weeks (even in the showers); and hazing by letter-winners (J-Club) was merciless, sometimes cruel. Professors addressed students as "Mister" for class roll call; class absences were recorded and reported. Lights on freshman floors went out at 11 p.m., bed checks courtesy of "Lurkin' Durken the Sneakin' Deacon" (Father Daniel Durken, later a favorite Scripture prof and director of the Liturgical Press). Students needed a "per" just to go to the El Paso in Saint Joe or the Fairgrounds Ballroom in Saint Cloud and had to sign out when they left campus and sign in when they returned. Punishment for excessive drinking: three- to five-day suspensions.

THE RATS

During interminable, relentless, snowbound winters, college basketball games transformed the old gym into thunderous, raucous, foot-stomping Rat Hall, redolent of cigar smoke, popcorn, stinky lockers, Ben Gay, and sweat. Many visiting coaches, taunted and mimicked by the student "rats," swore they would never play there again. The story perhaps is apocryphal. A middle-aged man apologized years later to former Saint Thomas coach Tom Feely for harassing him behind the bench during a game at Collegeville. "Were you a student at Saint John's?" asked Feely. "No, I wasn't," he replied, "I was on the faculty."

Saint John's remained a rugged, elbows-on-the-table, all-male enclave until 1963–64 and the first civilizing influence: forty-eight brave young women from the College of Saint Benedict were allowed to enroll in courses at Saint John's.

John Gagliardi

In 2000 Saint John's won the first three playoff games and was getting ready for the championship game against Mount Union the following Saturday. On Monday, Aaron Krych, Saint John's starting and starring tailback from Holdingford, came up to John in practice. Aaron told John he was in somewhat of a predicament. "What is it?" asked John.

Aaron answered, "Well, tomorrow I have an interview at the Mayo Clinic in Rochester for admission into their medical school next year. But if I go to the interview, I'll have to miss practice tomorrow, and I know we have a lot to do to get ready for the championship game on Saturday."

John replied without hesitation, "Aaron, you take that interview. Your getting into medical school is a lot more important than our football game." Aaron went to the interview and was told he would be admitted to medical school if he scored a touchdown. He had his chance in the third quarter but was stopped at the one-yard line. They let him into Mayo anyway.

SJU quarterback Ryan Keating (7) throws a five-yard touchdown pass to Josh Nelson (32) with 2:03 remaining in the game to give SJU a 29-26 win over Bethel and coach John Gagliardi his record-setting 409th career win on Saturday, November 8, 2003. The crowd of 13,000 fans in Clemens Stadium—named for Bill Clemens '42, a longtime fan and generous supporter of both colleges—was also record-setting. SJU went on to complete a perfect 14-0 season and win the national championship for the fourth time.

53

"Members of the mixed classes," admitted a writer for the *Sagatagan* yearbook, "generally conceded that the presence of the opposite sex was beneficial to most courses." Generally? Most?

The monks made their mistakes, to be sure, but far more often than not, they had that patient Benedictine understanding of human nature, of wanting no "bruised reed broken," with an emphasis on moderation, discretion, flexibility, humaneness. They saw not just boys but the men they would become. Father Walter wanted students to experience education as an exciting adventure, not a tedious exercise, perhaps one of the wellsprings for today's extensive study abroad program. Asked Father Arno Gustin, who came as eighteen-year-old Anthony from Mandan, North Dakota, in 1924 and was president of the university as the fifties turned to the sixties, "Who can pinpoint the depth and promise in the life of another person?"

"SAINT JOHN'S? WHERE'S THAT?"

It is a winter Sunday morning in 1958. I am an eighth grader at Saint Austin's School in north Minnesota, serving Mass for Father Adelard Thuente of Saint John's, who was helping out on weekends at our parish. I had unwittingly come into the crosshairs of the Johnny recruiting machine. As he removes his vestments after Mass, Father Adelard innocently asks: "So, Haeg, where are you going to high school?" (This was a vigorous, ruddy, muscular, straight-talking monk with a passion for dialectic, biology, embryology, ornithology, sports, philatelics, chinchilla breeding, cards, and wine. Years later I learned that in 1953 it was Adelard, himself a Johnny halfback in the thirties, who was one of the first to befriend the newly hired twenty-seven-year-old football coach, John Gagliardi.)

SJU's Jon Kaus (4) dribbles around a Bethel defender in Sexton Arena on Wednesday, December 8, 2004. The college basketball coach with the highest number of winning scores on any level in Minnesota, coach Jim Smith has over 630 wins in 41 seasons as a collegiate head coach. He has won MIAC titles in each of the past five decades and has repeatedly led his teams to NAIA and NCAA Division III playoffs.

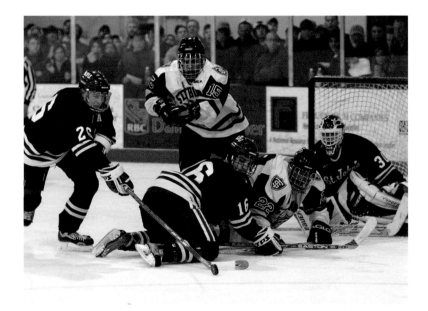

SJU hockey players Bille Luger (16) and All-American Darryl Smoleroff (26) try to clear the puck as All-American Adam Hanna (30) blocks the net in the last seconds of a 3-2 win over Saint Thomas on Friday, February 11, 2005. Saint John's won the MIAC regular season title for the third straight season, seventh time overall, and advanced to the NCAA playoffs for the fifth time. SJU hockey coach John Harrington has been at Collegeville for twelve seasons, has over 200 career wins, and was a member of the 1980 "Miracle on Ice" gold-medal U.S. Olympic hockey team.

"I don't know, Father, maybe De La Salle, maybe Benilde."

"Have you ever thought of Saint John's?"

"No, Father, where's that?"

A few weeks later our assistant pastor, Father Nick Cody, piled four of us into his car and drove us to Saint John's to have Father Adelard give us the grand tour. We drove past the pine curtain, the road Father Adelard had traveled as sixteen-year-old Walter thirty-two years earlier. It was a bitterly cold, crystal-clear January day, the campus buried in fresh snow. A wooden chrysalis of scaffolding encased what was becoming Breuer's bell banner. Adelard led us down a shoveled path to the gym. I remember distinctly coming in out of the cold and hearing a flood of voices, cheering, yelling, three cross-court basketball games in progress; I had never seen and felt such condensed energy come out of nowhere, in the midst of nowhere. Then to Engel Hall, Adelard's science building—he was a professor of biology—was that a fetus in a bottle? To the refectory—Adelard personally raiding the refectory pantry for cold cuts, pickles, mustard, potato chips, milk, and, of course, the pièce de résistance, Johnny bread.

That fall my father, who first met Benedictines at his boyhood parish in Richfield, drove me to campus, handed me my suitcase from the trunk of the car, shook my hand with understated love, and drove away. I looked around. Now what? I heard a distant whistle. I wandered down to watch the end of prep varsity football practice. The senior center, who I later learned was Roger Quinn, removed his shoulder pads and tossed them at me. "Freshman?" he asked. I nodded. "Carry these up to the gym." I had become a Johnny. That spring, as I gazed out of a third-floor Quadrangle window during Louis Senta's history class, I watched a crane remove one of the huge bells from the twin towers for transfer to the new Breuer banner. Two years later, on Palm Sunday, Adelard was found dead of a heart attack at age fifty-two.

CLASSES, 2004

Steve Humphrey, Joe Heininger, Fathers Alfred, Conrad, Adelard, Dunstan, Walter, Martin, and so many beloved others are all gone now. Are they? It is Monday morning after Thanksgiving 2004. Father Nathanael Hauser leads a late-morning class discussion on nineteenth-century European art with sixteen Johnnies and ten Bennies in the art center at Saint John's. "You don't need a teacher now," he says, "you just need a friendly guide to help you understand what was going on in Europe at this time." He compares Renoir's "The Party" with a conventional sixteenth-century religious painting. "Why did these two artists paint these pictures? How are these two paintings the same? How are they structured? How does this show psychological realism, which so interested the impressionists? Why are there so few 'religious' paintings in the nineteenth century? How did the industrial revolution make impressionism possible? Remember what we discussed about ready-to-use tubes of paint and portable easels?"

I remember distinctly coming in out of the cold and hearing a flood of voices. I had never seen and felt such condensed energy.

A First-Year Symposium class happily poses at the end of the course and the beginning of summer.

I line up with Johnnies and Bennies to take "The Link," the shuttle bus, to Saint Ben's and head for Dr. Robert Hesse's calculus class. He paces, works his chalked hand through his thatch of wayward, black hair, attacks the blackboard. "We are now going to measure the area on the axis under the curve. You are going to have to start thinking backwards to do this." And then, soberly, a time-honored warning, "We've got two weeks before finals. *(Pause.)* This is the time you should be studying for them. If you wait until the night before, you may pass the exam but you won't learn anything, please?" Then across campus to join Dr. Madhu Mitra and her senior English class of twelve Bennies and nine Johnnies gathered in a circle to discuss how we read. Books are not just a mirror of reality; they have their own reality that enables you to enter another world. Can one be a critical reader of the text and also, childlike, let the mysteries of the text work on you? Does critical reading diminish the pleasure of reading? There are three minutes left in the class. Dr. Mitra looks around the room at her students with an open, inviting smile. "What do *you* think?" she asks. "Tell me."

Just as Father Cornelius Wittmann must have done 147 years ago in that "poor and miserable" house, she pauses and waits for the answer.

Junior Colt Edin caught unawares in the company of Tolstoy's Prince Andrew, Natasha, and Pierre on a barefoot summer afternoon. Later in the summer Colt got honorable mention at the annual meeting of the Animal Behavior Society in Salt Lake City for his undergraduate research on differences between the prairie voles of Tennessee and Illinois.

The ice is out of the lake and on the shore as Richard Ice and his communications class welcome spring with an afternoon session on a grassy slope leading down to the lake.

Crew
(St. John's)

Most wore shirts—oversized,
shabby-aquarium-green
singlets that the light

off the water at once
filled, making
the bodies inside

visible: their lack
of fullness, what
eventually they would come

into, briefly
the body seemed what it
never is

—ignorable,
a small concern.

But the boy at the bow was shirtless:

how bells at evensong,
though this was morning, leave
changed the air—

Facing the others, he watched them
pull in unison their
course across and

over again the water,
as if to the rowing there were now
no struggling,

or it was as if—about struggling—
the only difficult part left
lay in settling

finally on a pattern for it.
Three strokes; four—

And the boy at the bow sang out to
them:

*What is dread
but that from which the soul
will be delivered?*

　　　　　To which *O what
is the soul?* the rest of the boys
sang back.

　　　　　　　　—Carl Phillips

Carl Phillips, "Crew (St. John's)," *The Rest of Love* (New York: Farrar, Straus and Giroux, 2004). Reprinted by permission.

CHAPTER 5

Plowing the Fields, Scattering Good Seed upon the Earth

Hilary Thimmesh, O.S.B.

THE HISTORY OF THE PARISHES AND MISSIONS of Saint John's Abbey over 150 years is the story of a surprising number of our monks, both priests and brothers. The records show more than five hundred of us involved in some form of pastoral or mission service from 1856 to the present. Missions, parishes, chaplaincies in convents, hospitals, retirement centers, prisons, and military service are all included. How the Saint John's pastoral mission originated, grew, and touched the life of Catholics from Minnesota to the Caribbean Islands to Japan is the story outlined here. (Rather than burden the text with "Brothers" and "Fathers" I will note the distinction only when it is significant and not clear from the context.)

Countless human interest stories could be told were there room to tell them: Bonaventure Hansen in Nassau marching the third-grade pupils over to Saint Francis Xavier to be baptized en masse; Brothers Elmer Cichy, Gregory Eibensteiner, Michael Laux, Placid Stuckenschneider working with Father Egbert Goeb and the sisters from Saint Benedict's Monastery in the sixties to make the mission at Red Lake prosper; Agnes Ramler, longtime housekeeper for Anselm Ortmann, retired to her little house in Flynntown as Skat player and art critic in residence; Terence Carroll and his "mission on the subway," pleading with tears in his eyes that the abbey chapter not give up Saint Anselm's in the Bronx; Louis Traufler, like Chaucer's Franklin the soul of hospitality at Saint Aug's in East Saint Cloud, his door always open to confreres waiting for their ride back to Saint John's—a treasury of good people with their quirks, biases, blind spots, enthusiasms, good intentions, sacrifices.

The story starts in August 1856 when newly ordained Bruno Riss, twenty-six years old, was appointed the first Benedictine pastor of Saint Joseph with missions in Jacobs Prairie and Richmond. He was there two years, then went to Shakopee with his classmate Cornelius Wittmann. Writing in *The Record* in 1889, he described what it was like to go on a mission in those first years.

> Our calendar was prepared two months in advance in order that the larger congregations might have services on Sunday at least twice a year. According to the arrangements I was free to return to Shakopee every two weeks. For two years I made all these trips afoot . . . . Whenever we set out on a trip we stowed away in the fathomless depths of a carpet sack one altarstone, a Missal, a book of Gospels, a Breviary, vestments for Mass, candles, crucifix, altar wine for two weeks, altar breads—in fact all that

Father Cornelius Wittmann figures as a teacher and a pastor throughout his long monastic career: first teacher in Stearns County, first faculty of newly incorporated "Saint John's Seminary" in 1857, wood carver on the side, pastor of several Minnesota parishes, part of the founding community of Saint Martin's Abbey in Lacey, Washington; venerated elder when young Novice Angelo Zankl pushed his wheelchair to church and refectory in 1921, the year of his death.

◀ Happy school children troop past the church in Saint Joseph on a fall afternoon. The original church was a log cabin. The present fieldstone and granite church was completed and consecrated—the first in Minnesota—in 1871. Saint John's monks have continued to serve the parish with Father Gregory Miller as the present pastor.

was needed; moreover, some linens and—snuff. When all had been well packed away, this baggage weighing some sixty pounds was fastened to the end of a substantial stick; this was slung over the shoulder and we plodded over hills and through swamps, in every season, exposed to biting cold and vexatious mosquitoes, from station to station for six-to-eight and occasionally twelve-to-fifteen miles a day. . . . Every day we had different fare, different water, different lodgings infested with all kinds of vermin; then after a short rest we moved on to the next station. Such was pioneer missionary life.

Bruno was one of three Benedictine priests from Saint Vincent Abbey in western Pennsylvania who arrived in Minnesota in May 1856. Eight others joined them in the next four years. They were sent to found a new monastery, indeed, but their primary task was pastoral; they came as missionaries to a new territory rapidly filling with German Catholic immigrants. As Alexius Hoffmann, chronicler of the first half century, puts it: "They came, established themselves near Saint Cloud and at once began to develop missionary activities, as that was the immediate purpose for which they had been invited." (Unpublished MSS. in Saint John's Abbey Archives, 38.)

One of these priests, Alexius Roetzer, found the pioneer missionary regimen literally killing and went back to Pennsylvania to die of pneumonia in 1859. Of the other ten, one served as prior of the fledgling monastery, and one served as the faculty of the newly chartered Saint John's Seminary. These two also did part-time pastoral work in places like Sauk Rapids, Saint Augusta, and Luxemburg near Saint Cloud. The other eight were engaged full-time in sacramental ministry to Catholics in the little settlements springing up in the middle part of the state or around Shakopee farther south or in Saint Paul at the Church of the Assumption.

Of the two men wearing crosses in this picture, the shorter one is Bishop Rupert Seidenbusch. To his right, a head taller, stands Abbot Alexius Edelbrock. A cavalcade of parishioners on horseback rode out to welcome the bishop for the dedication of the new church at Meire Grove on July 20, 1886. Alexius Hoffmann notes the paradox that the early settlers customarily put a penny in the Sunday collection—one who put in a nickel was asked if he wanted change—but treated their pastors generously and built churches that cost as much as $90,000.

Stearns County, Benedictine Country

Diocesan clergy assumed responsibility for the Shakopee area in 1869. Stearns County became Benedictine country. Starting with Saint Joseph and Saint Cloud, the monks reached out to a growing cluster of Catholic settlements in eastern and central Stearns County. Richmond became a parish in 1861, New Munich in 1864, Saint Martin in 1872, Meire Grove in 1874, Cold Spring in 1878. Others became parishes in the eighties and nineties: Farming, Oak Station (renamed Freeport in the nineties to avoid confusion with Osakis in the train schedule), Albany, Avon, Saint Rosa. Saint Mary's Parish in Saint Cloud was Benedictine from 1856 until the church acquired the status of cathedral of the diocese in 1937. A dozen other missions, some of which became parishes, were served by Benedictines for a time—places like Spring Hill, Saint Nicholas, Saint Wendel, and towns on the route of the Saint Paul and Pacific, later the Great Northern, like Sauk Centre, West Union, Osakis.

The towns and rural communities that grew up around these missions were almost exclusively Catholic until well into the twentieth century and were to be the subject of fictional treatment by Sinclair Lewis, J. F. Powers, and Garrison Keillor, and sociological study by various scholars. These communities preserved many of the characteristics of their Old World origins. It was a testimony to their faith that in town after town they built splendid churches with spires to be seen for miles across the rolling farmland. It is also true that no town lacked its saloon, sometimes located across the street from the church to provide immediate relief after long sermons.

Not everyone considered the presence of monks an unmixed blessing. Know Nothing agitation peaked when the Benedictines arrived in Saint Cloud. Bruno Riss notes that people in Saint Joseph at first objected to having monks imposed on them. In one pioneer parish some of the more athletic faithful got on the roof of the rectory one night and blocked the chimney to smoke out a pastor they didn't like.

More typically, priests from Saint John's and sisters from Saint Benedict's Monastery in Saint Joseph worked together with parishioners to form solidly religious communities. Evidence of their influence was the extraordinary number of religious and priestly vocations from many of these parishes over the next century: 115 from Saint Martin, 111 from Richmond, 85 from Cold Spring, to name only the three largest.

Parishes in "The Cities"

A year after the monks arrived in Stearns County, Bishop Cretin entrusted to them the German parish of the Assumption in Saint Paul. The parish had been founded in 1854 to serve German Catholics. The head of the original band of five Benedictines, Demetrius di Marogna, was its first Benedictine pastor. In 1871 his successor, Clement Staub, laid the cornerstone

Assumption Church

Assumption Catholic Church has been a downtown landmark in Saint Paul since 1874. Its two towers, at 210 feet, were the tallest objects on the city's skyline when they were built, and they show up prominently in many old photographs of Saint Paul, photographs in which every other building has long since vanished. The massive limestone church remains very much a part of life in Saint Paul.

Benedictine priests from Saint John's Abbey served as pastors of Assumption Parish from 1857 to 1912. The parish, formed in 1854, was German. Presumably this was why Bishop Joseph Cretin of Saint Paul called in the Benedictines. A parish history written in 1931 states, rather mysteriously, that Father Demetrius di Marogna came down from the abbey in 1857 "in order to study the situation" at Assumption. Four months later he agreed to become its pastor. What he was studying isn't clear, but it may have been the parish's considerable debt.

The key Benedictine in Assumption's history was undoubtedly Father Clement Staub. As pastor from 1863 to 1873, he undertook the building of the great church, which became known as the "German Cathedral." It was a vast and costly project for a small frontier city like Saint Paul. By the time all the bills were toted up, the church cost over $100,000. Today, of course, a solid stone structure like Assumption would be all but unbuildable, no matter how many millions might be available to throw at the job.

It appears that Father Clement felt the full weight of the long building project. Wrote the anonymous 1931 historian: "Father Clemens [sic] had so overtaxed his strength during the months following the consecration [of the church in October 1874] that it was thought best for him to take a rest and withdraw for a time from the great strain unavoidably connected with the task of completing the church."

Abbot Alexius Edelbrock called Father Clement home to the abbey and appointed him prior. In 1877 he was appointed pastor of Saint Joseph's Church in nearby Saint Joseph. There he died in 1886. Assumption Church, listed on the National Register of Historic Places and one of Saint Paul's most significant and enduring works of architecture, may fairly be accounted his monument.

Larry Millett '69

Eugene McCarthy Recalls Mandan Parish

I went to Mandan to teach in the public high school after teaching at Tintah and Kimball in Minnesota. Mandan was a town of about seven thousand. There were a lot of German and Russian immigrants, and you would hear German spoken on the streets. Lawrence Welk had an orchestra that played at the pavilion on the river bottom. Abigail Quigley and I sometimes went there to dance. She was also teaching at the public school.

I was there two years. I taught two European history classes and three English classes and was the debate coach. I think the baseball coach, who was Catholic too, was worried that I'd try to replace him.

Father Hildebrand Eickhoff was one of three Saint John's priests at Saint Joseph's Church and grade school. He was very much in charge and managed the church and school and rectory. The others were Father Valerian Thelen and Father Othmar Hohmann, good German names. Father Othmar had been assistant to Father Clarus Graves, the drama coach, at Saint John's. Father Othmar put on a medieval morality play every year that I don't think Hildebrand cared much for.

Hildebrand was very interested in local politics and was always involved in fights with the public school board. He was interested in what was being taught there because there were many Catholic students. He wanted Catholics to teach history. He was pleased that they had teachers like me. He said let the Protestants teach typing and business and the Catholics can teach history.

The principal was Catholic, but the superintendent was Protestant. Hildebrand called him a "cheeseknifer," which I guess was some kind of German term. It wasn't meant as a compliment. Hildebrand used to give a series of Lenten evening lectures about history at Saint Joseph's. He carried Queen Elizabeth back and forth, figuratively speaking, as he corrected the historical record.

Eugene McCarthy '35
as told to Albert Eisele '58

of the present Church of the Assumption. Abbot Boniface Wimmer from Saint Vincent Abbey in Pennsylvania and Rupert Seidenbusch, first abbot of Saint John's, were in attendance. Saint John's cared for the parish until 1912, when we were given charge of another Saint Paul parish, Saint Bernard's.

The pioneer Benedictines also founded two parishes in Minneapolis. Saint Boniface began as a mission from Assumption parish in 1858, became a parish in 1861 and, except for one short break in the early 1870s, continued as a Benedictine presence in northeast Minneapolis until 1998. Saint Joseph's Church dated from 1875 and continued in our care until the old church and rectory were demolished in 1976 to make way for I-94.

Other historically Benedictine parishes in the metropolitan area were Saint Boniface in Hastings, founded in 1880 and merged with Holy Angels to form a single parish, Saint Elizabeth Anne Seton, in 1987; Saint Mary's in Stillwater (1880); and Saint Bartholomew's in Wayzata (1916). The only church in the metropolitan area currently in Benedictine hands is Holy Name in Medina, a small outlying parish until it became a mecca for area Catholics under the charismatic leadership of Arnold Weber, pastor from 1980 to 2001.

DULUTH, BISMARCK, AND PLACES IN BETWEEN

Our monks moved north in the 1880s under the expansive direction of Abbot Alexius Edelbrock—to Duluth, to North Dakota, to the Ojibwe in northern Minnesota.

The population of Duluth mushroomed in the 1880s, and Alexius responded to the need for more churches there with plans for a monastery, hospital, and school. The Benedictine sisters opened Saint Mary's Hospital in 1887, just in time to accept the abbot as their first patient on the same day that he blessed the new Saint Clement's Church down the street. Years later Grand Marais and Grand Portage on the north shore of Lake Superior were entrusted to our care.

Four hundred miles due west of Duluth, priests from Saint John's went to Bismarck in 1881 at the request of Abbot Martin Marty of Saint Meinrad Abbey, now bishop of the Dakota Territory. From Saint Mary's, Bismarck, Paul Rettenmaier visited missions up and down the Missouri. From Saint Joseph's across the river in Mandan, Martin Schmitt ranged west to towns along the new Northern Pacific line. In 1885 the Benedictine sisters turned a Bismarck hotel into Saint Alexius Hospital, and a third priest, Bede Northman, joined the two already in the area.

The history of Saint John's monks in North Dakota over the next century involves many relatively brief pastorates at many places throughout the state. One longer pastorate was at Saint Joseph's, Mandan, in diocesan hands from 1886 until 1910, when the bishop of the new diocese of Bismarck traded it for Saint Mary's in Bismarck, which he made his cathedral. Saint Joseph's stayed a Benedictine parish until 1947, long enough for Mr. Eugene McCarthy, alumnus and future U.S. senator, to teach history in the Mandan public school from 1938 to 1940 with the blessing of Hildebrand Eickhoff, pastor.

Mission to the Ojibwe

In 1875 Rupert Seidenbusch, first abbot of Saint John's, was made bishop and named vicar apostolic of the Vicariate of Northern Minnesota. This was a vast territory reaching from Saint Cloud to the Canadian border and from Wisconsin to the Missouri River. It included two Ojibwe reservations, White Earth and Red Lake, with a combined population of about four thousand. Bishop Seidenbusch encouraged his successor, Abbot Alexius Edelbrock, to send missionaries to work among them. In 1878 young Aloysius Hermanutz, good at languages and inspired by monastic tradition, volunteered to go to White Earth. Escorted by the abbot, he and two sisters from Saint Benedict's Monastery arrived there on November 5. On the second Sunday of the month Aloysius read the gospel in the Ojibwe language.

Aloysius had found his true calling. He labored at it until his death in 1929, and he set the standard for other Saint John's missionaries who followed him, beginning with Thomas Borgerding and Simon Lampe at Red Lake in 1888. Sister Owen Lindblad's *Full of Fair Hope* (1997) tells the history of the century-long Benedictine mission at Red Lake, where sisters, brothers, and priests collaborated in pastoral care, farming, and conducting a grade school. This was where Virgil Michel came to recover his health in 1931 and regretted the need to leave after a year.

A number of predominantly Indian parishes separate from the reservations grew out of this missionary effort—places like Ponsford, Naytahwaush, and Beaulieu (pronounced Bow-lee-oh)—but the character of the pastoral

Father Aloysius Hermanutz and an unidentified sister had their picture taken with some of the men and women of the White Earth reservation in 1883. Unlike Red Lake, White Earth was an open reservation with a mixed although predominantly Ojibwe population.

Making shakes to roof houses at Red Lake produced lots of shavings. Father Thomas Borgerding looks on in this 1909 photo while one man wields the draw knife and another lends moral support. Father Thomas devoted sixty years to pastoral work among the northern Minnesota Ojibwe missions, forty-one of those years at Red Lake.

Otto Zardetti, a Swiss theologian, became the first bishop of the new diocese of Saint Cloud in 1889. Zardetti had preached at the consecration of the abbey church in 1882. Alexius Hoffmann says he made a good impression with his courtly manners and elegant German. He left Saint Cloud in 1894, when he was named archbishop of Bucharest. The four monks pictured with him all figure largely in Saint John's history. From left to right they are John Katzner, Alexius Hoffmann, Peter Engel, and Chrysostom Schreiner.

The least expected pastoral commitment of Saint John's Benedictines had nothing to do with Minnesota but led to Saint John's largest missionary effort.

mission changed as pioneer conditions yielded to railroads, towns, and settled communities. As the Vicariate of Northern Minnesota was divided into two and then three dioceses—Saint Cloud and Duluth in 1889, Crookston in 1910—the new bishops had parishes to care for and not enough priests to go around. Saint John's Abbey had a relative abundance of priests—fifty-five in 1889—and by now it was taken for granted that many would support the abbey with income earned in parishes. (There was, of course, no income from missions and new foundations; quite the contrary.) Thus the abbey accepted the care of Saint Joseph's in Moorhead in 1883; Barnesville in 1894; Detroit Lakes in 1900. A string of parishes running north from Detroit Lakes on County Road 59—Callaway, Ogema, Waubun, Mahnomen, Bejou—were assigned to Saint John's by the new bishop of Crookston and tagged "Pater Noster Row" at the abbey.

Things were different in Stearns County. The new bishop of Saint Cloud, Otto Zardetti, a Swiss national of refined taste, looked out across his diocese in 1889 and found that he had priests in only two Stearns County parishes. All the rest were in Benedictine hands. His tastes did not include a fondness for monks; when parishes were eventually reassigned to his satisfaction, he wrote that "all counties except Stearns are free from the religious" (quoted in Colman Barry, *Worship and Work,* 217). A ruling from Rome in 1893 assigned a limited number of parishes to Saint John's in perpetuity, a right that we quietly relinquished a hundred years later.

THE BRONX AND THE BAHAMAS

By far the least expected pastoral commitment of Saint John's Benedictines had nothing to do with Minnesota but led to Saint John's largest missionary effort. New York's Archbishop Michael Corrigan befriended Alexius Edelbrock when the abbot resigned in 1889 and gave him a pastorate in the rural Bronx where he could start a monastery. A condition was attached: Saint John's Abbey would accept the Bahamas, an ecclesiastical charge of New York, as a mission field. Alexius accepted the pastorate despite Abbot Bernard Locnikar's explicit refusal to commit the abbey to taking care of the Bahamas. Having made that clear, the abbot sent three priests to join Alexius, two of them for the parish, one for the Bahamas. The parish, Saint Anselm's, was founded in 1891 with a four-story rectory big enough for a priory and plans for a large church in the Byzantine style.

As the area became completely urban, the parish flourished and even spawned a second Benedictine parish, Saint Benedict's, in 1923. These became Saint John's largest parishes, with as many as nine priests in residence at the two of them in mid-century, a touch of Saint John's far from home for Benedictine Oblates and others, as I was to discover for myself during graduate study in the fifties and sixties. The challenge of serving in the inner city and the anomaly of sending half a dozen or more priests from Minnesota to supplement the clergy of one of the largest metropolitan dioceses of the country led the chapter to relinquish both parishes in 1976.

The Bahamas mission also dated from 1891, when Chrysostom Schreiner, on his way to San Salvador for a look at Columbus's landfall, ran aground on a reef off Conception Island in bad weather as night was coming on. In this frightening situation he made a vow to devote the rest of his life—he was thirty-two—to missionary work in the Bahamas if spared. Paul Rettenmaier, whom we last saw in Bismarck, was with him in the little boat that got them to shore in the morning but did not feel constrained by the vow and returned to the solid ground of Minnesota. A year later Abbot Bernard himself went down for Christmas and took tubercular Father Rupert Kiefer with him. Others followed, some for their health, some to work in the two Catholic parishes in Nassau or the one on Andros Island.

Abbot Alcuin Deutsch broadened the scope of the Bahamas mission after the First World War by sending enough priests to reach out to towns and settlements throughout the islands. These were jack-of-all-trades missionaries who constructed churches with their own hands, pulled teeth, delivered breech babies, and shared the poverty and the joy of the people they lived with. The future structure of the church in the Bahamas was decided in 1933 when Bernard Kevenhoerster was made bishop and appointed vicar apostolic of the Bahamas. His successor in 1949 was Paul Leonard Haggarty, also a monk of Saint John's, under whom the Bahamas became a diocese in 1960.

In 1946 Saint John's founded Saint Augustine's Monastery in Nassau and Saint Augustine's College, a secondary school for boys. The school achieved a high reputation early on and grew to a stable enrollment of over nine hundred boys and girls. The monastery attracted local vocations at first and gave promise of taking root in the Bahamian culture, but in the end only one stayed and no more came. In 1999 Nassau became an archdiocese, Saint Augustine's College was separately incorporated, and a small crew of Benedictines, including George Wolf, who had come to the Bahamas immediately after his ordination in 1944, remained to tidy up the affairs of the priory. It was a muted ending to a mission in which more than a hundred Saint John's monks had played a part since Chrysostom Schreiner's midnight vow on a stormy sea.

Chrysostom Schreiner and a junior parishioner on the second floor gallery of "The Priory" adjacent to Saint Francis Xavier Church in Nassau. In 1893 Father Chrysostom acquired Dunmore House, a large historic residence situated on a hill overlooking the harbor, and renamed it to serve as a rectory and the center for Benedictine activity in the Bahamas. When Saint Augustine's Monastery was established in 1946, it was carefully not called a priory in order to avoid confusion with the Priory, which by that time had become Bishop Bernard Kevenhoerster's residence as vicar apostolic of the Bahamas.

According to a memorial plaque formally placed in the Cathedral of Saint Francis Xavier in Nassau by Archbishop Patrick Pinder in July 2005, Fathers Fintan Bromenshenkel and George Wolf and Prior Mel Taylor, left to right, were the last of 126 monks of Saint John's to serve in the Bahamas over a span of 114 years. They are pictured here at Saint Augustine's Monastery, mission accomplished.

A different kind of mission was involved in the four Saint John's foundations that became abbeys. Technically, only one of them was a mission, although the earliest, Saint Martin's Abbey in Lacey, Washington, grew out of an invitation from the bishop of Nisqually to staff the new German Catholic parish, Holy Rosary, in Tacoma. William Eversmann went there in 1891. Wolfgang Steinkogler joined him. On their recommendation, Abbot Peter Engel sent half a dozen monks headed by Oswald Baran to start a monastery and school on land outside of Olympia in 1895. The monastery became an independent priory in 1904 and an abbey in 1914, with Oswald as its first abbot.

Saint Peter's Abbey in Saskatchewan grew out of a plan to create a German Catholic colony on the rich farmland opened to immigration by railroads in the new century. By a kind of providential coincidence, Saint John's found itself at the same time involved in the fate of a struggling Benedictine priory in Illinois. Abbot Peter Engel sent seven monks, some from Saint John's, some from Illinois, to Saskatchewan in May 1903. Officially the move was a transfer of the existing Illinois monastery to Canada, but once situated they adopted a new name, Saint Peter's Priory, in honor of Peter Engel. Eight years later the priory became an abbey and in 1921 an abbey nullius, the abbot in effect serving as the bishop of a diocese. Its first three abbots were former monks of Saint John's, the third—Severin Gertken—serving from 1926 to 1960.

Saint John's was also called on to assist some abbeys in trouble: Sacred Heart in Oklahoma, Saint Mary's in North Dakota, Santa Maria de Montserrat in the Philippines. Renamed and relocated, Saint Gregory's, Shawnee, Oklahoma, had a long period of stability under Mark Braun, college dean at Saint John's, who was appointed abbot in 1932. Saint Mary's at Richardton became Assumption Abbey under another Saint John's monk, Cuthbert Goeb, appointed prior in 1928, elected abbot in 1932. An effort to bolster the Benedictines in the Philippines was interrupted when two Saint John's monks, Boniface Axtman and Owen Tekippe, sent to teach in San Beda College in 1940, were interned by the Japanese at the outbreak of the war in the Pacific. After the war they were joined by several other monks from Saint John's, who assisted in getting the Benedictine community at San Beda back on its feet.

Father Kenneth Russell talks with some of the students at San Antonio Abad in Puerto Rico. By the early sixties the original plan to offer schooling for a hundred boys had developed into a boarding school for about 250 boys in grades 7 through 12. The monastery became an abbey in 1984.

Abbot Baldwin Dworschak got a new tie and a happy welcome when he visited Colegio del Tepeyac in 1958. With him are Fathers John Eidenschink, Prior Odo Zimmerman, and Aldo Cadena.

Benedictines in China, Mexico, Puerto Rico

In China, Aidan Germain was sent to join the faculty of the new Catholic university in Peking in 1929. After a year Terence Carroll replaced him. In 1932 Abbot Alcuin, then president of the American Cassinese Congregation, sent Basil Stegmann to Peking to survey the situation. At the urging of Pius XI, the university had been founded by Saint Vincent Archabbey in the name of the congregation ten years earlier, and when it sputtered along without adequate funding or staffing, the pope held the order remiss, as he told Abbot Alcuin in an unpleasant audience in 1933. The Society of the Divine Word, a missionary order, took over in Peking, and the monks came home to find other ways of supporting the church in China during the turbulent half century that followed. Much more recently we have supported Chinese students, clerical and lay, in the school of theology, as I've noted in chapter 1.

After World War II Abbot Alcuin spun off new foundations at a remarkable rate. Saint Augustine's Monastery in Nassau has already been noted. The Abadia del Tepeyac began with four monks going to Mexico in 1947 to take charge of the Colegio del Tepeyac, a school for boys and girls. Clarus Graves was the first prior, Berthold Ricker the second. Both were later priors at Saint John's. Encouraged by the archbishop of Mexico City, the monks acquired land near the school and built a monastery. In 1971 the community, now largely Mexican, elected Placid Reitmeier as its first abbot, a position he held until resigning shortly before his death in 2000.

Tokyo and Shakertown

In 1946 a Puerto Rican landowner proposed that Saint John's build an agricultural and trade school for local boys with his support. That is how the Abadia de San Antonio Abad got its start. The local bishop urged the monks to build a monastery with the school and gave them charge of Holy Name Parish in Humacao with its thirty-seven thousand members and its mission stations in the hills. Fathers Basil Stegmann and Julian Simon and Brother Joel Blekum arrived there in 1947. Others followed. Sisters from Saint Benedict's Monastery opened an elementary school in the parish. The free school for a hundred boys got underway in 1950. Monastic growth was slow, but the foundation became an abbey in 1984 and elected José M. Rodriguez Santiago as its first abbot.

In 1946 Saint John's acquired an outpost on the other side of the world when Hildebrand Yaiser, a monk of Beuron Abbey and a longtime missioner in Tokyo, gained Abbot Alcuin's support for a monastic foundation there. Aloysius Michels, a chaplain in the Pacific area during World War II, joined Hildebrand and his compatriot, Joseph Schmerbach. Their church, Saint Anselm's, completed in 1955, eloquently reflected the monastic ideal by its purity of taste and design, but the monastery's site on an urban railway hummed with activity twenty-four hours a day. In 1999 the archdiocese took over the parish, and the community moved about 120 miles west of Tokyo to a site near Fujimi Nagano, Ken, for the sake of a more contemplative style of monasticism.

A foundation of Abbot Alcuin's that did not work out as planned was Saint Maur's interracial monastery in Kentucky. Alexander Korte proposed the venture in 1946. A racially mixed group of priests, clerics, and brothers moved into historic buildings at Shakertown near Bowling Green in August 1949. The abbot named the new priory Saint Maur's, and the bishop designated it as his diocesan seminary. The monastery became independent in 1963. Four years

It also snows in Japan, as Father Edward Vebelun, one of the Saint John's monks at Fujimi, demonstrates. But if winter comes . . . In the lower photo he mows the lawn while three monastic retreat participants help him with yard work at Trinity Benedictine Monastery. The retreat was an introduction to monastic life for young Japanese men and included prayer with the monastic community and presentations on Benedictine spirituality.

The age-old monastic instinct to share the riches of the gospel, to baptize and catechize, to care for souls, took shape from the start of Saint John's history.

later the seminary moved to Indianapolis, and the year after that most of the community went there too. A group continued at Shakertown as Saint Mark's Priory. Under the aegis of the American Cassinese Congregation, Saint Mark's was canonically dissolved in 1988, Saint Maur's in 2001.

Since Alcuin Deutsch's retirement in 1950, Saint John's has not undertaken a new monastic foundation. The abbots who followed him—Baldwin Dworschak, John Eidenschink, Jerome Theisen, Timothy Kelly, John Klassen—directed significant support to the existing foundations but gradually found themselves concerned with retrenchment. Parishes in New York, in the Twin Cities, in northern Minnesota were turned over to other hands. Mexico and Puerto Rico grew into autonomous abbeys. The mission to the Bahamas came to a close as the diocese and then the archdiocese of Nassau developed under bishops from the region. Holy Trinity Monastery in Japan continues as a dependent priory of Saint John's and has been instrumental in promoting a loose confederation called the Benedictines of East Asia and Oceania (BEAO).

A cluster of historically Benedictine parishes in Stearns County and Holy Name in Medina keep the monastic community attuned to pastoral service. Chaplains continue to serve hospitals, retirement centers, and correctional institutions in the state. The lifestyle of the great parish rectories—the older ones built with a few spare bedrooms to accommodate visiting clergy overnight in the age of buggies and bad roads—has passed into memory along with housekeepers and assistants. Did the first monks make a pledge to serve in the missions? Alexius Hoffmann seems to say so. Whether they did or not, the age-old monastic instinct to share the riches of the gospel, to baptize and catechize, to care for souls took shape from the start of Saint John's history. In time it came to embody Benedictine outreach and hospitality on a vastly broader scale than Bishop Cretin could have foreseen when he sought some German-speaking priests to minister to Catholic immigrants in Minnesota Territory in 1856.

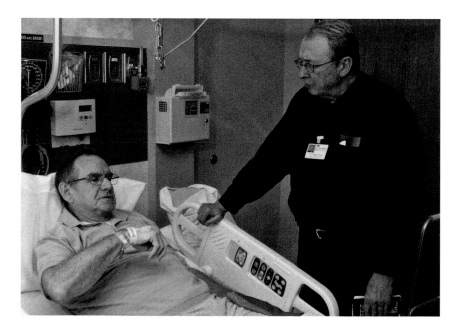

Monks of Saint John's have served as chaplains in hospitals and nursing homes since Father Bede Northman went to Saint Alexius Hospital in Bismarck in 1885. Here Father Roger Botz, chaplain at Saint Cloud Hospital since 1985, chats with Bob Fulton, a member of the CSBSJU chemistry faculty.

Keeping the Word of God

Blessed are those who hear the word of God and observe/keep it. (Luke 11:28)

What does it mean to *keep* the word of God? The original word in the Gospel is used to describe a man guarding his castle (v. 21) or a security person protecting an important person.

Hubert Humphrey, Vice President of the United States, came to Saint John's for a special event. His helicopter landed on the tennis courts, and he was led by the secret service on a path carefully set out beforehand here to the abbey church. The exact same path was taken on his return to the helicopter, and he was guarded against any possible unruly people or potential assassins.

In a similar fashion we are called upon to keep the word of God, our faith.

It is not just a matter of observing that the word of God is there in a book or of keeping it under wraps in a safe place.

We must be willing to guard and protect it with our lives, if necessary, and to live in a manner that shows our commitment to the word of God and our response to the demands it makes on us.

The word of God is not just another book. It is the life of God given to us, and we are called upon to preserve and nourish it with all the gifts we have been given.

Prior Raymond Pedrizetti, O.S.B.

At Saint Boniface parish, Cold Spring, in the care of monks from Saint John's since its founding in 1878, Father Matthew Luft baptizes the newest member of the parish while the pastor, Father Cletus Connors, dressed in all of the liturgical colors simultaneously, enters into the spirit of the summer bazaar. At the church of Saints Peter and Paul, Richmond, in the care of the monks since 1856, Father Stephen Beauclair, pastor, talks with children.

CHAPTER 6

Saint John's and the Liturgical Movement: A Personal View

R. William Franklin

THE STORY OF SAINT JOHN'S ABBEY in its first 150 years is for me all about the liturgical movement. In this essay I want to offer a memory of what it was like to be drawn into the last phase of the modern liturgical movement and what the contributions of the abbey in this area have meant to me.

In the practice of Celtic spirituality these days, people reflect upon a "thin place" where God dwells with us. For thousands of people, Collegeville has been such a "thin place" in all sorts of ways. For some it has been the place where God called them to monastic life or to a life of ordained priesthood. For so many young people, Collegeville is the place where they were introduced to the wonders of learning or discovered their career or met their spouse.

For me, Collegeville and the liturgical movement were the door into a Catholic tradition that could be humane and liberating. I was privileged, as an outsider, to be formed by a generation of heroic monks who through their vision of the spiritual power of the liturgy not only transformed my views but really changed my life. They also permanently altered the religious landscape of the United States. More than any other person, this essay focuses on Dom Virgil Michel, a Collegeville monk of the early twentieth century, who placed Saint John's Abbey in the mainstream of the liturgical movement and who in turn inspired the generation of monks I had the privilege to know.

Filled to capacity, the church becomes a vibrant setting for liturgical celebration with the participants themselves providing the color and warmth for which the space was designed.

A convincing demonstration of the power of sacred art to transform a place of prayer was Brother Clement Frischauf's painting of the apse of the 1882 church to glorify Christ, the Ruler of All, while angels stand in awe before the sacred mystery of the altar.

The Liturgical Movement

The phrase "liturgical movement" was first used more than a hundred years ago to describe the rediscovery of the centrality of the Eucharist in the life and teaching of the Catholic Church and to describe a campaign for the full and active participation of Catholic laypeople in frequent celebrations of the Eucharist. Comprehension by the laity of all that was happening at the Eucharist was the key to participation and the key to the liturgical movement. Participation and comprehension were necessary reforms, because before the liturgical movement took hold, the laity were silent, stationary spectators at worship. Lay passivity in the liturgy unfortunately abetted passivity in the worldly duties of the Christian as well. The liturgical movement sought to remedy this situation by encouraging two reforms:

1. To provide a fuller and more distinctive place for the ministry of the Word in the celebration of the Eucharist;

2. To encourage full and active participation in the Eucharist by all the people of God, as in the early church, by providing vernacular translations and by liturgical education.

In time the liturgical movement transformed the face of Christendom, not just the Roman Catholic Church. By the 1960s the Catholic Church spoke with a new voice. Priests celebrated Mass in the language of the people for the first time in over a thousand years, and altars stood in the midst of actively participating congregations rather than in remote sanctuaries.

Lutheran Churches found their way back to well-trodden sixteenth-century ground, to the equal standing of word and sacrament. Throughout the world the Eucharist supplanted Morning Prayer and Evensong as the chief form of Anglican worship. To the Methodists, the liturgical movement communicated a

Sunday evening college student Mass on the mall.

newfound sense of the corporate nature of the church, demonstrating that by frequent and even weekly celebrations of the Lord's Supper, congregations could be built up into active communities of service and love.

From the perspective of modern history, the triumph of the liturgical movement in many world families of churches represents a major contribution of Christianity to the cultural achievements of the twentieth century, for this renewal of worship by the people and for the people must be seen as part of a larger cultural dynamic, a cluster of parallel movements in politics, the arts, and labor relations opposing the individualizing tendencies of the democratic and industrial revolutions in the name of community.

The Benedictines and the Liturgical Movement

Benedictine monasticism was central to the rise and growth of the liturgical movement. Reading through the Rule of Saint Benedict, we are struck by how many of its features form the basic themes of the liturgical movement: the importance attached to worship; the necessity of meaningful labor; the carefully calculated moderation of Christian authority with freedom and diversity; the balance of the needs of the individual Christian with the aims of the larger community.

The international character of Benedictine monasticism allowed the leadership of the liturgical revival to spread from abbey to abbey and from country to country. In the period after World War I, the liturgical movement gained significant following not only in France and Germany but also in Belgium, Austria, and Holland, so much so that in the 1920s it could gain explicit recognition by the Vatican in the reign of Pius XI, the first pope to use the term "liturgical movement." By then its American home had become Saint John's Abbey.

A First Phase

Saint John's Abbey first felt the influence of the German liturgical movement in the 1890s under Abbot Bernard Locnikar. For Abbot Bernard, the distinctive mission of the Collegeville monks on the frontier was the promotion of liturgical life and the improvement of church music. Manuals on worship and Gregorian chant were imported from Germany to Minnesota in 1891–92; the feasts of the church year began to be celebrated with much greater solemnity in the Saint John's abbey church; and the Divine Office was accompanied with Gregorian chant for the first time in 1893.

Under Abbot Alcuin Deutsch (1877–1951), the abbey church at Saint John's was redecorated following German Benedictine concepts of liturgical art: the altar was moved out from the wall and surrounded by vivid and glistening color in order to highlight the central place of the celebration of the Eucharist in spiritual life and in the rhythm of prayer. In 1921 Abbot Alcuin encouraged a thirty-year-old native of Saint Paul, Father Virgil Michel, to take up the liturgical mission for which he became known. In 1924 Virgil was sent to Rome and to Germany to study what the Europeans were up to. His mission was to determine how to transplant successfully to America what had heretofore been essentially a European development.

Bernard Locnikar became abbot at a troubled moment in Saint John's history and had only a few years to live. He is easily overlooked in the shadow of Abbots Alexius, Peter, and Alcuin. Yet he made a permanent mark on the community by his attention to rubrics, monastic ceremony, liturgy, and music. He had the organ loft extended and an organ installed; he sent a monk to Germany to study organ and chant; he introduced a form of Gregorian chant in all services; he directed attention to careful performance of the Divine Office, use of the monastic choir robe—the cuculla—on feast days, and promptness at the Work of God. (Exclusion from the daily haustus—a beer before supper—was the penalty for coming late.) Peter and Alcuin built on his foundation.

Virgil Michel (1890–1938) was a man of many parts. Here he is pictured in a formal portrait for his ordination in 1916. His doctoral studies at the Catholic University of America, his European study of the liturgical movement, the twelve whirlwind years between 1926 and 1938 when he was founder, promoter, professor, writer, traveler, college dean—all this was yet to come when he posed calm and clear-eyed on the eve of becoming a priest.

VIRGIL MICHEL

Virgil Michel was born in 1890 and died in 1938. He was raised in a large Catholic family in Saint Paul. He came to the prep school in 1903, entered the novitiate of Saint John's Abbey in 1909, and professed his solemn monastic vows in 1913. When he returned to Collegeville from his studies in Europe in 1926, he drew on the resources of this unusually large monastic community to found two projects that became permanent forces for the revival of worship in the United States: the journal *Orate Fratres* and the Liturgical Press. Both implied a commitment to mass communication as a legitimate medium for the instruction of the Catholic public. In stressing that the liturgy of the church must be permeated from beginning to end by the ideal of community, the American Benedictine fixed on lay participation as the supreme key to renewal, without which there could be no Catholic reemphasis on the experience of fellowship in worship.

Orate Fratres appeared on the First Sunday of Advent in November 1926. Its forty-eight pages, by 1930 sent out monthly from Saint John's Abbey to three thousand subscribers in twenty-six countries, rapidly became the voice of the liturgical movement in the English-speaking world. The content of the articles

Liturgical Press

The symbols of the evangelists—ox, eagle, lion, man—were executed in bronze at the entrance to the Liturgical Press by Brother Placid Stuckenschneider, cartoonist for the Pacific Theater edition of Stars and Stripes in World War II and illustrator at the Liturgical Press for three decades.

Not until 1972, when I was hired as an editor at the Liturgical Press, did I realize that for readers around the world "Collegeville" is synonymous with expressive liturgy, the Benedictine monastic life, and publications for the popular, pastoral, and academic market. Thousands of footnotes identify "Collegeville: Liturgical Press" as the source for citations.

Father Virgil Michel, who insisted that the congregation is not an audience but a community that has a priestly role in the liturgy, realized that the liturgical movement would become a part of parish life only if a publisher provided material that focused on the riches of the church's liturgy. The Liturgical Press began in 1926, when it published *Offeramus*, a booklet in which the Ordinary of the Mass was arranged for congregational participation.

Following Father Virgil's untimely death in 1938, the Press was managed from year to year by Fathers Rembert Bularzik, Gregory Roettger, William Heidt, or Ronald Roloff, until Father William Heidt was appointed director in 1951. He continued until 1978. Fathers Daniel Durken (1978–88) and then Michael Naughton (1988–2001) followed him. Peter Dwyer, whose father, John Dwyer, was business manager from 1952 to 1986, became the director in 2001.

Nearly eighty years later the original mission continues as the Press publishes journals, Mass guides, bulletins, books, and electronic products in four principal subject areas: liturgy, theology, Scripture, and monastic studies. The Press provides parishes with liturgical books and ministry materials, and academics and libraries with textbooks and reference works. Via phone, direct mail, and website, the Press markets its eight hundred titles throughout the English-language world and is developing a Spanish list as well.

Among the Press's "bestsellers" across the years are: *The Collegeville Bible Commentary; RB 1980: The Rule of St. Benedict in Latin and English with Notes* (published on the occasion of the sesquimillennium of the birth of Saint Benedict and his twin sister Saint Scholastica); *A Short Breviary for Religious and Laity; The Church's Year of Grace; Our Parish Prays and Sings.* Father Donald Cozzens' *The Changing Face of the Priesthood* (2000) has sold more than 42,000 copies and has editions in French, German, Portuguese, Italian, Spanish, and Czech.

Early publications in booklet size like *Offeramus* rolled off the press in the abbey print shop, founded in 1889, but the Liturgical Press houses no presses nowadays. Today the low-profile campus building with the granite façade adorned with bronze symbols of the evangelists bustles with the editorial and production activity of a staff of nearly sixty, who seek, in the words of the Press's mission statement, "to proclaim the Good News of Jesus Christ through various media and to deepen the faith and knowledge of a richly diverse church."

Mark Twomey '59

and editorials Virgil Michel wrote for *Orate Fratres* from 1926 to 1938 sought to enable the laity to unite in heart and mind with the priest's words and actions at the altar.

A major task of *Orate Fratres* in its early years was to explain the doctrinal content of the prayers of the Mass. The austere restraint and symbolic imagery of liturgical language was unfamiliar to many of the laity, and Michel as editor clarified the theological underpinnings of the formal prayers of the liturgy.

From the beginning, *Orate Fratres* made the case that intelligent congregational participation is closely related to knowledge of early Christian texts. And perhaps even a greater revolution, Virgil Michel wanted his journal to reorient lay instruction along the lines of a thoroughgoing biblical catechesis. He also strove to make liturgical music more appealing and held up the vision of a singing church; in a singing congregation he saw the Holy Spirit of God nurturing human hearts. Finally, from 1933 on he began quietly to advocate a liturgy in the language of the people, evening Masses, and an altar away from the wall and close to the congregation. All of these were unusual, even revolutionary suggestions in 1933.

The Liturgical Press, also founded in 1926, pursued similar goals through its Popular Liturgical Library. The library supplemented the articles of *Orate Fratres* through the production of practical parish resources. During the twelve years of Virgil Michel's directorship, the Popular Liturgical Library sold seven hundred thousand pamphlets at a cost of ten to thirty-five cents each. The two most popular of these, *Offeramus* and *Our Mass*, made active participation of the Catholic laity a reality for the first time in the history of the American church.

To encourage singing, the Liturgical Press published *The Parish Kyriale*, a booklet containing the texts and notations of fourteen Gregorian chant Masses arranged for parish congregations. The entire booklet was handset, note by note, at Saint John's Abbey to make it possible to keep the price at ten cents and thus within the reach of the average American Catholic.

The most radical departures took place in the last eight years of Virgil Michel's life. During the Great Depression *Orate Fratres* and other publications of the Liturgical Press emphasized the social action implied in worship and prayer. Virgil Michel looked out across a land grown hard, cynical, and sinister. One-fourth of American families were on relief. Against this background, *Orate Fratres* and the Liturgical Press addressed unemployment, the reduction of the individual to a depersonalized cog in the workplace, and the economic disparities of capitalism. In these years Virgil Michel presented the liturgy as the school in which people could learn to live in a just community.

The doctrine of the Mystical Body of Christ frames all Virgil Michel's social thought. To him it meant that all worship and work, all human and Christian life, should be thought of in terms of the Christian's organic union with Jesus Christ and with others in Christ. In the supernatural community of "the mystical Christ" is to be found the pattern and inspiration for all social living. This thought permeates Michel's writing on social justice: the communal structure of the Mystical Body of Jesus Christ is the best model for all economic organization. The very momentum of living the liturgy developed an overwhelming conviction in him that a genuine liturgical life flows into the whole of culture and human relationships, that Christians must as a result seek "a reconstruction of the social order."

To Virgil Michel it meant that all worship and work, all human and Christian life, should be thought of in terms of the Christian's organic union with Jesus Christ and with others in Christ.

Abbot Baldwin Dworschak took part in Vatican II as president of the Benedictine federation to which Saint John's belongs. He is pictured here with Father John Eidenschink, on his right, and on his left Mr. James Kritzeck, prep school '48, Islamist and medieval historian, his uncle Leo Dworschak, Bishop of Fargo, and Father Godfrey Diekmann.

This insight of Virgil Michel's is the greatest contribution of Saint John's Abbey to American Catholicism. He saw and implemented in every way at his command the impulse that leads from participation in worship to involvement in the search for peace and justice in the world. There were practical results at Saint John's in the 1930s: the Institute for Social Study was designed to train lay leaders in the implementation of social principles, the fostering of credit unions, grocery cooperatives, and rural life associations. Bernard Evans deals with this topic further in the next chapter.

Quite understandably, there were many critics of Saint John's, from morticians disturbed at a new emphasis on simple funerals to bishops who banned *Orate Fratres* from their seminary libraries and Collegeville monks from their dioceses. One critic was Sister Antonia McHugh, president of the College of Saint Catherine in Saint Paul, who wrote: "The Liturgical Movement centered at Saint John's, which aims to diffuse social charity and understanding through increased lay participation in the official worship of the Church, is something with which I will have nothing to do. The thought of connecting the psalms with socially activated prayers is too irritating to be considered. The whole commotion is doubtless of German origin." To Irish Catholics on the East and West Coasts, the national liturgical conferences, held annually after 1945, were "a meeting of a bunch of German monks out in the Midwest."

The Influence of the Liturgical Movement

In the end Virgil Michel urged Christians who had been given a radical new vision of human life through the liturgical renewal not to withdraw into a movement apart but to take an active place in their local parish church. And this is precisely what happened. The liturgical movement spread to Catholic parish churches and dioceses, and then to the parishes and dioceses of other American denominations as well.

Orate Fratres supported the remarkable growth of the liturgical movement in American parishes. By 1945 it reached five thousand subscribers; by 1955, nine thousand. The Liturgical Press continued to operate out of a room in the

The liturgical movement spread to the parishes and dioceses of other American denominations as well.

basement of the campus auditorium. In 1960, Liturgical Press sales reached a high of eighty thousand books. *The Short Breviary for Religious and Laity,* which went through four editions from 1940 until its revised fourth edition in 1975, was an especially noteworthy volume. It adapted the Roman Breviary to the needs of the Catholic layperson. *The Short Breviary* was anything but short. It contained sixteen hundred pages of scriptural and liturgical extracts. Tens of thousands of lay persons from all across America bought it. By 1980 more than forty thousand copies had been sold.

The revolutionary abbey church completed in Collegeville in 1961 concretely embodies the corporate ideals of the liturgical movement. Bauhaus architect Marcel Breuer used concrete, steel, and glass to provide the monastic community with a great open church where monks and laity could gather together for corporate worship. Breuer's design unifies monastic choir, altar, and congregation into one space for one great community of worship, not divided by class or station, through the rhythmic repetition of starkly modern elements. The emergence of this great church was the final achievement of the

Godfrey Diekmann—A Personal Memoir

When our class manifestly failed to understand his point, Father Godfrey would bang his head against the blackboard, searching for inspiration. We would then try harder to understand.

The time was the late 1950s, and the class had to do with liturgy and the sacraments. We few lay undergraduates felt privileged to be included in a class made up mostly of Benedictine clerics and other seminarians.

Godfrey was in his early fifties. His style was flamboyant and he looked like Moses. The material was largely drawn from nineteenth-century German theologians with polysyllabic names starting with "S." I wasn't sure what the course was about, but I was sure that it verged on heretical. My meager grasp of Thomism was extra logical and mechanistic and certainly allowed no room for symbolism in understanding the sacraments. I gave Godfrey a hard time, asking hostile questions that began, "Surely, Father, you can't mean . . ." He once asked me after class if I disliked him personally. I assured him that my opposition was purely intellectual. He endured my eighteen-year-old arrogance with patience and good humor.

Toward the end of the semester, I converted. How could anyone have seen sacraments any other way than the way Godfrey saw them? He seemed to be the font of all theological wisdom. Surprisingly, he liked me too.

Twenty years later I was back in Collegeville for a month with a family and a borrowed house on Big Watab, about to move to England. Godfrey undertook to tutor us all on the merits of Romanesque over Gothic architecture. In the interval he had become famous as a leader of the liturgical movement and an expert at the Second Vatican Council. He was a leader of ICEL, the body responsible for English in the liturgy.

Godfrey's knowledge of cathedral architecture was more experiential than theoretical. He loved the vitality and exuberance of the Romanesque. Later that year, on his way south from an ICEL meeting in Edinburgh, he stopped to see the cathedral in Peterborough. When we met him at Kings Cross station the next day, he said that he hoped that our guest room was as good as the cell he had begged at the Peterborough jail the night before. By the end of the weekend, my first wife and I had toured Oxford under Godfrey's tutelage along with Brother Dietrich Reinhart and Father Alberic Culhane and had been taught that the Anglo-Saxon chapel at Iffley was the highlight of the region's architecture.

In the eighties, with members of my family, I twice visited Godfrey in Jerusalem. His enthusiasm for the holy places exceeded even his love of the Romanesque. He introduced us to his countless friends among the Syrians, the Ethiopians, and most of the other branches of Christianity. We braved hostile Palestinian stares and gun-toting Israeli settlers to see little-visited biblical sites. When he was too tired to go himself, he deputed Father Thomas Wahl to take us.

In the nineties Godfrey was old and increasingly infirm but no less enthusiastic. The tide of the Council was ebbing, and the church was in some disarray, but Godfrey remained optimistic. When we were living in England, I saw him only once or twice a year. I relied on his long, rambling Christmas letters (with illegible marginal notes) to try to keep up with his enthusiasms.

And finally two years ago, at age ninety-four, Godfrey died. Certainly my most important teacher and perhaps the most famous monk of twentieth-century Saint John's, he was never pretentious and never, ever dull.

Thomas Joyce '61

Godfrey Diekmann (1908–2002) made vows as a monk of Saint John's in 1926 and was ordained a priest in 1931. He completed his doctoral studies in Rome in 1933 and taught a highly regarded course on early church writers at Saint John's and in summer courses elsewhere until 1994. He was once famously barred from lecturing at the Catholic University of America along with Hans Küng and two eminent Jesuits, John Courtney Murray and Gustave Weigel, a distinction he treasured.

<blockquote>
The Constitution on the Sacred Liturgy of the Second Vatican Council vindicated the work of Virgil Michel and the liturgical movement.
</blockquote>

Benedictine liturgical ideals preached and practiced in Collegeville with increasing awareness and sophistication since Bernard Locnikar was abbot.

The Constitution on the Sacred Liturgy of the Second Vatican Council vindicated the work of Virgil Michel and the liturgical movement in its call for a return to the sources of liturgy in the early church and for the adaptation of liturgy to modern conditions. Thus began a thorough revision of the liturgical books of the Roman Catholic Church and also new publications that supported the equally revolutionary call for a revised role for the laity in the Decree on the Apostolate of Lay People, one of the final Council documents. Translations of Belgian, French, and German liturgical tracts, missals, and essays poured from the Liturgical Press to make even larger the range of resources available to Catholic dioceses and parishes in the Popular Liturgical Library. The Liturgical Press also published sources of worship and liturgical piety for the other American denominations that were undergoing a renewal stimulated by the liturgical movement.

A Final Phase in the Twentieth Century

From the end of the Second Vatican Council to the end of the twentieth century, *Orate Fratres,* renamed *Worship,* became the principal way that Saint John's Abbey guided the liturgical movement in what now must be called its last phase. Through this period a remarkable team of monks—Godfrey Diekmann, Michael Marx, Aelred Tegels, and Kevin Seasoltz—guided the magazine. As an assistant professor of history, an Episcopalian, and a Southerner who had arrived at Saint John's from the history department of Harvard University in 1974, I was taken in by this group of men as one of the writers and editorial associates of *Worship,* and from this point I can offer an eyewitness account.

After Virgil Michel, Godfrey Diekmann is the name most people would associate with Saint John's and the liturgical movement. He symbolizes the continuity in Collegeville of what might be described as the "radical" phase of the movement. Father Godfrey was, in fact, Virgil Michel's successor as editor of *Worship,* and he was a *peritus* or advisor on the liturgy at the Second Vatican Council. During the postconciliar period, Godfrey ensured that *Worship* would continue to be a bimonthly review exploring the structures of Christian worship and the problems of liturgical renewal.

To this mission Godfrey contributed an expansive catholicity of spirit after the Council. He wanted *Worship* and the liturgical movement generally to be completely comprehensive and liberal in its examination of fields related to worship, contemporary in its treatment of theological and pastoral concerns, and fiercely analytical in its appraisal of the impact of new movements, such as the women's movement, on the liturgical life of the church. He also made sure that *Worship* monitored closely the Vatican's implementation or non-implementation of conciliar decrees related to the liturgy.

Michael Marx symbolizes the ecumenical spirit of the liturgical movement and of *Worship* in the years after Vatican II. Less well known today than Godfrey Diekmann, he was in fact the guiding spirit behind *Worship* for thirty years. Michael Marx was born in 1920 in Saint Michael, Minnesota, and was educated in Collegeville and in Rome, where he spent all of the Second World War studying at the Benedictine College of Sant' Anselmo. Father Michael was deeply influenced by the persecution of Jews in Fascist Italy. He deeply regretted not being able to rescue the Jews of Rome who faced deportation and death. Out of these experiences Michael embraced the insights of a variety of religious tradi-

Michael Marx (1913–1993) made vows in 1936 and was ordained priest in 1941. He gained a degree in sacred theology during a stay in Rome that was prolonged because of World War II and returned to Collegeville with an Italian accent. The proper answer to any question put by him in the dreaded "hot box" orals before major orders was "Sacramental." During his Italian sojourn he perfected the art of the seemingly bland inquiry that undermines a whole structure of conventional thought. His staid exterior concealed a revolutionary.

tions and new movements. I remember visiting his room in his last days, and his bed was piled high with feminist biblical criticism, which he forcefully encouraged me to study!

Michael worked with scholars from around the world engaged in the study, revision, and renewal of Christian liturgy, who in consequence were engaged in the search for Christian unity. For thirty years he shaped *Worship* so that its liturgical scholarship transcended denominational divisions and served all the churches. He was convinced that the twentieth-century convergence in the reform of worship, resulting from the liturgical movement, powerfully served the cause of Christian unity. While he was guiding *Worship,* most of the major Protestant churches throughout the world became involved in the revision of their liturgical books, and Michael brought *Worship* into these currents of activity. He made *Worship* an editorial force to be respected in the Christian world. He was both a gentle and demanding personal force who allowed scholars to get to know one another through their contacts with him and to come to share a common approach to Scripture, ancient texts, and new research. For him there was at the very heart of the liturgical movement a call to see Christianity as a shared faith that can never be the possession of any one generation or any one century, a faith expressed in a Eucharist that binds into one solidarity all Christians despite their separate denominational affiliations.

Abbot Jerome Theisen and Bishop Robert Anderson apparently regarded something as going without saying when this photo was taken on December 6, 1983. Their congenial relationship paved the way for planning an Episcopal retreat center at Saint John's by the end of that decade.

Michael Marx used Benedictine hospitality to forge this ecumenical dimension of the liturgical movement in the last third of the twentieth century. In 1967, Saint John's founded the Institute for Ecumenical and Cultural Research, which enabled scholars of many traditions to live and study in Collegeville for an academic semester or a year. Michael had a regular table in the abbey guest dining room, where he invited these ecumenical guests to meet members of the monastic community or the Saint John's university faculty. Out of these lunches grew not only scholarship and publications for *Worship* but Christian friendship and mutual exchange that influenced the course of Christian scholarship and liturgical reform in the American churches for decades.

An Ecumenical Project

Along with Abbot Jerome Theisen, Michael was one of the principal monastic supporters of an ecumenical project that might be considered one of the final achievements of the liturgical movement, namely, the Episcopal House of Prayer at Collegeville. On September 16, 1989, three hundred Minnesota Episcopalians and Benedictine monks and sisters gathered to break ground for the House of Prayer on five acres of abbey land leased to the Episcopal Diocese of Minnesota without fee. For the previous ten years, hundreds of Minnesota Episcopalians had gathered at Saint John's for retreats, seminars, and worship services. In 1980–81, the assistant bishop of Minnesota, the Right Reverend William Dimmick, had lived and worked out of Saint John's Abbey. Now for the first time since 1533, at the start of the Reformation, a large Anglican diocese and a Benedictine monastery in communion with the Roman Catholic Church pledged to live, work, and pray together in a new way.

The House of Prayer was dedicated in 1991 and expanded significantly at the end of the twentieth century. It is a place set apart to plan for a renewal of the parishes and the diocese, the same goal as that of the liturgical movement.

The Episcopal House of Prayer at Collegeville might be considered one of the final achievements of the liturgical movement.

We realized that the language of faith and theology is ultimately a language of prayer.

Names reminiscent of the long ties of Anglicans and Benedictines were suggested for this house: Canterbury House, reminding us that the mother church of the Anglican Communion at Canterbury was founded by Benedictine monks in 604, or Bede House, reminding us of the Benedictine foundation of the theological tradition of the Church of England.

But over the course of the 1980s and 1990s we realized that none of these names was adequate. We realized that the language of faith and theology, of Scripture and sacraments—the living stones of the House of Prayer—is ultimately a language of prayer. Saint John's monks and Episcopalians living and working together came to the same conclusion as the liturgical movement: that the necessary work of theological reflection, of Scripture analysis, and of social criticism all follow from and are secondary to the basic work of God, the speaking to God in prayer. The name "House of Prayer" is an affirmation that it is in the prayer of the church, the liturgy, which Catholics and Anglicans share, that the way is opened up between heaven and earth, past and present, fusing the oppositions that we make between Protestant and Catholic, men and women, gay and straight, black and white, Native American and European.

The House of Prayer is a final twentieth-century symbol of the work of the liturgical movement in Collegeville, an outward and visible sign that God calls us to participate in the great rhythm of life, the breathing in and the breathing out of the Holy Spirit, emphasizing the dynamic relationship of prayer and justice that has been revealed in singular and numerous ways in the "thin place" of Collegeville in the twentieth century.

The wooden structures of the House of Prayer with its common space, private rooms, and chapel become part of the natural setting on a corner of the campus just beyond Flynntown.

Founding Collegeville Institute for Ecumenical and Cultural Research

Kilian McDonnell, O.S.B.

Institutional ecumenism at Saint John's started in the 1950s with the unofficial dialogue between Lutheran and Catholic seminarians initiated by Father Paul Marx and Jack Eichhorst. As a young theology student, I was a part of it. In the late fifties Father Colman Barry organized one of the first ecumenical meetings in the United States between Protestant and Catholic theologians. It was held here at Saint John's.

So ecumenism was in the air when I attended a theology school discussion about the possibility of teaching Protestant theology to our undergraduate students. I was opposed. Why take from the little time we had for teaching them Catholic theology? I lost. Then the faculty decided that since we were committed, we should train someone who could do it professionally. The faculty looked around the room and said "Kilian."

I told Abbot Baldwin that I thought I could get grant money, as it would be unusual at that time for a Catholic to be studying theology under Protestant professors. I sent out a two-page proposal to ten foundations. Eight of them declined, and two responded positively. When Patrick Butler read my proposal, he called Father Walter Reger to ask about Kilian, and then the Butler Foundation in Saint Paul made a grant of $5,000. I did my doctoral studies in Germany. Every year I wrote a long letter to Patrick Butler about my life and studies. I made the letters as interesting as possible, including new theological movements, significant ecumenical personalities, the relevance of the courses I was taking. Though I never received a response, I did the same every year.

After I received my doctorate in sacred theology, I came home and called Patrick Butler, saying I would like to come and thank the Butler family personally. I went to Saint Paul and had lunch with him and Aimee and Peter Butler and found that they had multilithed my letters from Germany for their friends. At the end Patrick Butler said, "Where do we go from here?" I thought the heavens had opened. But I simply said that I should go back to Saint John's, talk with my confreres, and I would get back to him.

After consulting with others at Saint John's, I explained to the Butlers that the churches of the United States were out of the missionary stage (when bricks and mortar were important) but were not out of the missionary mentality. We were still borrowing our research from the mother countries. What the churches needed was a post-doctoral research institute. Patrick Butler said, "Don't call me, I'll call you." After a year I still had not heard from him, so I disobeyed him and telephoned, saying the churches were at the crest of a wave of ecumenical enthusiasm. If the Butler family wanted to help, now was the time. He told me to come down. When I got there he gave me $250,000.

Fathers Florian Muggli and Gervase Soukup were helpful with building suggestions. Father Colman Barry, then president of Saint John's University, went with me to see Bishop Peter Bartholome. In presenting the project to the monastic chapter, I proposed that the research center should be called the Institute for Ecumenical and Cultural Research and should not be a Catholic institution. We Benedictines would lose control, but the institute would operate better if it were ecumenical not only in purpose but in structure. The chapter generously agreed. After I had engaged architect Marcel Breuer and let the bids, the cost of the buildings furnished came to $350,000, so I returned to Patrick Butler, suggesting that we might put up half of the institute and worry about the other half later. But he said, "No, if we are going to do this, we should do it." He gave another $100,000.

I assembled an ecumenical board of directors after consulting Fathers Walter Reger, Colman Barry, Michael Blecker, and other monks. Peter Butler, Colman Barry, and Godfrey Diekmann were among its first members. We still had to provide the scholars with studies in the Alcuin Library. Patrick Butler granted the institute $50,000 to create the eleven studies. In planning for the dedication ceremony, we wanted to bring to Collegeville the two top ecumenical leaders at the international level, Bishop Jan Willebrands of the Vatican Secretariat for Christian Unity and Dr. Eugene Carson Blake of the World Council of Churches in Geneva. Patrick and Aimee Butler made it possible. At this point I asked Abbot Baldwin for another monk to assist me, and the abbot offered Ephrem (Philip) Kaufman, who joined me as associate director.

The state charter was granted in 1967, the institute was dedicated on May 26, 1968, and the first scholars arrived in the fall of that year. To date over four hundred scholars from Africa, Europe, Asia, South and North America have been residents. Besides myself, Morris Wee, Robert Bilheimer, Patrick Henry, and Donald Ottenhoff have served as executive directors. It is obvious that the institute owes its existence to the vision and unusual generosity of the Butler family, not only at the beginning but, together with other board members, during the years since.

Kilian McDonnell, O.S.B.

Patrick Henry, executive director of the Institute from 1984 to 2004, with Don Ottenhoff, the present executive director and former senior editor of The Christian Century.

CHAPTER 7

Virgil Michel and the Collegeville Community: Liturgy and Social Justice

Bernard Evans

Here was a place where persons interested in liturgy and justice and rural life found a supportive environment.

When I accepted Saint John's invitation to be the first occupant of the Virgil Michel Ecumenical Chair in Rural Social Ministries, it was a homecoming. I was a seminary student in the sixties, and Saint John's provided the context from which I rejoiced in the Second Vatican Council and despaired at the Vietnam War.

In the intervening period I spent two years with the Peace Corps in Turkey and ten years on the staff of the Catholic bishops' Campaign for Human Development. I was privileged to help shape one of the most exciting social justice initiatives in the U.S. Catholic Church. The campaign sent seven million dollars each year to local self-help projects to build economic strength and political power among America's poor. It engaged the church in structural change shaped by principles of justice. When some affluent Catholics and a few bishops questioned this work, I enrolled (at the urging of Father Colman Barry) in a doctoral program at the Catholic University of America.

When a generous gift from the Butler Charitable Trust enabled Saint John's to establish the Virgil Michel Chair a few years later, it seemed like the right place to blend my interests in academics and social change. The chair was made possible by a tradition at Saint John's that attracted such people as Leonard Doyle, Emerson Hynes, and J. F. Powers. Here was a place where persons interested in liturgy and justice and rural life found a supportive environment. It was an environment shaped in part by Father Virgil Michel's ideals and the social movements he furthered.

For almost twenty-five years this chair has focused on social justice from a Catholic perspective, not only in the classroom but in advising the bishops on Catholic social teaching bearing on agriculture, the environment, and rural issues. Its work in rural social ministries connects it with rural life programs, such as the National Catholic Rural Life Conference. Its ecumenical thrust shapes the chair's engagement to achieve social change through such endeavors as the Joint Religious Legislative Coalition, a coalition of Muslim, Jewish, Protestant, and Catholic faith communities devoted to lobbying Minnesota legislators on social justice issues. The Virgil Michel Chair's work is rooted firmly in the heritage of Saint John's involvement with social movements.

Arleen and Emerson Hynes were a rare phenomenon at Saint John's, a lay faculty couple, when they married and began their idyllic rural life at Kilfenora, the home they built near Collegeville station, in the 1940s. Here they are pictured before going to Washington, D.C., in 1960.

Emerson Hynes at Collegeville

In 1938 Emerson Hynes was happy to accept Father Virgil Michel's invitation to teach ethics and rural sociology at Saint John's University. He meant to spend a lifetime of living and teaching at his revered alma mater, so he tramped the fields and woods looking for land for our ideal, rural home. He found it on the hilltop along the gravel road between Saint John's and the Collegeville railroad station, now the Lake Wobegon Trail for hikers and bicyclists.

During summer of 1941, Emerson and a host of good friends, including Father Walter Reger (mentor), Father Emeric Lawrence, and Father Martin Schirber, put the Benedictine motto "Ora et Labora" into practice as they worked on the cinder-block home we called Kilfenora.

As our family grew to ten wonderful children (two girls and eight boys), we eagerly carried out our intent to live off the land: to heat the house with our trees, preserve our garden vegetables, can our neighbor's beef, rely on milk and butter from our cow, Lucia, and bake our daily bread. We were delighted with our lifestyle and the stimulating conversations with our Benedictine friends and with our neighboring friends: J. F. Powers and his wife Betty, sculptor-artist Joe O'Connell and Jodie, artist Don Humphrey and Mary, translator Leonard Doyle and Betty—in short, what J. F. Powers called "The Movement." A rich life.

We did not leave Kilfenora and Saint John's because the abundant life became sterile but because as legislative assistant to Minnesota Senator Eugene McCarthy, fellow alumnus of SJU, Emerson could work on national legislation furthering the common good. In 1960 we moved to suburban Virginia near Washington, D.C. Emerson died there in 1971. However, our hearts never abandoned Kilfenora and Saint John's.

Arleen Hynes, O.S.B.

THE SOCIAL MOVEMENTS

While these movements spanned the mid-twentieth-century decades, they are especially identified with the thirties. The period of the Great Depression, with its bank closures, bread lines, and desperate farmers, seemed to call social movements into existence. By this time U.S. Catholics had moved beyond an immigrant need to demonstrate patriotism. A growing Catholic social consciousness took form, emboldened by pronouncements such as the following from the bishops' National Catholic Welfare Conference in 1931: "The real authors of violent and bloody revolutions in our times are not the radicals and communists, but the callous and autocratic possessors of wealth and power who use their positions and their riches to oppress their fellows." Catholic interest in social change also drew energy from the high-profile public policy work of Monsignor John A. Ryan, a Minnesota native, whose efforts over the previous two decades bore their greatest fruits in the 1930s.

Several persons who were introduced to Saint John's by Virgil Michel became involved in the social movement of the thirties. He became known as a leader of the liturgical movement who grasped its social implications. He put the fundamental principle simply in *Orate Fratres*, the liturgical journal he founded, in 1935: "The common offering made by them [the early Christians] to God became at the same time a common act of love and charity to the poor and the needy, so that in one and the same collective but unitary action they worshipped God directly and served Him indirectly in their fellowmen" (9:543).

The *Catholic Worker*, begun by Peter Maurin and Dorothy Day, encouraged lay Catholics to live out their personal responsibility for the poor through daily acts of compassion and mercy. Many Catholics of the time believed that the cooperative movement expressed the communitarian ideals of Christian morality in a way that capitalism, with its competitive nature, could not. Pius XI's harsh assessment of capitalism and his call for a new economic order encouraged new experiments with cooperative principles like Nova Scotia's Antigonish Movement.

These social change efforts were promoted throughout rural America by the National Catholic Rural Life Conference. Formed in 1923, by mid-century the conference became the Catholic voice for rural life issues, with a particular focus on questions concerning food and agriculture. But while the various social movements shared the goal of promoting social and economic reform in the United States, they represented two distinctly separate views about the best way to achieve change.

Monsignor Ryan's success in influencing national economic policy was rooted in a conviction that the struggle for social justice must be waged in the area of systemic, structural change. Economist Ryan believed that the self-serving power of businesses in the capitalist system could be checked only by an equally powerful social, political force. That force would be found in the State, especially the federal government. The church's Catholic Action Movement, strongly championed by Pope Pius XI, shared Ryan's views but called for committed and well-formed Catholic laypersons to work for reform throughout society. This systemic social-reform approach was seminally present in Pope Leo XIII's 1891 encyclical, *Rerum Novarum*; it became a moral imperative in the post-Vatican II encyclicals of Paul VI and John Paul II.

Another approach to social reform put the accent upon changing individual persons. It held that the spiritual and moral renewal of persons was the primary and necessary way to change society's institutions and structures. The emphasis here reflected elements of European Christian personalism and demanded personal reform and commitment, love of neighbor, and voluntary action. Societal change would result from the example of Christian love, and not be derived through legislative or institutional change. This personalist approach was articulated in a most uncompromising way by Catholic University of America sociologist Father Paul Hanley Furfey. Others who reflected this view included Peter Maurin and the early leaders of the Catholic Worker Movement, many of whom found nourishment in the liturgical revival.

SAINT JOHN'S AND THE MOVEMENTS

In the middle decades of the twentieth century, several persons embodied Saint John's connection with the period's social movements. Emerson Hynes (philosophy) brought into the classroom the Catholic social encyclicals that had been developed up to that time, notably Leo XIII's *Rerum Novarum* and Pius XI's *Quadragesimo Anno*. Father Martin Schirber (economics), in a joint effort with the National Catholic Rural Life Conference, promoted the study of rural issues, especially those related to agriculture. Sylvester Theisen (sociology) took a leave from Saint John's to work with the United Nations' Food and Agriculture Organization. Many Saint John's alumni gratefully recall Dr. Theisen's courses on Catholic social thought and on developmental issues related to world population growth. The teaching and programmatic work of these three faculty members reflected in part John A. Ryan's approach to systemic change.

Father Virgil, a member of the faculty and monastic community, represented the alternative approach described earlier as "personalist." His contribution to the social movements stemmed from his understanding of the liturgy. The liturgical movement, he argued, sought to bring lay Catholics into active participation in the liturgy, especially the Eucharist. The result of informed and active liturgical engagement would be an ever-deepening lay awareness of fellowship in the Mystical Body of Christ. This recognition would lead to the further realization that salvation was not to be perceived in isolation from other

J. F. Powers won the National Book Award in 1962 for his novel Morte d'Urban, *with its trademark two-edged description of the diocese of Ostergothenburg and the Order of Saint Clement. On the strength of the award he and Betty moved to Ireland and wrote books there, she* Rafferty & Co., *he* Look How the Fish Live. *They returned to the States in 1975 and Jim became a writer-in-residence at Saint John's. Joe O'Connell, Garrison Keillor, and he formed a warm friendship. On Sunday Jim preferred to occupy a seat in the empty balcony of the church, where Joe often joined him and where the sound of the sermon was indistinct.*

J. F. Powers at Collegeville

My father's connection with Saint John's began in the early 1940s and arose out of his informal affiliation with the Catholic Green Movement, which flourished around Collegeville, thanks to Abbot Alcuin Deutsch, Father Virgil Michel, and a loose-knit community of Catholic families. Facing a prison term for refusing induction into the army in 1943, he attended a retreat at Saint John's, about which he later wrote: "I will not forget the plain chant and that cemetery under the July sun. The brothers who work in the fields." His correspondent was Sister Mariella Gable of Saint Benedict's, who, in fact, produced the tie that ultimately fastened him to the Benedictines for good: her protégée, my mother, Betty Wahl.

"I am filled with what I choose to call Benedictinism," he boasted to Mariella; but neither she nor my mother were convinced. Both recognized that it was the religious community's implicit criticism of the world that attracted him, not communal life lived in what he called "Big Missal Country." Still, after three decades of wandering, hardship, and loneliness, my parents returned to Saint John's, where my father taught writing and put bread on the table. It amounted to a homecoming, especially for my mother, who positively bloomed, finally able to grow a garden and attend daily Mass and feel part of the world here and beyond. My father, himself, let slip the occasional note of satisfaction, especially at Christmastime: "Even I was impressed," he wrote in 1976. "Abbot John got off a first-class sermon."

Katherine A. Powers

Leonard Doyle came to Collegeville after World War II and held a position as a typesetter and translator at the Liturgical Press. He and Betty Finegan were married in 1948, the same year that the Liturgical Press published his translation of the Rule of Benedict. Two paragraphs about qualities to be desired in an abbot from chapter 64 of Doyle's translation of the Rule speak to the personalist roots of Benedictine community.

From Leonard Doyle's Rule of Benedict

"Once he has been constituted, let the Abbot always bear in mind what a burden he has undertaken and to whom he will have to give an account of his stewardship, and let him know that his duty is rather to profit his brethren than to preside over them. . . . Let him exalt mercy above judgment, that he himself may obtain mercy. He should hate vices; he should love the brethren. . . .

"In his commands let him be prudent and considerate; and whether the work which he enjoins concerns God or the world, let him be discreet and moderate, bearing in mind the discretion of holy Jacob, who said, 'If I cause my flocks to be overdriven, they will all die in one day.' Taking this, then, and other examples of discretion, the mother of virtues, let him so temper all things that the strong may have something to strive after, and the weak may not fall back in dismay."

members of this Body. He anticipated by thirty years the Second Vatican Council's observation that God has chosen us not as individuals but as members of a community. Awareness of one's membership in a community of believers—in a saved community—carried implications for how we live our entire lives.

Virgil Michel believed that the liturgical spirit should have an impact on the restructuring of society, but it is not clear how he thought this link between liturgy and social life was to be realized when the latter includes working for social justice. He strongly promoted Pius XI's encyclical *On Reconstructing the Social Order,* the only modern papal encyclical seeking to outline a program to reshape societal structures to reflect a Christian social order. He criticized unrestrained capitalism: "It is an economic system that is the combined product of the high-powered individualism of the modern world and the supremacy of material ownership above all other human rights" (*Economics and Finance,* [1936], 20). Yet he did not believe that Christianity provided a detailed plan for social reconstruction. He even felt that the Catholic Action Movement, so dear to the hierarchy, failed to grasp the necessary relationship between personal conversion and societal reform. He was convinced that a viable Catholic Action effort must include the liturgical life, which alone could instill in Catholics the love for others and the sense of solidarity that are prerequisites for legislative and systemic change.

In 1931–32 Father Virgil recuperated from overstrain by joining in the life of the Red Lake Indian Mission in northern Minnesota, and when he returned he was more intent on defining the connection between liturgy and social justice. In 1935 he began the Institute for Social Study, which enabled Catholic laymen to attend weekend conferences at Saint John's for liturgy and study. The institute had a primary goal of helping participants apply principles of Catholic social teaching to contemporary problems.

Virgil Michel was also actively involved with the National Catholic Rural Life Conference (NCRLC). He had reservations about large urban parishes and about society's steady transformation into an urban population. In an *Orate Fratres* article in 1938, he asserted that rural life might be the

Alphonse Matt, Sr., stands to the right of Virgil Michel in this 1938 photo of participants in a campus meeting of the Institute for Social Study. Emerson Hynes appears in the top row at the extreme right. Matt became editor of *The Wanderer,* the Catholic weekly paper founded in 1867 as *Der Wanderer,* in 1967. He and his father, Joseph Matt, editor of the paper in the 1930s and 1940s, were strongly interested in the liturgical movement and its social implications.

best environment for nurturing community and solidarity among people. The NCRLC seemed to him to be a place where these concerns could be addressed with a spiritual focus that could lead to social change. His support of NCRLC led to jointly sponsored rural-life summer schools at Saint John's in the forties, a cooperative effort that continues today. In the last two decades the Virgil Michel Chair and NCRLC have co-sponsored Theology of Land Conferences at Saint John's.

Virgil Michel was an ardent supporter of the cooperative movement and invited its leaders to lecture at his Institute for Social Study. He spent three weeks in Nova Scotia studying the Antigonish Movement. He maintained that cooperatives were one piece of the effort to bring economic reform and that the cooperative movement and credit unions deserved Catholic support. Shortly before his death he began designing a series of courses to explore the relationship between the cooperative movement and the liturgical revival.

The founders of the Catholic Worker Movement had an ongoing rapport with Virgil Michel, who was among their earliest supporters. He corresponded with Peter Maurin over their differences regarding personalism. Maurin and Dorothy Day were occasional visitors on the campus, and Father Virgil visited the Catholic Worker house in New York City. In 1934 he sent Dorothy Day copies of all the publications of the Liturgical Press to help the Catholic Worker integrate liturgy into its program of social action.

Lasting Influence

Saint John's contribution to the social movements of the mid-century is best represented in one person: Virgil Michel. Others contributed to aspects of social reform during this period, but none had his broad and lasting impact. He saw the connection between liturgy and justice. If Virgil Michel's efforts to link liturgy and justice were not reflected in Vatican II, they are boldly present in the document of the 1971 World Synod of Bishops issued just five years after the council adjourned. In *Justice in the World,* the bishops remind us that the church does not exist for itself, but to reach out to the world in service and justice. In words reminiscent of Virgil Michel, the synod affirmed that the Eucharist forms the community and places it at the service of all people.

As I conclude this essay, I am preparing to leave for North Dakota to discuss land ethics at a gathering of Protestant bishops. The ecumenical character of this dialogue about caring for the earth and building a more just society promises to be interesting and challenging. I hope it demonstrates as well that what Virgil Michel sowed continues to grow.

Saint John's association with Dorothy Day began in 1934 when Abbot Alcuin Deutsch sent her a contribution of $10 and recommended to Virgil Michel that he acquaint himself with her "excellent little paper." Two short notes from Dorothy Day reflect her friendship with Virgil Michel as well as her matter-of-fact poverty: "eviction held off till June; am in bed with a cold." In an earlier letter to Abbot Alcuin she remarked that "I think it is very significant that God always sends us enough to keep going on, with nothing left over, so that we can still rejoice in the poverty we are privileged to share with Him."

Dorothy Day

April 16, 1936

Dear Father Virgil:

Thank you for your continued support of our work. We are all looking forward to your visit to us in the summer.

You will notice that the farm is 71 miles out but it only takes 1 1/2 hours to get there by train and we hope you will spend a few weekends with us not to work but to rest.

Please pray for us all.

Sincerely yours in Christ,

Dorothy Day

January 31, 1937

Dear Father Virgil:

We should be most happy if you can speak on Wednesday evening, February 17th at The Catholic Worker office. I am certainly sorry that I am going to be away at that time as I am making my usual spring trip of a month—this time to cover parts of the South. You remember that I was not in the office before when you called and here it is happening again.

You will be happy to hear that our eviction has been postponed until June. This must be just a short note as I am in bed with a cold.

Sincerely yours in Christ,

Dorothy Day

CHAPTER 8

Nursery of the Arts

Robin Pierzina, O.S.B.

I am determined to have our monasteries [be] not only schools of religion and of science, but also nurseries of the fine arts, in order to develop a better taste for these things and to keep from our people the American mercenary spirit which thinks of nothing but how to make a living, because necessity demands it, and example encourages it. . . .

Art must go hand in hand with religion, to give the exercises of religion that external splendor, dignity, and sublimity which make them more meaningful . . . . It is the duty of monasteries to foster, to promote, and to spread art, especially religious art . . . . I am fully convinced that a monastic school which does not promote the fine arts as well as science and religion is very incomplete, and that, in the beginning, the want of scientific learning is more excusable than neglect of the arts.

Abbot Boniface Wimmer, July 1849

DESPITE THE CHALLENGES OF FRONTIER LIFE in central Minnesota and despite the ever-present threat posed by the "American mercenary spirit," Abbot Boniface's entreaty and promotion of the arts did not go unheeded by the pioneer monks and leaders of Saint John's. From the community's earliest days and throughout the past fifteen decades, the arts have animated the lives, the lifestyle, and the vision of the Saint John's community.

Artistic expression, especially music and drama, enjoyed a significant role in the educational development of Saint John's. In the 1860s, advertisements for Saint John's College identified "Music—Piano, Violin, Brass Instruments, and Vocal Music" in the curriculum; by the mid-1880s four professors gave instruction in music, and "5 pianos, 2 organs, flutes, violins, guitars, and citherns" were in service. The first formal commencement (known as "Exhibition Day") in June 1868 included some hours of music by the college band, violin solos, a treatise on history, comic pieces in both English and German, and the drama *Harvest Storm;* for lack of an adequate indoor performance space, all were presented on an improvised outdoor stage, which, claimed chronicler Father Alexius Hoffmann, "savored of the best features of the early

The instruments if not the instrumentalists can be identified in this 1885 brass quintet. They are from left to right a euphonium, an E-flat alto horn, two cornets, and a sousaphone. The full band numbered twenty members when it played on Thanksgiving in 1887.

◄ "This music crept by me upon the waters," says Ferdinand, prince of Naples, in *The Tempest*. For music upon the waters at Saint John's the musicians presented what they called gondola concerts from boats on the lake standing close to shore. Here a guitar and flute duo perform while a third person holds the music. In this 1905 photo Adrian Schmitt is the guitarist and the duck boat is the gondola. The other performers are not identified, although one is a monk and the other probably a student.

Brother Paul Richards evokes a perfect vowel from a junior member of the Boys Choir. Founded by him in 1981, the choir will celebrate its silver anniversary in Saint John's sesquicentennial year.

There were never enough violins to satisfy Father James Kelly, director of the orchestra, who stands to the left in this 1947 photo. The orchestra made its first appearance on Thanksgiving Day, November 26, 1885. Choral maestro Gerhard Track was its last director. It passed into history when he left Saint John's in 1969. Today a symphony orchestra under the direction of David Arnott includes more than sixty student musicians from both colleges.

Saint John's–Saint Benedict's Chamber Choir poses in formal dress in the choral rehearsal room of the renovated and expanded 1928 auditorium building. Axel Theimer, the director, is not in the photo, but he has put his signature on choral music and ensemble accompaniment since he came to Saint John's in 1969.

Grecian theatre." In the mid-1870s, in addition to the classical and commercial curriculum, "Cecilian music was cultivated." A few years later a singing society was organized, and according to a *Saint Cloud Daily Times* correspondent, "The boys take to it like kittens to milk."

Since its earliest decades the Saint John's calendar has been punctuated with musical and dramatic performances by its students and staff. The arts were also advanced through the organization of various literary associations promoting the mastery of oratory and debate and the cultivation of language and literature, as well as through many musical ensembles. In 1953, anticipating the later coordinate relationship between the College of Saint Benedict and Saint John's University, the presentation of *La Boheme* brought together the students and staff of the two music departments as well as members of the Benedictine communities. Father James Kelly prepared the university orchestra and male chorus; Sister Firmin Escher directed the female chorus; Sister Clarus Himsl, along with the home economics department, oversaw the women's costumes; Father Bartholomew Sayles worked with the Saint John's Preparatory School singers, while Father Dominic Keller, who for years brought much drama to the university and monastery, took charge of the staging, sets, and men's costumes. Today Brother Paul-Vincent Niebauer, using skills and insights honed in years with the Franzen Bros. and other circuses, brings distinction to the prep school stage while blurring the distinction between a three-ring circus and a monastery.

The brass band that had celebrated the first Exhibition Day expanded in subsequent years; an orchestra was also in place by the beginning of the twentieth century. In the following decades creative and enthusiastic students, faculty, and monks formed a wide variety of musical groups. A dance band specializing in the sounds of the Big Band era was formed in 1948; twenty-five years later college students were still presenting concerts under the name of the "Moonmisters." Cyril Paul and his university Latin American combo won the Minnesota centennial college talent contest in 1958. In the late 1970s Fathers Don LeMay (piano) and Gordon Tavis (violin) were staples of Johnny homecoming entertainment. Recitals and concerts, by soloist and ensembles, both students and staff, have been the norm throughout Saint John's history.

Vocal music, from the ancient Gregorian chant in the monastic choirs to the contemporary voices of student or faculty groups, flourished as well. Beginning in the late 1950s, under the direction of maestro Gerhard Track and continued by Axel Theimer to the present day, the

University Men's Chorus has raised choral music at Saint John's to a high level. Brother Paul Richards and the Saint John's Boys' Choir have delighted audiences and advanced music programs in central Minnesota in the quarter century since the choir was formed. Gregorian chant was the love and life's work of Father Gerard Farrell; with the introduction of English into the liturgy in the 1960s, Fathers Henry Bryan Beaumont Hays and Jerome Coller composed a substantial number of new hymns; and Father Robert Koopmann, pianist and organist, excels at inviting the con-

gregation to raise its collective voice in song. At the turn of the twenty-first century, Father Anthony Ruff introduces a new generation to the riches of sacred music and the liturgy through the National Catholic Youth Choir.

PHOTOGRAPHY, PAINTING, SCULPTURE

In the last decades of the nineteenth century, Father, then Abbot Peter Engel began to experiment with photography. Numerous monk and lay photographers followed him over the next century. In the last years of the twentieth century, Brother Simon-Hoa Phan began to experiment with filmmaking and later to record community events digitally. Painting and sculpture have also flourished at Saint John's as evidenced by the exceptionally fine large figure of Christ on the cross carved by pioneer Father Cornelius Wittmann, the rural scenes painted by Father Raphael Knapp before 1920, and the work of such painters and printmakers as Gordon Goeteman, Bela Petheo, and Jim Hendershot of the art department.

The art center, designed by Hugh Newell Jacobsen and completed in 1991, symbolizes the historic importance of the fine arts at Saint John's, not only in the fields of photography and filmmaking but also in sculpture and ceramics, drawing and painting, calligraphy, and the study of art history, architecture, and design. For some monks, such as sculptor and photographer Father Hugh Witzmann, the study and the making of art have been lifelong pursuits; for others, such as painter Father Jerome Tupa, art has been a second career. For alumnus and artist-in-residence Richard Bresnahan, art is indeed an expression of the soul on fire: while exercising the utmost sensitivity to environmental stewardship, he produces pottery of exceptional quality and mentors others in the same approach and commitment.

Artists and artisans have given form and direction to Saint John's in many other ways as well. Consistent with Saint Benedict's observation that "then are they truly monks when they live by the labor of their hands" (Rule, ch. 48), pioneer masons, carpenters, and woodworkers exercised their craft, first building the monastery, classrooms, and church, and then furnishing or adorning each

The new library (1901) featured a third-floor photo studio with a big skylight to let in floods of natural light. Two students posed there with cameras and props in 1902. Father Angelo Zankl recalls that the darkroom had a red glass window. Before 1920 he assisted in developing the pictures that photographer Father Fridolin Trembreul took in this studio.

Pioneer Cornelius Wittmann did not regard himself as an artist but as a woodcarver. Nonetheless this austere, delicately molded face of Christ crucified skillfully draws on the artistic tradition as well as the traditional piety of his native Bavaria. The 96-inch corpus is carved in oak and was probably originally painted to weather the seasons in an outdoor shrine.

Two styles of church art jostle one another here as the monks in the pews focus their attention on the altar along with Brother Clement Frischauf's Beuronese angels while a plaster statue of the Sacred Heart keeps devout watch over the monks in the choir stalls.

Brother Clement Frischauf, a monk of Seckau Abbey in Bavaria, came to Saint John's in 1929 to paint the apse of the church. He stayed until his death in 1944. His work was more than mere redecoration; it underlined the sacred character of the monks' daily worship and meals. In the monastic refectory he painted murals illustrating themes from the Rule of Benedict. In the church he replaced the original decorative patterns on the plaster walls of the apse with a semi-circle of twelve seraphim veiling their faces in awe before the altar. The *Christus Pantocrator* rules as *Via* (Way), *Veritas* (Truth), and *Vita* (Life) in the vault of the half-dome above. Here the artist puts finishing touches on a lunette of Mary as Mother of God.

of the spaces. Faith and craft have been combined in artistic expressions ranging from Brother Gabriel Bieniek's humble, handmade rosaries to the bold initials on the west façade of the Quadrangle: IOGD *(in omnibus glorificetur Deus)*. The sublime *Christus Pantocrator* painted by Brother Clement Frischauf in the apse of the former abbey church, now the Great Hall, echoes the prayer that God may be glorified in all things.

WOODWORKING

Carpentry and woodworking, in particular, have been significant parts of the community's history. Brothers Andrew Unterberger and Leo Martin were instrumental in the construction of the first abbey church. Other monks and laymen such as Peter Eich would transform carving and carpentry into art. Rare is the day, for example, when the quality of the meals of the monastic refectory exceeds that of the handsome tables on which the meals are served. Father Raphael Knapp was the likely designer of the monastic refectory (ca. 1918) as well as the chairs, crafted in the mid-1920s by Theodore Dillenburg, a master woodworker who taught Brother Hubert Schneider.

Beginning in the early 1930s and throughout six decades of faithful service, Brother Hubert would transform Saint John's oak planks into fine woodwork, including thirty thousand feet of oak and maple for flooring in the Breuer monastery. More recently, Brother Gregory Eibensteiner and his lay colleagues Larry Notch and Michael Roske have continued the tradition as they produce furnishings for the college and monastic communities, with Brother Christopher Fair now joining them. Saint John's alumnus K. C. Marrin '71 also was influenced by Brother Hubert as he applied his own talent to the fabrication of tracker organs and to the production of copies of the Saint John's cross.

Art and academics were joined early in the history of Saint John's. Following his ordination in 1916, Father Gilbert Winkelman began a career of thirty years of teaching in the university, including courses on architecture, mechanical and freehand drawing, and engineering. He helped found a school of architecture in the 1920s and was dean of the department until 1946. Among those earning a bachelor of architecture degree from Saint John's was Ray Hermanson '38, who, in addition to serving as the "court architect" for Saint

Carts return to the pit near the present radio tower hill to bring more clay to the brickyard kiln in front of the 1870s Saint John's College. The upper floors of the main building are visible in the background. More than a million bricks were made on site in the quarter century following construction of the first brick building, the smokehouse, in 1866.

John's for many years, also collaborated with Marcel Breuer on campus construction during the 1950s and 60s.

Art and publishing have also been partners for many decades at Saint John's. The Liturgical Press was established in 1926, and thousands of books, pamphlets, and periodicals from the Press have been graced by the graphic work of numerous monks, including Father Joachim Watrin and Brothers Placid Stuckenschneider, Frank Kacmarcik, David Manahan, and Joachim Rhoades.

A century after Abbot Boniface insisted that "art must go hand in hand with religion," art, architecture, and liturgy were animating the Collegeville community as never before. Gerald Bonnette '53, a creator of religious artwork, came to Saint John's in 1950 "to study art and get a Christian education." At the same time that Abbot Baldwin Dworschak was inviting noted architects to assist Saint John's in the construction of a new abbey church, the university introduced a degree in sacred art. Father Cloud Meinberg, who earned a degree in architecture before entering the monastic community, taught courses in architecture and sacred art, was directly involved in the design and planning of the new abbey church, and also designed tables and chairs still in use that captured the beauty and daring design of the era of the 1950s Buick.

ARCHITECTURE

Architecture, expressing concretely Benedictine stability and a sense of place, may claim pride of place among the creative endeavors of Saint John's during its first 150 years. Inspired by the natural beauty of God's creation, the monks of Saint John's resolved that the work of human hands would also be crafted with care and reverence. From the first decades, boldness in scale and design has marked the buildings of Saint John's; quality has been prized, if not always pursued, throughout the community's history. Boulders and bricks were the building materials of choice for the young foundation; concrete and granite would be added to the palette a century later. Each was consistent with an understanding of Benedictine stewardship that emphasizes the enduring value of simple yet sturdy construction.

The first buildings of the Indianbush, solid as they were, reflected the basic, immediate needs for sheltering the first residents and embarking on a mission

Twenty-eight-year-old Hubert Schneider came to the monastery in 1930, made vows as Brother Hubert the next year, and worked in the carpenter shop, as the woodworking shop was called, for the next sixty years. He was in charge of it from the late 1930s until 1970. He died in 1995 universally regarded as a wise and holy man for his gentle disposition, the quality of his work, and his unwavering charity and patience.

Father Raphael Knapp designed several campus buildings early in the new century. He was also a painter. His rural scenes are now valued because they record the local countryside as it was early in the twentieth century. His master work was to design furniture for the monastic refectory after World War I—a massive reading stand facing the abbot's table from the middle of the long room, dark-stained oak tables which he himself decorated with hand-carved ornamentation in deep relief, and chairs so well designed for sitting at table that no one has ever suggested replacing them.

Raphael Knapp, O.S.B. *The Tony Walz Farm near Saint Joseph*. Oil on canvas. 11" x 14". 1920.

of education. The modest dimensions of the buildings may also have hinted at the tentative nature of life on the edge of the prairie. If, however, in the minds of the founding monks, there were any doubts about the long-term future of Saint John's, such hesitation found no expression in the building program of Abbot Alexius Edelbrock. He envisioned a Quadrangle and church of colossal scale—among the larger structures west of the Mississippi at the time—and with the assistance of resident designer Father Gregory Steil, his vision took form. When the various wings were completed, some thirty years after the community's founding, the Quadrangle could easily accommodate six hundred students, although enrollment was barely a third of that number. Initially, many rooms stood vacant; but the vast Quadrangle would be grown into, serving the monastery and its schools well into the twentieth century—and then undergoing significant renovation to extend its life into another century. Though he had dreamed of a church for twelve hundred worshipers, Abbot Alexius was forced to limit the space to one accommodating only four hundred; financial constraints, driven by the needs of the schools, took precedence over the monastic community's needs, as they would continue to do for more than a century.

Frequently, especially among the pious, when disasters occur, interpretations are offered suggesting that a divine message is being communicated, and, often enough, the message is to change course. Such thinking may have influenced Saint John's building plans following the resignation of Abbot Alexius in 1889 and a devastating tornado in 1894. The imposing scale and European heritage represented in the design and layout of the Quadrangle gave way to smaller, free-standing structures; a small American town began to appear around the Quad during the tenure of Abbot Peter Engel. During the first quarter of the twentieth century, Father Raphael Knapp oversaw much of the architectural development of Saint John's. He is credited with the design of numerous buildings from 1915 until 1978, including Luke Hall, Joe Hall, Frank House, Engel (now Simons) Hall, the plumbing and old laundry (now paint) shops, Devil's Tower, and what may have been the first skyway in Minnesota, a bridge connecting the Quadrangle and Wimmer Hall (the former library).

The monastic community, the student population, and the farm herds expanded and flourished under the leadership of Abbot Alcuin Deutsch. Growth of the physical plant, however, other than a splendid new powerhouse with an industrial-size smokestack, would not be addressed until the 1950s, when Abbot Baldwin led the community into its second century with a building plan as bold as that of Abbot Alexius. It would be inaccurate and unfair, however, to discount Abbot Alcuin's contribution to the arts and architecture at Saint John's.

Early in Abbot Alcuin's tenure, two major buildings were completed: Benet Hall, which was planned by Abbot Peter, and the auditorium/music building. Renovation of Benet Hall in the 1990s made it preferred housing for studious juniors and seniors. Its ornamented exterior was and is a handsome addition to the inner campus and harmonious with the Quadrangle, to which it is connected. In 1928 the construction of the auditorium provided a home for the fine arts and a stage for hundreds of performances, recitals, lectures, and convocations that would sustain the community through the dark days of the Great Depression and the world at war. Like Benet Hall, the exterior of the auditorium, including the original stained-glass windows depicting literary and musical masters, gives evidence of careful design but not ostentation. Until the Benedicta Arts Center at the College of Saint Benedict opened four decades later, the auditorium would function as the primary venue of the fine arts for the Collegeville community and for generations of students.

In the 1930s and 1940s, having an abundant supply of young monks and an even more abundant supply of boulders, Abbot Alcuin engaged master stonemason John Pueringer to build massive stone walls, stairs, arches, and even a fountain on the grounds. Many of these handsome structures were removed in later years as the inner campus was developed. In the 1990s, however, sculptor Tadd Jensen reintroduced the art form as he provided the exposed concrete foundation of Joe Hall with a fieldstone sheath and created new stone walls over the Watab/Stumpf Lake causeway and at the main intersection opposite the Warner Palaestra.

Father Jerome Tupa went to France to study French and came back knowing both French, which he teaches, and painting, which he does with *éclat* in bold colors on large canvases.

MARCEL BREUER AND FRANK KACMARCIK

Along with the transition in leadership from Abbot Alcuin to Abbot Baldwin came a major shift in the architectural character of Saint John's. In the

Frank Kacmarcik and the Sisters of Saint Benedict's Monastery

Frank Kacmarcik was associated with Saint John's for fifty-four years, briefly as a college faculty member in sacred art, then as a freelance graphic artist and consultant in design. He entered the monastic community as a cloistered oblate in 1988, a status that left him free to continue consultancies around the country. It would be hard to exaggerate the degree to which he shaped the Collegeville environment for half a century through his association with the Liturgical Press, his collaboration with Marcel Breuer and other architects, his life membership on the design committee, which he invented, and the sheer force of his take-no-prisoners approach in matters artistic and monastic.

The relationship of the sisters of Saint Benedict's Monastery, Saint Joseph, Minnesota, with Frank Kacmarcik began in late 1978, when he was invited to review the initial plans for a modest renovation of our 1914 Sacred Heart Chapel. As liturgical consultant, Frank was asked to journey with us into the unknown territory of updating this sacred space. Frank met the community at a monastic chapter meeting on April 6, 1979, and made the first of many presentations to us.

The chapel renovation was an experience of the paschal mystery for us. What began as a maintenance project became an architectural and spiritual work of art. Throughout, the common good of the community was held in balance with Frank's artistic integrity. We learned to appreciate the importance of detail in the design process and the centrality of the assembly in our sacred spaces. Frank respected the integrity of the original structure and diligently preserved major pieces in the new design.

Thanks to the persistence of the renovation committee and the continuous involvement of the community, Frank was challenged to reflect feminine, monastic, and artistic elements in his proposed designs. The rejection of his first drawings of the predella, the platform on which the altar stands, was offered with this comment,

"This is a women's monastic community, Frank; warm it up!" When Frank came back, he commented, "I have a design you will really like; some 'warm' steps!" To this day I cannot walk up from the Gathering Place to the Sacred Heart Chapel without uttering a prayer for Frank and his gracefully curved "warm steps" (see illustration page 114).

As Frank showed pictures of our chapel to religious communities across the nation, he applauded the planning process and the commitment of the sisters of Saint Benedict's Monastery in Minnesota. I thanked Frank for these affirmations and challenged him to "tell our sisters" what he was proclaiming to others. His response was, "You know what I think of your project!"

Not every sister in the community liked Frank; his blunt honesty did not always garner him friends. At times it was difficult to distinguish between his deep humility and arrogance. However, he was and always will be lovingly respected for his understanding of liturgical worship and his deep commitment to good design. After twenty-five years of worshiping in our renovated chapel, we continue to appreciate the simple yet sublime beauty of this sacred space.

Colleen Haggerty, O.S.B.

1950s and 1960s the heart of the campus passed from the nineteenth-century Quadrangle and church to a strikingly modern collection of twentieth-century structures. The twin towers bowed to a monumental bell banner. Warm, red brick buildings formed the background for cool, unadorned, gray/blue brick and concrete buildings. Even the orientation of the inner campus shifted—from an east/west to a north/south axis. In the span of only ten years, Saint John's dedicated Mary Hall, perhaps the most unremarkable building on campus, and the Marcel Breuer abbey church, an icon of modern architecture.

If the community can take pride in being called prophetic for the quality of its abbey church, it must also acknowledge responsibility for the major shortcomings of its prep school dormitory. Ironically, the same community that planned a building that would anticipate the changes in the church dictated by the Second Vatican Council failed to recognize the societal changes that would so soon make the huge, open dorm of Saint Michael Hall outmoded.

Throughout the second half of the twentieth century at Saint John's, no voice was more dominant in the realm of design than that of Frank Kacmarcik, who served as a consultant in architecture and design from 1952 until his death in 2004 and who was admitted to the monastery as a claustral oblate in 1988. When the design committee was established in the early 1970s and charged with the responsibility of attending to the overall aesthetics and quality of the buildings, furnishings, and visual symbols of the Collegeville community, Frank would be a charter member and always vigorous voice. Less combative than Frank but with no less design sensitivity, Brother Alan Reed continues the long line of monastic members knowledgeable about contemporary architecture and also supportive of simple, enduring design solutions at Saint John's.

RENOVATING HISTORICAL REGISTER BUILDINGS

The frugality and simplicity of lifestyle urged by Saint Benedict have influenced the manner in which monastic communities use, reuse, or recycle their belongings. If pack rats (who are never lacking in a monastery) represent an aberration of simplicity, the renovation or restoration of buildings evidences an approach to property more in keeping with Benedict's exhortations. Saint John's penchant for upgrading and rearranging spaces dates to its early history. The first and fastest major renovation took place in June 1894, when a tornado substantially reduced the height of the old south wing of the Quadrangle and

Joe Hall edges toward its new location inch by inch. The move placed the last structure built with Saint John's brick next to the first, the smokehouse, out of sight to the right. The building started life as a carriage house in the 1890s, acquired a garage annex when the horseless carriage arrived, ejected the buggies and turned itself into a bunkhouse for unmarried workmen in the 1920s, dolled itself up and took an appropriate name—Saint Joseph Hall—when graduate students moved in forty years later, and after relocation in 1992 served as college student housing atop Richard Bresnahan's walk-in basement pottery.

transformed numerous wooden outbuildings into kindling. Later renovation projects would be less dramatic but not necessarily less destructive.

The harbinger of upgrades in the physical plant of Saint John's in the late twentieth century was the renovation of the student refectory. The growth of the student population and the transition from family-style dining and on-site preparation of meals to cafeteria service necessitated the expansion of the serving and seating areas of the campus dining service. To assist in the initial stages of renovation, students were invited to use mallets and sledgehammers to remove the plaster and expose the brick and fieldstone walls.

Changes in pedagogy, technological advances, code requirements, maintenance concerns, and aesthetics all contributed to the decision to embark on a major renovation of the Quadrangle in the late 1970s. Over the course of two years, the classroom/office spaces of the second and third floors were given the plaster-removal treatment and completely redone, air-conditioning and all. Twenty years later the administrative offices of the first floor, along with much of Wimmer and Luke Halls, were also renovated. Architectural critique and functional adequacy suggest that the Quadrangle may be Saint John's most successful building.

Renovation was not the only manner of reusing and recycling buildings on campus. Benedictine stewardship was also exercised through the physical relocation of various buildings. In the 1930s the original portion of the gymnasium (Old Gym; a.k.a. Rat Hall; a.k.a. Guild Hall) was mounted on logs and rails and moved a hundred feet west to its current location; subsequent expansion and upgrades have allowed it to serve as an athletic center for the prep school and university, a dining room for major events, and even as a meeting space for the United States Conference of Catholic Bishops in the 1980s.

The construction of Sexton Commons in the nineties occasioned moving another building. When the site was selected, the first Richard Bresnahan pottery studio and kiln and Joe Hall (once the bunkhouse for lay employees) stood on much of the footprint of the proposed campus center. A team of professional movers spent most of the summer of 1992 teasing the one hundred tons of Joe Hall onto steel beams and then, with painstaking care, inch by inch, transporting the brick building to the west side of the campus, where it was eased into place on top of a new walk-in basement studio for Mr. Bresnahan's pottery studio next to the 1866 smokehouse.

Master Plan Revisited

When Marcel Breuer was engaged to assist Saint John's in its building plans in the 1950s, he prepared a hundred-year plan for the community, one that would have led to the removal of most of the older brick buildings. Financial limitations and philosophical differences—it simply would not have been practical or prudent to raze the old buildings—resulted in that provision of the plan being abandoned in short order. This left the community without a coherent, long-range plan to guide its construction needs. When a plan to create much needed on-grade entrances to the abbey church, Great Hall, and auditorium was proposed—a plan that included the removal of two sixty-year-old maple trees—community dissatisfaction came to a head. Ill-advised building plans were vexing enough; cutting down trees was intolerable!

To do a new master plan, the community engaged Hugh Newell Jacobsen, Daniel Kiley, and George Rafferty, along with Lee Tollefson. In the summer of 1988 the first project based on Saint John's master plan was constructed: a new

Richard Bresnahan '76 shapes pottery for domestic uses from local clays and glazes in the Japanese karatsu tradition. Here he inspects work about to be fired in the wood-burning Johanna kiln, named for Sister Johanna Becker, his college mentor.

Lee Tollefson was the chief architect of Sexton Commons, the 1993 student center that combines bus terminal, bookstore, cafeteria, and pub in a hub location handy to dorms and classrooms. Bill Sexton, legendary forward of the 1953–1955 basketball seasons, was the lead donor, and the red brick structure, echoing the texture of the pre-Breuer campus, was named in honor of his family.

entry plaza, providing the desired on-grade entrances—and the maple trees are still standing.

Although Saint John's master plan continues to serve as the blueprint for campus development, the architectural roller coaster that had first appeared at the end of the nineteenth century reappeared at the close of the twentieth century. In the shadows of the substantial brick and Breuer buildings, smaller wood-frame residences dot the fringe of the campus. The Quadrangle that saw a small town grow around it now witnesses the development of suburban housing—building out rather than building up; building cheaply rather than for the long term.

Saint Benedict exhorted his monks to treat the community's property with reverence and to practice their crafts so as to give glory to God. Abbot Boniface Wimmer, apprehensive about the American mercenary spirit and a too-utilitarian approach to life, urged that monasteries be nurseries of the arts. Responding to these entreaties, the monks of Saint John's Abbey have fostered the arts and crafts as well as sensitivity to good architecture and design, thereby echoing the "good" work of the divine Creator (Genesis 1). At its sesquicentennial, Saint John's commitment to the "splendor, dignity, and sublimity" of art finds further expression in a host of plans and projects: sacred art and calligraphy have been united in *The Saint John's Bible*; the book arts and a commitment to preservation and conservation work continue in the Hill Museum & Manuscript Library and *Arca Artium;* and the construction of an abbey guest house affirms the community's commitment to hospitality and architectural excellence. "Thus God's creative work continues without cease" (Sirach 38:8).

"The Athlete"

The architect plays with blocks of Cold Spring granite to display the stages of his craft from basic to high tech.

Post and Beam — Cantilevered Post — Move over, Vitruvius! — The Athlete

Combined, the parts add up to a 17′ 5″ sculpture, "The Athlete," a gift to Saint John's in 1973 by the architect-artist and signed by him. Going him one better, the digital photographer suspends nine tons of stone in the air.

From the Preface of Illuminating the Word

This whole project is either utter madness or magnificent good fortune. A whole series of chance circumstances have unexpectedly come together to result in the commissioning of an entire Bible copied by hand. For the first time in about five and a half centuries, since Johann Gutenberg began to sell copies of the earliest printed Bibles, an otherwise entirely sane American institution has ordered a new Bible to be made by a process which most people would assume had been rendered obsolete by the invention of printing.

First of all, the setting is a Benedictine monastery. From the beginning, Christian monastic communities have been patrons of art and sponsors of the production of monumental Bibles. The earliest surviving complete Bible in Latin, the huge *Codex Amiatinus,* now in Florence, was made in one of the twin Benedictine houses of Wearmouth or Jarrow in northern England in the early eighth century. The great Carolingian Bibles of the ninth century were almost all prepared in the Benedictine monasteries of Tours. The vast Bury and Winchester Bibles of twelfth-century England were Benedictine commissions, as were many others, such as the Admont and Stavelot Bibles. The custom of creating and using vast manuscript Bibles runs deeply in the ancient Benedictine tradition.

Secondly, Saint John's is a major contemporary university. Books are and always have been at the core of scholarship. Saint John's has a first-rate modern library, its own publisher, and, most famously, the Hill Monastic Manuscript Library, now with some hundred thousand early manuscripts stored by photography and digital technology. It is equipped with the latest scientific techniques of research. In such a context it is reassuring and valuable to modern students to be able to reflect on the methods of communicating all written knowledge at a period when the universities of Europe were in their infancy. The survival and evolution of modern learning have descended directly through a huge epoch of manuscript culture. To those who have never seen a real manuscript, The Saint John's Bible will open a new world. For the experienced historians of books and of the Middle Ages, who cluster around the Hill Monastic Manuscript Library, the Bible will supply answers to countless practical questions on how medieval books were designed and made a thousand or so years ago. . . .

Finally, is it complete insanity to make such a book, by such a method? Yes, it probably is, in the sense that it is not necessary to spend so much time and money on something that could be made mechanically in a few moments. It has not happened for a long time. It probably will never happen again. It may be madness or imagination or simply faith that has driven this project, or a combination. Let us be glad that we live in a world where patrons and artists can seize a chance like this to participate in a book, a Bible no less, which will certainly outlive all of us.

Christopher de Hamel
Gaylord Donnelley Librarian, Parker Library
Corpus Christi College, Cambridge, UK

(Illuminating the Word. Collegeville:
The Order of Saint Benedict, 2005)

CHAPTER 9

Going Forth to Work till Evening Falls

Annette Atkins, Norma Loso Koetter, Zach Lewis

THERE HAVE BEEN EICHS IN COLLEGEVILLE for as long as there have been monks of Saint John's Abbey. In fact, the German Benedictine founders of Saint John's Abbey migrated to central Minnesota in the 1850s to minister to what would turn into a flourishing German Catholic community.

Marlin Eich, who, with his usual twinkle and laugh, identifies himself as a "professional putzer," is only the most recent of several generations of his family to work at Saint John's. Off the top of his head he can name seven other Eichs, including his father, who, over a century and a half, have helped keep Saint John's going. They worked in housekeeping and the laundry and on the farm. In his own forty years on the payroll, he's worked as a roofer, locksmith, carpet and tile installer, shoveler of snow on roofs, and clock repairer. He's best known, though, as a talented carpenter like Johnny, his father, and Peter, his great-grandfather.

Peter Eich worked his own farm next to the abbey and did carpentry for the abbey too. He helped build the "Old Stone House," the first permanent building on campus, as well as the first abbey church and the Quadrangle. He also designed, built, and decorated furniture. Art historian Rena Coen judged that one of his pieces "rises above mere serviceability to express the creative of the true artist."

There are so many local families who have histories intertwined with Saint John's that any attempt to list them would be long and partial. So, as some Oscar nominees should do, we won't start naming them but will only marvel at their number and their loyalty. The similarity of the names in the 1870 census rolls and a current local telephone book suggests that many of these German American families, like the monks, took vows of stability.

From its first days in central Minnesota, the abbey has depended on the hard work of the members of the monastery and their neighbors. The Rule of Benedict stipulates that all monks serve in the kitchen and that they work in the fields when necessary. A range of other duties—from guestmaster to infirmarian to porter at the gate—are assigned to individuals so that whatever needs doing is taken care of by the monks themselves. What happens when fourteen hundred years later monasteries send out missionaries, staff parishes, conduct schools, colleges, and seminaries? The actual tending of the flock and the making of meals, clothing, furniture, crops, roads, warm buildings; the cleaning of floors, sheets, and socks; the raking of leaves; the picking of apples—these become the work of lay brothers and lay workers.

Peter Eich (1834–1920) was a vigorous 30-year-old Civil War veteran when he claimed a tract of wooded land across a meandering stream from the claims that Bruno Riss and his fellow monks had staked out. The land he claimed has been in the family since then, separated from Saint John's by a bucolic lake when the monks dammed the stream in 1867 to provide water power for a grist mill and a saw mill. Carpenter and wood carver, Peter helped build Saint John's from the start. He is pictured in 1910 with his wife, Philomena, in whose arms sleeps Andrew Brinkman, son of Mary Gretsch Brinkman in white, daughter of Theresa Eich Gretsch in black, the second of Peter and Philomena's thirteen children.

◄ Invisible behind the windshield of the snowplow as winter comes on in late November is Louis Himsl, longtime member of the grounds crew and representative of the local Himsl family, who have been part of the community for more than a century.

Brother William Borgerding, the "Night Abbot" watchman/philosopher in a smiling daytime appearance in 1993.

Fourteen plasterers pose with the tools of their trade on the top floor of the uncompleted Quad in 1885. Ironically other workers a hundred years later systematically removed much of the plaster in the Quad to reveal the bricks these artisans so skillfully covered.

Older employees recall and comment on the sense of family that often intertwined the worlds of laypeople and Benedictines at Saint John's. They were bound together by their faith, their heritage, their language, and often by their humility and their spirituality. There have been many holy people at Saint John's; some of them have been these laypeople. They had families, religious and social lives, and aspirations separate from the abbey, however intertwined their worlds.

This essay is about (and for) the many talented, able, dedicated, and dogged brothers and laypeople who have for generations kept the place going day to day.

Historically, lay brothers and young monks preparing for ordination worked, cooked, made clothes, repaired watches, shoed horses, farmed the land, and helped build the buildings. They did whatever work needed to be done: switchboard operator, night watchman, engineer, nurse, butcher, cook, gardener. Brother Thaddeus "Taddy" Hoermann (1857–1907) spent his days carrying—and none too fast, reportedly—the mail and passengers from the abbey and college to the post office and train station in Collegeville.

IMPACT OF THE LAY BROTHERS

Lay brothers have cast long and warm shadows over the place. Brother Hubert Schneider made the working of wood into a high and holy art. His colleagues in the carpentry shop and most others who knew him are quick to say that if anyone here is a saint, it's Brother Hubert. Other brothers, too, had a big impact on the place; among them were Brothers Ed Zwack and Victor McMahon, who were plumbers; Ansgar Niess, the butcher, assisted by Brother Patrick Sullivan. Brother William "Willie" Borgerding managed the cattle herd until it was sold. He walked the halls and grounds of Saint John's for over

thirty-five years as the night watchman. The affection in which he's been held is memorialized in Brother Willie's Pub in Sexton Commons. For over thirty years Brother George Primus has carried on the monastic tradition of making and mending clothes for the monks. Before him Brother John Anderl ran the tailor shop with an iron hand and gloried in his job as fire chief, hat and all.

The German Catholic and monastic cultures that formed the abbey and the surrounding community were steeped in feudal and ecclesiastical ideas about status, hierarchy, obedience to authority, and humility. These ideas were challenged and reshaped by American ideas of democracy, equality, and individualism, but not in the second half of the nineteenth century in central Minnesota. In those years the centuries-old hierarchical patterns held sway.

In the European monastic tradition, the ordained monks and the lay brothers often came from different ranks or social orders and had different levels of education. Choir monks had to know Latin (as long as Latin was the language of the liturgy—which it was till the 1960s). Lay brothers did not. No Latin, no ordination. No ordination, no vote in chapter, which meant no voice in the election of the abbot or other formal business of the monastery. Priests and brothers often came to Saint John's, however, from the same or quite similar backgrounds, so their place in the monastic community did not reflect class, but their different roles and ecclesiastical status did have consequences in their monastic lives. Even the Breuer church building, which in so many ways anticipated the post-Vatican II changes in the church, shows the differences with the separate brothers' chapel in the basement and the lower stalls for the brothers in the main church. The differences sometimes rankled.

Brother Samuel Lickteig helped bridge the differences when he joined the monastery in 1950. He earned a BA before presenting himself for candidacy in the monastery, and after taking vows he was the first brother to teach in the prep school, which he did for forty years. Similarly, Louis Blenkner showed up

The Church Gable

Bricklayers and Carpenters

Tensions occurred between the bricklayers and the carpenters as the two crews topped off the façade of the old abbey church. As the carpenters prepared to add the wooden trim and roof, they found that the peak of the pattern of arches that formed a border for the gable was off-center. In chronicler Alexius Hoffmann's words, "The center arch on the front gable is more than its own width from center. Bad."

The carpenters protested having to top off a bad brick job and feared that future observers might conclude that it was the carpenters and not the bricklayers who had arrived at the top off-center.

This undated photo of unidentified hands in the butcher shop apparently antedated construction of the laundry.

at the abbey intending to be ordained, completed his PhD at the University of North Carolina, then decided on the brotherhood instead. He served as a long-time member and chair of the English department in the university.

Various ecclesiastical and social changes in the 1960s made it possible for Saint John's to abolish the canonical distinction between lay brothers and choir monks and brought priests and brothers together to eat, pray, and live as a single community. They can drink from either mugs or cups—whatever suits them; one report had it that only priests could use cups in the early days. Perhaps most importantly, brothers and priests now both vote together on community decisions, including the election of the abbot. A real milestone occurred when Brother Dietrich Reinhart became the president of Saint John's University in 1991. Two significant appointments had paved the way: the appointment in 1980 of Brother Linus Ascheman as headmaster of the prep school and, a few years later, of Brother Kelly Ryan as subprior. Brother Benedict Leuthner's appointment as corporate treasurer in the 1990s further demonstrated the new place of monks who are not ordained in the work of the community. A few vestiges of status differences remain, but they're shadows rather than real presences.

LAY WORKERS' ESSENTIAL ROLE

Monks do and did much of their own work, as the Rule requires. Even so, from the first and like most abbeys everywhere and for fourteen hundred years (1880 marked the fourteenth century since Benedict's birth), the Saint John's Abbey enterprise grew faster and in more directions than even a rush of vocations could have managed alone, so it employed laypeople. Although Abbot Alexius Edelbrock worried about the abbey's dependence on outsiders and the unspecified "inconveniences and disturbances" they introduced, lay workers played essential roles in the life and work of the Saint John's community. Neighborhood women took in laundry and mending for the monks and then for the students. John Pueringer, a talented stonemason who built his own house a mile from Saint John's, also did the stonework still visible—and recognizably his—on the west side of the Quadrangle near the entrance to the refec-

George Klein was on the Saint John's payroll in one capacity or another for seventy years. He liked working here. He said, "Saint John's don't pay much, but the work's steady."

Michael and Veronica Roske pose with their first five children, Joe between them, then left to right Philip, Mike, Jr., Katie on mother's lap, and Mary. The year is 1903 and their home is the Roske farm in what is now Flynntown. In the end there were five more children, then 64 grandchildren, then 194 great-grandchildren. Joe worked at the powerhouse on campus for forty-five years, becoming chief engineer. Hal followed in his father's footsteps but quit after forty-four years so as not to challenge his father's record. Hal's son Michael does fine cabinetry in the woodworking shop across the road from the powerhouse and can be spotted wearing the only mustache on the fire crew in the chapter 1 photo.

tory. Peter Eich and dozens of other neighbors helped raise the church and the Quadrangle. They were a community.

A few of the early skilled stonemasons hired to help with the abbey church and the Quadrangle building were Irish or Norwegian, but most of the lay-people hired by the abbey were German and German-speaking like the monks. Most were members of the Saint John's Parish. Their children attended school in Saint Joseph, taught by the Benedictine sisters, or the public school on the back road just south of the cemetery. A few of their sons attended Saint John's, later their daughters the College of Saint Benedict. More than a few of their sons and daughters joined one of the monastic communities.

Often the skilled laborers lived on their own farms nearby and worked at the abbey when needed. The farm workers and those who didn't have their own places nearby or who came from elsewhere, as employees increasingly did in the twentieth century, needed to live on campus. In the 1920s the abbey provided accommodations for lay workers in the "bunkhouse," a made-over carriage house, later called Joe Hall, after Saint Joseph the Workman. In 1930 the bunkhouse housed several dozen workers, including Coach George Durenberger, just two years out of Saint John's himself, and Professor Herbert Payne, who directed the orchestra. These men represented a new category of laymen who worked in the university. If the farmhands and plumbers and carpenters were the colleagues of the lay brothers, the lay faculty members of the college and of the prep school were, by virtue of their education, the colleagues of the priests.

In Flynntown, just north of the campus (named after Edward Flynn, the coach who established football as a conference sport in the 1920s), workers with families rented houses from the abbey. George Klein, who worked as carpenter, farm boss, second foreman, and, after retirement until his ninetieth birthday, ticket-taker at campus athletic events, lived for fifty-five years in the same house in Flynntown. He died at 101 in 1989. He recalled working for $2.00 a day, with free lights, water, rent, and fuel and considered it a "comfortable living." The last laypeople to live in a Flynntown house were Betty and Jim Powers, both writers, he a Saint John's regents' professor, she the sister of Father Thomas Wahl. She died in 1988; he moved across the road into a little stucco house on the site of what had been the Roske farm in an earlier generation, and their old house was razed for new student parking. John and Peggy Gagliardi have lived for nearly fifty years just west of Flynntown and remember the community that their neighbors formed.

Other employees rented houses from the abbey near the cemetery. Bob and Louise Pflueger lived in one. He drove the dray truck for Saint John's, and she did laundry. Their children, including Herb Pflueger and Jane Pflueger Simon and several others, worked at Saint John's when they were in high school. Herb took a job at the Liturgical Press and stayed until his retirement in 2000. Jane started at the Liturgical Press in 1960, then moved to the registrar's office, where she has worked for nearly forty years. After the Pfluegers moved out, the abbey fire department used the house for fire-fighting practice. The only reminders that people lived there are the apple trees planted by the Pfluegers, and a garage. The Huschle sisters, Catherine and Marie—their mother was an Eich, and they were abbey seamstresses for years—were the last to live on that back road, in the only house that still stands, empty for the present.

Today the lay employees live in a wide radius from the abbey—in Avon, Albany, Holdingford, Luxemburg, Saint Joseph, Saint Cloud, Saint Anna,

Betty and Jim Powers stand at the door of their Irish home around 1970. They took one of the old stucco houses in Flynntown when Jim later accepted a position as writer-in-residence at Saint John's during Father Michael Blecker's presidency. Jim survived Betty and moved to the old Roske house across the road when a parking lot was needed where the stucco house stood.

Frances Pond was the first woman to be employed in an office at Saint John's when she became Father Godfrey Diekmann's secretary in his capacity as editor of *Orate Fratres*— soon to become *Worship*—in 1952. Her fellow Coloradan, art historian Sister Johanna Becker, had just become the first woman to be appointed to the Saint John's faculty.

Donald Forbes, director of the bookstores at both Saint John's and the College of Saint Benedict, joins Cindy (Janssen) Dirkes, assistant director, and Ann (Schleper) Jonas, book buyer, at Cindy's desk, textbook central for Saint John's. The family names—Janssen, Dirkes, Schleper, Jonas—go back for generations in local history.

Frail and pious Brother Gabriel signed up for a haircut in the monastery barber's last slot for the day: "Brother Gabriel—if alive." After his name a brother candidate wrote: "If not, J. Fred Simms."

Clearwater, Cold Spring, Rockville, in the country, on one of the lakes; an increasing number of lay faculty live in the Twin Cities to accommodate dual-career partnerships, changes in educational patterns, or city hunger. The workforce is increasingly diverse in religious preference, national origin, family ties, and loyalties. Even so, German Catholic families from Stearns, Benton, and Sherburne Counties continue to provide a large number of workers at Saint John's Abbey, University, Prep School, and the Liturgical Press.

Some employees find out about jobs through ads in the newspaper or on the Internet, but a much larger number still find out from friends and relatives who currently work at Saint John's. Five generations of Gillitzers/Dullingers have helped to keep the place going. Betty Hennen works in the library, her mother in the dining service, and her brother too. Dan Vogel is a forest technician; his mother, Elaine Vogel, was the secretary for the president and the abbot for over thirty years. Jean Stottlemyer was in life safety for seventeen years and in the physical plant for eight years; she heard about the job from her father, who worked here for twenty-four years. Even a surprisingly large number of faculty members have connections with Saint John's or Saint Ben's.

Those commonalities and the long and intertwined histories of so many lay and monastic people mean that working at Saint John's is for many people something different from working elsewhere. Many current employees report that they work and stay here because of the community feel, the sense that this place is different from others, the connection to the college and the abbey, the beauty of the grounds, the atmosphere, and the Benedictine values. Even the non-Catholics report feeling at home in this Catholic place. Some people leave for higher wages or other opportunities, but an amazingly large number of people stay put. For a long time.

Nonetheless, there have also been tensions in the relationships. After the first generation or two, European notions of place and deference fissured and then gave way to more American ideas of democracy, and lay workers—kitchen and workshop, farm and college—joined forces to improve their conditions. Like many laborers in the United States, these workers made common cause with one another to bargain collectively with the management—in this case the abbey. Unlike other laborers of the time, however, they did not adopt a union structure or vocabulary, but the medieval language of the guilds—self-governing and independent skilled workers.

THE SAINT JOHN'S WORKERS' GUILD

In 1943 forty-eight laymen, led by Julian Botz, manager of the abbey print shop, and Emerson Hynes, a faculty member in sociology, and inspired by Catholic social teaching of the time, including Pope Pius XI's 1931 encyclical *Quadragesimo Anno*, formed the Saint John's Workers' Guild to give the lay employees a voice in dealing with the abbey.

Like other benevolent societies common in immigrant and religious communities—Sons of Norway, Lutheran Brotherhood, Knights of Columbus, for example—the guild looked to the social needs of its members. All lay employees, including women after 1963, were invited to join. Not all did. Out of the dues it collected, the guild bought door prizes for meetings, sent cards to sick members, made charitable contributions, hosted holiday parties, distributed holiday turkeys, honored longtime employees. Like a union, the guild charged its workers' relations committee to meet with an abbey committee "to establish policies concerning wages, hours, working conditions, and work standards to

The Workers' Guild, February 19, 1948. Joe Roske, powerhouse engineer, sits in the front row with his jacket open. Steve Humphrey stands in the back second from the right. One could name a dozen other dignitaries in this photograph, men like Ted Schreiner in the cardigan in the fourth row, switchboard operator at the front door, or Ralph Meyer and Joe Douvier, right end of the front row, Ralph in charge of orchards, Joe the mailman and driver to the Collegeville station.

be maintained," as reported in the Saint John's *Record* in 1953. Over time the guild won paid vacations, paid funeral leaves, higher wages, and college tuition remission for their children. Many of these benefits were long battled for and hard won and paid for with lower wage increases.

Sometime in the 1960s, the faculty peeled off from the guild and formed its own employee group (now with the faculty of the College of Saint Benedict called the Joint Faculty Assembly). The administrative employees, too, followed suit and formed the Administrative Assembly. In 2001 the guild reformed itself into the Support Staff and Guild Association (by a contested vote, the name Guild was retained). All three organizations do various kinds of community building, and each lobbies and negotiates on behalf of its constituents around a budget that is still ultimately under monastic control and subject to monastic approval.

Several dramatic changes have reshaped the abbey community in the last half century. The monastic population has changed in composition (older and more varied in background) and dramatically decreased in size over the last half century. This has meant that more and more laypeople have been needed to keep the enterprises going. The monks have become a small minority in their own place. Moreover, Saint John's, long a legally constituted corporation, has become a diversified enterprise of several divisions and has suffered all the strains of modern corporations. It struggles with many of the commercial, social, and political issues that any business must face. It cannot be a world unto itself behind a sheltering Pine Curtain. The university accepts government money and its strings. It must apply rules equitably and enforce the law fairly. The culture of law and business has seeped in.

Even so, it is not only a corporation. It is still something else, as the three of us who collaborated in writing this chapter can testify. Norma Koetter is from one of those German American families from Stearns County who have persisted. Four members of her family have worked—and she and one brother still do—for Saint John's or Saint Ben's. Annette Atkins came to Saint John's on a one-year appointment and has stayed for more than a quarter century. Zach Lewis, a pre-med student from southwestern Minnesota, is incredibly loyal to Saint John's and, like many alumni, is more fond of it than many

Longtime employee Ralph Meyer went to the business office to hit Father Ignatius for a raise. Ignatius took a long drag on his cigarette and then explained at some length how the abbey just couldn't afford to offer anything at the time. After seeing how crestfallen this hard worker was, Ignatius leaned toward Ralph and in lowered voice said, "Listen, Ralph, I tell you what. We'll give you a five-cent-an-hour raise, but don't tell any of the others." Ralph replied, "Don't worry, I'm just as ashamed of it as you are."

Rich Ruprecht, baker, puts loaves of bread into the 1964 Middleby-Marshall revolving oven while David Schoenberg, director of the dining service since 1983, looks on. The typical batch is sixty loaves. Half an hour in the oven and voila! the local staff of life, Johnny Bread. Average production a week is a thousand loaves. At Thanksgiving 240 turkeys are roasted, 120 at a time.

graduates are of their alma mater. Norma might prefer a higher salary, and Annette has chafed at the maleness of the place. Both might want to be considered more a part of the community, in which we're sometimes treated like guests, no matter how long we've been here. Nonetheless, each of us has had chances to go elsewhere but didn't. We're still here.

Saint Benedict's respect for the work of the hands is part of what makes Saint John's special. Other Benedictine ideas, too, infuse the place. The Benedictine priests and brothers may be centrally responsible for the articulation of those values, but the Benedictinism of the larger Saint John's community has been expressed, in addition, by generations of able, faithful, and valuable lay workers as well.

Sister Jordana Mayer, one of the German Franciscan women who made up a self-contained religious community on campus and did all the food preparation for monks and students from 1913 to 1958.

This essay is based on the work of many others: Colman Barry, *Worship and Work: Saint John's Abbey and University 1856–1992* (Collegeville: Liturgical Press, 1993); Thomas Whitaker, O.S.B., "The Brothers of Saint John's Abbey," in three parts, in *Scriptorium*, Vol. 13/1; 13/2; 14; The United States Manuscript Population Census Enumerations, 1870, 1880, 1900, and 1930; *St. John's Workers' Guild Cookbook* (Collegeville: Saint John's University, 1986); Saint John's *Record*, June 26, 1953, p. 2; Minutes of Guild Meetings, 1951–1960, 1961–1974, Saint John's Abbey Archives; Rena Coen, *Painting and Sculpture in Minnesota, 1820–1914* (Minneapolis: University of Minnesota Press, 1976) 64. The *Sagatagan* in its many forms also provides useful information.

In addition, we're grateful to the many people who consented to oral interviews, who took the time to write responses to our questions, and who allowed us to ask a multitude of questions: Lois Angulski, Rita Auer, Mo Beilke, Tracey Birr, Glen Breth, Barb Brinkman, Polly Chappell, Viola Dullinger, Marlin Eich, Jeff Eiynck, Susie Eiynck, Cyndi Ernst, Sara Folk, Carol Fries, Jeanne Furst, Peggy Gagliardi, Bernice Hadley, Gloria Hardy, Betty Hennen, Ginger Hoffman, Carol Johannes, Mary Kaasa, Mary Beth Kemper, David Klingeman, O.S.B., Rob Koch, Marilyn Koltes, Benedict Leuthner, O.S.B., Debbie Linn, Rene McGraw, O.S.B., Shaun Melling, Janet Merdan, Nancy Mitchell, Fredric Petters, Lori Pfannenstein, David Philippi, Dietrich Reinhart, O.S.B., Fred Reker, Gregg Ressemann, Jane Simon, Columba Stewart, O.S.B., Jean Stottlemyer, Gordon Tavis, O.S.B., Vincent Tegeder, O.S.B., Leila Utsch, Cindy Ann Van Vickle, Dan Vogel, Lois Warnert, Brian Welsh, Rachel Wolinski, Lorraine Ann Zierden.

Raphael Knapp, O.S.B. *Twin Towers from Flynntown.* Oil on canvas. 8" x 14'. ca. 1920.

The Sages of Collegeville

Agnes Ramler's vocation was to be a parish housekeeper, which she did for many years with grace and wit. Then she retired to a tiny house in Flynntown, took in a college boarder, and made herself part of the local scene by her interest in everyone from the monk plumbers who came to remedy clogged drains in her house to artists attracted by the Breuer church. From the latter she gained an appreciation of the heroic cast-bronze John the Baptist—gaunt, hollow-eyed, formidable—that stands inside the front doors, gesturing toward the baptismal font. Interpreting the sculptor's symbolism to a visitor ready to buy the gesture toward the font but put off by the elongated, corded neck of the Baptizer, Agnes explained, "That's where the art comes in."

Marilyn Douvier, long in charge of the information desk in the Great Hall, had sold a Greyhound ticket to an elderly monk who, once on the bus, forgot where he was going and why. After he was returned to the abbey, the prior rebuked Marilyn for selling a ticket to a monk who was not in his right mind. Marilyn retorted, "How am I supposed to know which ones are in their right mind?"

Jack Rassier said: "I was a kid of sixteen and was sent to the woods to split wood for firewood. I picked up a twelve-pound maul and a couple of wedges and started off. [Brother] Ansgar stopped me and said, 'Take an eight-pound. You are going to miss the wedge and break the handle with the big maul.' Assuring him I had split wood before, I proceeded to start splitting wood and really wanted to impress him so I took extra hard swings. After a short time I missed and broke the handle right off. By the time I picked up the head of the maul, Ansgar was standing there with the eight-pound maul. I thought I was going to be fired, but he handed me the maul and said, 'Now don't miss again.' I split wood for six years with that same maul with the same handle and did not have a nick on it."

CHAPTER 10

Two Benedictine Communities Seeking God Together

Jana and Charles Preble

BENEDICTINE HOSPITALITY CAPTIVATED OUR HEARTS and lured us to settle in central Minnesota. Charles had first visited Saint John's in the early 1960s and was welcomed there for a visit with Father Godfrey Diekmann. Then in 1978 we and our ten- and twelve-year-old daughters accepted the invitation of Sister Jeremy Hall, who had been Jana's theology professor in Christian spirituality at Creighton University, and came as her guests to visit at Saint Benedict's Monastery. During that visit she and her close friend Father Michael Marx of Saint John's "recruited" Charles, in the hope that he would one day be a fellow at the Ecumenical Institute.

We didn't follow up on that opportunity, but instead in 1986 we decided to move here. We write as "innocent bystanders" who continue to be welcomed into the lives of the monks of Saint John's and the sisters of Saint Benedict's day in and day out as worshipers, as friends of men and women in both Benedictine communities, and as former "common law" monastic people who, after fifteen years here, finally decided to take the leap and formalize our relationship with the Benedictines as Oblates of Saint Benedict.

Prior to our move we purchased an old farm house convenient to both Saint John's and Saint Ben's and learned later that Father Gilbert Winkelman of Saint John's Abbey had designed it. Like others we know who are transplants to central Minnesota, once settled we asked many questions about the origins of the area's cultural richness: How is it that the arts flourish so in the midst of the farmlands? How is it that educational institutions came to such excellence here? How is it that such an ecumenical spirit prevails in a Roman Catholic county? How is it that generous, openhearted hospitality is so prevalent?

The more we asked these kinds of questions, the more the same answers seemed to recur—answers such as "The Benedictines brought this" or "This is the Benedictine influence." These answers came in conversations, not with the monks and sisters so much, as with people who are not members of the Benedictine communities at Saint John's Abbey and

In February the monks are guests of the sisters of Saint Benedict's Monastery to celebrate the feast of Saint Scholastica. In August the monks return the favor with a cookout on the monastery lawn. Here Fathers Alberic Culhane and Don Talafous chat with Sister Mary Anthony Wagner, while Sister Christine Manderfeld and Abbot Jerome Theisen, recognizable by his hairline, converse in the background.

◀ The steeple of the Church of Saint Joseph, served by Saint John's monks since 1856, and the dome of Sacred Heart Chapel of Saint Benedict's Monastery together with the conical spire of the main building of the College of Saint Benedict create a Benedictine skyline for the town of Saint Joseph.

Of the twelve children of Luke and Margaret Gertken, born between 1877 and 1902 , eleven joined the monasteries of Saint John's and Saint Benedict's. Seated left to right are Alban, who died as a deacon, Innocent, Margaret, Severin, who became abbot of Saint Peter's Abbey, and Norbert. Standing in coif and veil are Veneranda, Assumpta, Devota, Waltrudis, Gemma, and Urban. In white are the future Sister Cecile and Agatha, who became the Collegeville postmaster.

Bernard and Louise Weber, lifelong members of the Saint Martin parish, had ten children, six of whom entered religious life as Benedictines at Saint John's Abbey or Saint Benedict's Monastery. Seated with their parents are Sister Marcella and Alice. Standing left to right are Sister Helen, Father Otto, Sister Bernadette, Jerome, Father Arnold, Raymond, Elizabeth, and Sister Jane. The family gathered for Father Arnold's twenty-fifth anniversary of ordination in 1977.

Saint Benedict's Monastery, people who have lived in many parts of the world and know they have found treasure hidden in a field here.

Many of us came here from other places and discovered the treasure emanating from the Benedictine heritage of central Minnesota. Others had been formed in the Benedictine parish schools or colleges in the area and were hardly aware of the values assimilated in the process of their education. Only gradually they began to realize that the richness of heart and mind, the appreciation of balance and culture, the care and concern for others were the product of life in families and in schools under the influence of the two Benedictine communities in central Minnesota. Born in the extreme poverty both communities experienced in their first years, in confusion over governance and finances, in excruciating labor under difficult conditions, the efforts of the two Benedictine communities eventually grew into a longstanding collaboration in ministry and education that has been mutually enriching and has benefited many.

Forming Benedictine Parish Communities

The Benedictines' work in schools and parishes resulted in the Catholic faith becoming firmly established in generations of families, and nearly seventy families have given children to these Benedictine communities. It didn't take us long to figure out that six Weber siblings joined the two communities to serve in various ministries at home and in distant missions and that almost a dozen Gertkens blessed both communities with the gift of music and chant. Sometimes monks and sisters from the same family engaged in ministry together, as when Sister Claudina Locnikar and her brother, Father Florian Locnikar, were at Saint Mary's mission at Red Lake between 1910 and 1916, or when Brother Gregory Eibensteiner and his sister, Sister Lavonne Eibensteiner, were at White Earth in the 1960s.

A few years before we moved to Minnesota, we discovered the Benedictine missions while we were traveling across the northern part of the state, but it wasn't until much later that we knew these were part of Saint John's and Saint Benedict's outreach. Not long after the beginning of their work together in central Minnesota, the call came from the north for the establishment of missions and schools at White Earth and Red Lake. In 1878, knowing nothing of native culture, customs, or language, Father Aloysius Hermanutz from Saint John's and Sisters Lioba Braun and Philomena Ketten from Saint Benedict's went north to begin their work at White Earth.

It was not an easy time for the Ojibwe or the Benedictines. The mission was a place of severe poverty, and the monks and sisters were given only ten dollars to cover all their expenses for the winter. They suffered much in buildings where snow sifted in through cracks in the walls and winter temperatures dropped to forty degrees below zero. The Indians paid no board or tuition. In the early days the only support for the work there came from the two monastic communities and the Ludwig Mission Society of Bavaria. Later the mission received aid from the federal Indian Agency and from Katherine Drexel of Philadelphia.

The Benedictine partnership on the Red Lake reservation began in 1888 when Father Thomas Borgerding and Father Simon Lampe were sent there from Saint John's. Two Benedictine sisters from Saint Joseph, Sister Amalia Eich and Sister Evangelista McNulty, started a school at this new mission. The work grew quickly there. By 1889 a parish house and a small log school for forty children were built. Sisters at Red Lake received no salary for the first thirty-five years but were supported by the motherhouse in Saint Joseph. By the 1930s the sisters received a stipend of $100 a year. However, this diocesan stipend was not sent to the mission but rather to the convent in Saint Joseph. Although Saint John's and Saint Benedict's supported the missions by providing personnel and funding, great self-sufficiency was required of the missionaries.

Work with the Ojibwe took place not only on the reservations but also in Stearns County. In the 1880s Saint John's and Saint Ben's cooperated in establishing boarding schools funded by the government to teach Indian boys and girls a useful trade. These were called industrial schools. They closed when government funding to religious institutions was withdrawn by Congress in the 1890s.

MISSIONARY TRADITION OVERSEAS

It used to surprise us when we learned about many members of both communities in missions thousands of miles from Minnesota, but we've learned that Benedictines have a long history of missionary work in cultures other than their own. For example, collaboration of the two communities occurred in China and then in Japan. Monks from Saint John's were among Benedictines from several congregations who established Peking Catholic University in China in 1922. In 1933 six Benedictine sisters from Saint Benedict's Convent opened the first Catholic college for women at Peking University. Later the sisters were forced to flee from China to Formosa and then to Japan. In the meantime Saint John's started Saint Anselm's Monastery in Tokyo after World War II. In 1950 women's Benedictine life was born in Japan when sisters from Saint Ben's founded a community in Hokaido. The monasteries are not located close together, but they have kept up cordial communication.

In the Caribbean, Saint John's established a foundation in Puerto Rico in 1947, and within a few years sisters of Saint Benedict arrived from Saint Joseph to operate a ten-room parish school there. In the same postwar period Saint Benedict's started a monastery and school in Nassau. In 1946 the monks from Saint John's who had been missionaries in the Bahamas for many years formed a monastic priory, Saint Augustine's Monastery, and a high school.

The educational ministry of the two communities continues today in parishes, schools, missions, and in the partnership of Saint John's University and the College of Saint Benedict at the undergraduate level. The graduate school of theology at Saint

From BIST to SOT: 1958–1978

The Benedictine Institute of Sacred Theology (BIST) was founded at the College of Saint Benedict in 1958 in response to Pope Pius XII's wish to promote the study of theology by religious women. Sister Mary Anthony Wagner was director of the program, with assistance from Father Paschal Botz at Saint John's. Sister Angelo Haspert, a member of the first class, recalls what it was like.

We were all Benedictine women taught by all Benedictine monks, scholars. We were women from a variety of Benedictine communities throughout the United States. I think in our first year we numbered twenty-seven from twenty-five motherhouses, and we did feel very special. I am not alone in feeling this.

During our first year we lived apart from the rest of the community at Saint Benedict's Convent. I think we prayed

Mary Anthony Wagner, O.S.B.

with the community, but we had our meals apart and slept in dormitories with private rooms, set aside for this community of women. For the first year this was probably a good thing because it allowed us to intermingle with one another, to get to know one another.

What we heard in the classroom rolled over into our conversations at mealtimes—arguments, lively discussions, questions. Though we were all Benedictines, I was impressed at the various expressions of the Rule in our daily life. At the same time I was also impressed by the uniformity of interpretation, dedication, and commitment to living out the Rule of Saint Benedict. To read, reflect, reread, discuss, question, and pray over what we learned in the classroom—all related to the Benedictine way of life—was a gift, a privilege, a joy.

In 1963 the program moved to the Saint John's campus with its extensive monastic and theological resources in order to be certified to offer the master's degree in sacred theology. The first graduates received their degrees in 1964. By 1978 the graduate program offered degrees in several areas and was formally organized as the School of Theology (SOT).

John's is also the result of collaboration as it evolved from an institute of theology started on the campus of Saint Benedict's Monastery, the Benedictine Institute of Sacred Theology. The first dean of the graduate program of theology at Saint John's was Sister Mary Anthony Wagner, a sister of Saint Benedict's Monastery.

Saint John's Abbey gave early support to the work of Saint Benedict's in the development of health care. A match in the temperaments and ideals of Abbot Alexius Edelbrock and Mother Scholastica Kerst led to the establishment of two hospitals. At the same time that joint missionary work with the Ojibwe was getting underway in northern Minnesota, Abbot Alexius assisted the sisters in acquiring a hotel in Bismarck, North Dakota, in 1885, which they converted into the only "state of the art" hospital between Saint Paul and Portland. They named it Saint Alexius Hospital. The sisters had also been working to establish Saint Cloud Hospital, and in 1887 they established in Duluth a third hospital, again a cooperative effort between Abbot Alexius and Mother Scholastica. By coincidence the abbot entered Saint Mary's, the sisters' new hospital in Duluth, as their first patient.

MONASTIC SPIRITUALITY AND MINISTRY

Mutual ministry between Saint John's and Saint Ben's has grown through the years. Abbot Alcuin Deutsch offered encouragement and support when the sisters undertook restoration of the full Divine Office in the 1930s. Mother Rosamond Pratschner enlisted Father Ulric Beste, an authority on canon law, in raising Saint Benedict's to pontifical status and establishing the Congregation of Saint Benedict in 1947. From the beginning the priests of Saint John's Abbey provided sacramental ministry for the sisters. One priest, Father Henry Borgerding, was their resident chaplain for twenty-nine years!

There has, however, been an evolution in this relationship from the days when eucharistic liturgies were entirely in the hands of the priests. Sisters tell us that in these times it is the sensitivity of the monks to the concerns of the women for whom they celebrate sacraments that has done much to encourage positive relationships between the two communities. In conversation with some of the monks who have been celebrants for the sisters, they tell us of what they have learned about liturgy in their dialogues with the sisters, and they seek mutuality to whatever degree possible in the celebration of sacramental worship.

The monks and sisters also support each other in their community retreats. Saint John's opened the door to the wisdom of women when they invited Sister Jeremy Hall to be the first woman to give a retreat for the monks. They tell us that she was the first woman to eat in the monastery dining room. In other conversations we learn of less obvious but very rich collaboration between the two communities—

deep spiritual friendships, spiritual direction given by sisters to monks and monks to sisters, academic support and mentoring for graduate studies, and artistic companionship.

MONASTIC INTERRELIGIOUS DIALOGUE

It is apparent that the mutual support of the two communities in the service of God's creation flows from their life of prayer, which reaches out to the needs of all human hearts that seek God, whether they call God by that name or not. Abbot Timothy Kelly and Sisters Katherine Howard and Johanna Becker are pioneers in the Monastic Interreligious Dialogue between world religions. Saint Benedict's and Saint John's became involved in this dialogue in 1978. Both communities had long histories of connections with the East through their missions in China and Japan. One of the sisters had studied under a Zen master in Japan, and this prepared her in a unique way for the dialogue. Others both at Saint Ben's and Saint John's became interested, including Abbot Timothy. They had many rich experiences in exchanges with Tibetan Buddhist nuns and monks, some of whom visited Saint Benedict's and Saint John's while Abbot Timothy (before he was abbot), Sister Katherine, and Brother Aaron Raverty all visited the Buddhists at Dharamsala in India at different times. Members of the dialogue were part of a special meeting with the Dalai Lama at the 1993 Parliament of the World's Religions in Chicago. They find participation in the dialogue a mutually enriching way to work together for world unity and peace.

Venerable Ngawang Chonzin and two other monks visited the Benedictine monasteries of Minnesota in 1995.

What began as a parochial attempt to serve Catholics in central Minnesota has become a ministry of support for any who seek to live the values of love, simplicity, social justice, and nonviolence. Many women and men have embraced Benedictine values in life outside the monastery and abbey and live as Oblates of the two communities, seeking God in mutual support of one another and their monastic sisters and brothers.

Of course, the partnership of the communities of Saint John's Abbey and Saint Benedict's Monastery has had its ups and downs. Institutional relationships can get prickly, as is true in families with long histories together in one place. In the 1950s a priest from Saint John's told one of the sisters at Saint Benedict's, "It's a man's world." Without missing a beat, she retorted, "That's why so many of us are waiting for the next world!" To us, though, respect for the life of Christ lived according to Saint Benedict's Rule is evident in the care and concern of the two communities for each other—not only in their work together but also in their sharing of each other's sadness and joy as their history continues.

Throughout their history a Benedictine theme has been the establishment of monastic centers that contribute to the life of an area. The monks of Saint John's and the sisters of Saint Benedict's have accomplished that in many places. Will there be other, new collaborative endeavors? Autonomy is important to both groups, but so is interdependence, and that seems evident in the comings and goings between the two communities, the friendships, the conversations about the continuing search for balance in a life in which fewer people do more work. This reciprocity is reminiscent of Saint Benedict himself and his sister Saint Scholastica, who, as the story goes, talked through a stormy night and came to a new understanding of love in the shared seeking of God.

CHAPTER 11

The Design and Construction of Saint John's Abbey Church

Victoria Young

"Truly an Architectural Monument in the Service of God"

> The Benedictine tradition at its best challenges us to think boldly and to cast our ideals in forms which will be valid for centuries to come, shaping them with all the genius of present-day materials and techniques. We feel that the modern architect with his orientation toward functionalism and honest use of materials is uniquely qualified to produce a Catholic work.[1]

So wrote Abbot Baldwin Dworschak of the Benedictine Abbey of Saint John the Baptist to twelve of the world's leading architects on March 7, 1953, inquiring whether one of them would be interested in preparing a comprehensive plan for the expanding abbey. From this group emerged Marcel Breuer, the Hungarian-born, Bauhaus-trained architect, then practicing in the United States. Breuer's architecture was bold and modern, and he had a preference for shaping space with concrete. Although the Benedictines might have considered a historical style of architecture for their project, perhaps a Gothic or Romanesque revival, they decided from the start to create their own tradition with forms expressive of their particular place in time. At the heart of their monastic project was the abbey's church. They were keenly aware of the importance of this structure and requested that their architect design "a church which will be truly an architectural monument in the service of God."[2]

Selecting the Architect

By 1950 Saint John's Abbey was the largest Benedictine abbey in the world, home to 306 monks, as well as nearly 1,000 college students, seminarians, and prep school students. They had outgrown the brick, German-inspired buildings of the previous century, built on the familiar Quadrangular layout of European monasteries. In August 1951, Abbot Baldwin Dworschak appointed a seven-member building committee to study the ways in which the physical character of the abbey and university could be improved.[3] After a year and a half of deliberations, the committee reported that the most urgent demands included more space to house the aged and infirm fathers and brothers; guest rooms for visitors; a library, administrative offices, and classrooms for the university; and a larger church for the worshiping community.

Realizing that their new monastery could not be built in the manner of the nineteenth-century complex, completed by monk

The campus was bursting at the seams—monastery, college, prep school—in 1952. Just visible on the left is a new college dorm, Saint Mary's Hall, and on the right the new diocesan seminary. Needed were more monastery rooms, a larger church, a prep school campus, expanded college facilities, an entrance road from the proposed I-94 exit.

artists and monk laborers, the Benedictines sought the advice of an architect in order to evaluate the feasibility of their ideas. The abbot charged building committee member Father Cloud Meinberg and Frank Kacmarcik, instructor in the university's art department, with the composition of the letter of invitation as well as the list of architects to receive it. The recipients of the letter were leaders in comprehensive planning or in religious architecture. Although the committee felt some pressure to select a Saint John's alumnus, in the end they extended their search beyond Collegeville to formulate a list of twelve architects, including five Europeans—Hermann Baur of Switzerland, Albert Bosslet and Rudolf Schwarz of Germany, Robert Kramreiter of Austria, and Thomas W. Sharp of England—as well as seven American-based designers—Pietro Belluschi, Marcel Breuer, Barry Byrne, Walter Gropius, Joseph D. Murphy, Richard Neutra, and Eero Saarinen. Unfortunately none of the Europeans ever had a chance to obtain the commission. The building committee contacted them mainly out of concern that the invited Americans might not be interested, only to find that five of them would be pleased to visit Collegeville.[4]

Richard Neutra of Los Angeles came first, bringing his architect son, Dion. During his stay Neutra did not promote any one architectural style but instead made it known that he was interested in staying true to the spirit of architecture in the temperate zones. One of the monks immediately interpreted this to mean

Ham Smith—no one seems to have called him Hamilton—joined the Breuer firm on Eero Saarinen's recommendation in 1953 to assist with the Saint John's project. Robert Gatje, not pictured, soon joined him in the firm and after Breuer's death in 1981 wrote Marcel Breuer: A Memoir, *with a firsthand description of the early planning. The church was the centerpiece of the Saint John's project, but a comprehensive campus plan was the first need. Here Smith and Breuer study a drawing of the campus plan on site.*

Ham Smith's Description of Breuer's Approach to Design

One of Marcel Breuer's strengths was the ability to generate a shaping concept. For the Saint John's abbey church, that concept was inspired by historic traditions of church building, in which structure, enclosure, and architectural expression were realized as a unity. Breuer's translation of this tradition into contemporary building technology involved design possible only in poured-in-place architectural concrete. The church sidewalls and roofspans made of this sculptural material are formed as deeply folded pleats, which remain undisguised in finish on interior surfaces modulating the large spatial volume they enclose.

Inherent in this monolithic system of construction is a degree of continuity between walls and roof such that the whole enclosure could be supported free of the ground on piers. The spaces between these piers open on confined cloister gardens, allowing the admission of natural light.

One big idea, however powerful, does not define an abbey church. Other concepts of hardly less significance were developed in memorable meetings with the community, in many of which both Breuer and I participated.

The north-facing orientation of the new church, respecting preservation of the old church for other uses, created the need for a means of introducing daylight deep within its interior. Breuer's solution was the bell banner positioned to reflect south light on and through the glazed tracery of the entrance wall.

As do many vital solutions, this one of an elevated concrete plane pierced to frame the cross and again to house bells transferred from the old church served a second purpose. A "spire" symbol for-our-time resulted, announcing Saint John's from a distance.

The concrete structure supporting the elevated banner is formed of parabolic arches, which deliberately contrast the pleated geometry of the church sidewalls and bridge over the entrance plaza and the baptistery.

The community decision to have the main entrance to the church reached only after passing through the baptistery formalizes the significance of that sacrament. Architecturally, a skylit, atrium-like space was generated, which contrasts and intensifies the volume of the nave.

The bell-shaped plan of the church grew out of an intent to have the altar in clear view of all in the church. Key in realizing this was the community's decision to move the altar well forward of traditional location against a reredos wall. The resulting spatial independence made the altar central to the monastic choirs and enhanced its relationship to the congregation. This sense of closeness was reinforced by a seating balcony, which made it unnecessary to extend the nave more distant from the sanctuary.

Another program decision called for a vertical axis ascending above the altar and culminating in an opening through the roof. The lantern covering this penetration was shaped to be structurally integral with the pleats and to admit daylight filtered through stained-glass lights.

Breuer's personal stamp is on all these defining elements, as it is on other aspects of design: crypt-level chapels, pews and other furnishings, and the baldachin over the altar. The palette of finish materials was also his: waxed brick and granite pavers for floor surfaces, and dark-stained oak for doors and frames.

The Saint John's abbey church is a building fully realized, and I regard it as Marcel Breuer's finest achievement.

Ham Smith

International Style architecture, like Neutra's 1929 design for the Philip Lovell Health House in Los Angeles, and stated that Saint John's might not want the International Style. To this Neutra replied, "I certainly am not a representative of the International Style—Mr. Gropius is that."[5]

Walter Gropius, founder of the Bauhaus and designer of its International Style building in Dessau (1925), arrived at the abbey during the last day of Neutra's visit, and the two shared breakfast before Neutra left. Like Neutra, Gropius pored over all aspects of the site and its extant buildings. He talked to the committee about good planning and about the proper use of materials and only brought out examples of his own architecture at the very end of his visit.

Two weeks later Joseph Denis Murphy of Saint Louis arrived. Murphy was invited in order to accommodate a small number of the monks who thought that a Catholic architect should be selected for the commission.[6] Others questioned his ability to unite engineering and architecture in a strong finished product, and his designs of churches did not impress the committee.

The next visitor was Marcel Breuer. Breuer's domestic work had come to the attention of Frank Kacmarcik on a visit to the Museum of Modern Art in New York City in 1949, where he saw Breuer's "House in the Museum Garden." Breuer discussed his theory of modern architecture, telling the monks that he would seek out "the expressive nature of the design," no matter what the building type, in his desire to create a "new tradition" of architecture in which the "rhythm of space is that of its structure."[7]

There was one highly qualified architect yet to visit the abbey, the Chicago-based designer Barry Byrne. Byrne had a strong involvement with the liturgical movement in America and had published

The typewritten working document "The Story of the Church" composed by Bob Gatje and Ham Smith with comments inked in by Marcel Breuer.

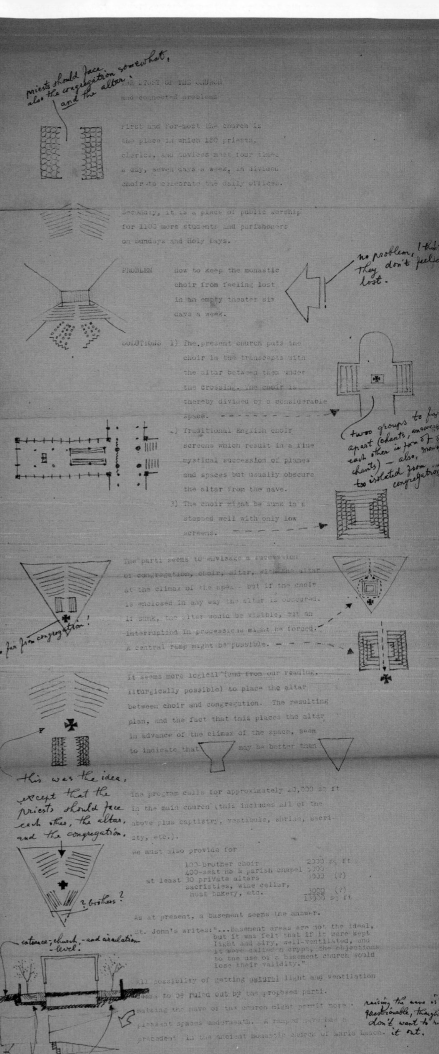

 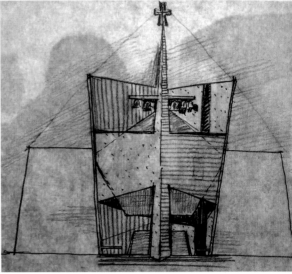

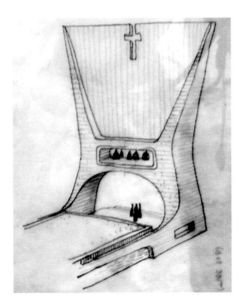

Banner sketches

several articles on church design in *Liturgical Arts,* as well as completing several liturgically recognized churches. Yet the committee decided in favor of Breuer on April 23, 1953. Breuer spoke the language of functionalism and modern materials that the Benedictines sought. Most important, however, was his unassuming, attentive style and his youth, as well as his readiness to discuss and follow up on his designs.

THE COMPREHENSIVE PLAN AND DESIGN OF THE CHURCH, 1953–1958

While the monks were convinced that Breuer's domestic sensibility could positively inform designs for the monastic and university residences, they were most concerned with his understanding of the church's complex religious program, a combination of monastic space and regular parish space all fabricated in light of new liturgical reforms. Breuer and his team of architects, including Hamilton Smith and Bob Gatje, began their dialogue with the Benedictine community on their first official visit to the site in June 1953. They studied reports, examined the extant buildings, talked with the monks, and observed them using their space.[8] To gain familiarity with the religious component, they read the Rule of Saint Benedict and essays on liturgical architecture.[9]

The shape of the church needed to reflect the liturgical reform in which Saint John's Abbey was a leader, and Smith and Gatje prepared the "Story of a Church and Connected Problems" to analyze the situation. Five solutions were presented. The first answer was to build in the manner of the old church: a Latin-cross plan with the choir in the transept arms. Breuer vetoed this version because of the great distance between the two divisions of the choir. Next, the associates offered a traditional English layout with a screen separating the laity from the choir, the monks' stalls arranged perpendicularly to the screen in three parallel rows, and the altar positioned at the easternmost end. This layout obscured the altar from the nave and therefore was not practical for a church that wanted to include the laity in the worship service. The third solution called for

1953 interior sketch

a square-shaped choir below grade, with low screens separating it from the rest of the church, an impractical solution because it did not help to define the overall form of the church. The fourth option organized the space in a triangular shape, with a succession of congregation, choir, and altar, but this created problems with circulation, and again the altar was located, as Breuer noted, "too far away from the congregation."

Finally the office hit upon the answer. They decided to place the altar between the choir and the congregation, combining a trapezoid (for the congregation) and a square (for the choir). This shape quickly gave way to a single trapezoid, a form Breuer had used before in other architectural types that gathered large numbers of people, such as theaters and conference halls. As a liturgical space, the trapezoidal shape could shelter and unite the large number of monks and laity who made up the Saint John's community. Breuer moved the trapezoidal-shaped church to several different positions in the plan of the new monastery before securing its place on the east side of the overall plan, on a north-south line in front of the old monastic church, the only large open space available.[10]

Breuer and his associates presented their comprehensive plan for the campus as well as a design for the church to the community on January 28, 1954. (See model of plan in chapter 3, page 35.) Their plan called for replacement of most of the campus's twenty-two buildings, using a process of shadow planning, in which seventeen new buildings would be built in the shadow of the old, which would then be demolished. The plan eliminated the enclosed Quadrangle of the nineteenth-century monastery but provided an open quadrangular area in front of the church. Although according to the terms of the architectural competition Breuer was not guaranteed the right to design any of the buildings in the comprehensive plan, the Benedictines proceeded to commission him to design a residential wing for the monastery, finished in 1955, and three years later a college dormitory, Saint Thomas Aquinas Hall.

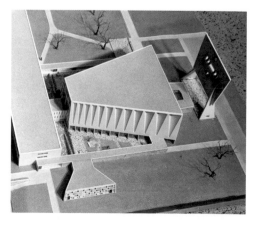

1953 exterior model of abbey church

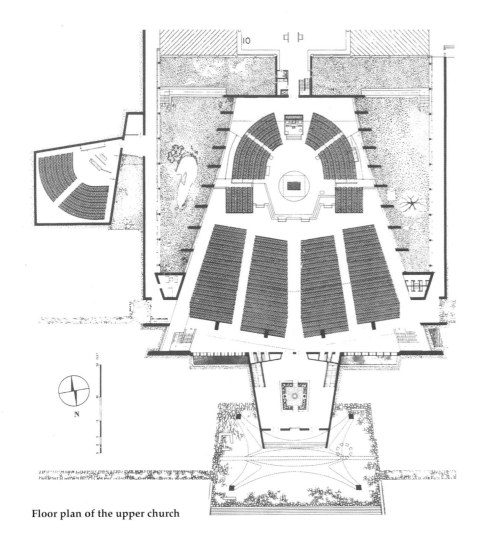

Floor plan of the upper church

Baptismal font

The 1953 church plan showcased Breuer's understanding of concrete, a material he thought facilitated "the most interesting developments in structural design. . . . For here the material not only acts as the support of the building, but also as the enclosure, the form."[11] Breuer's final design for the church, completed in 1957, included several of the key elements of the original design, such as the trapezoidal shape and the bell banner, the most creative element of the design. Architectural inspirations for the banner included churches Breuer saw on his travels through the Greek islands and the American Southwest.[12] He worked through several versions of the banner before deciding on its final form, a trapezoid supported by four legs, two of which straddle the baptistery. As Breuer scholar Isabelle Hyman has noted, this change to a dual support was the result of his time in Paris working on the UNESCO project, where he had a constant view of the Eiffel Tower.[13]

Just as he had done for the UNESCO Conference Building design, Breuer consulted with the Italian engineer Pier Luigi Nervi to find the solution for Collegeville. In the abbey church he employed folded-plate construction in the long east and west sidewalls of the trapezoid, while treating the ends as flat walls—the north wall comprised of large expanses of stained glass set into rectangular concrete tracery and the south wall made of concrete block with small openings to allow light to filter through to the interior. To bring in additional light, the side walls were lifted off the ground to rest on a series of pencil-thin piers framing plate-glass windows, as if to suggest that the entire concrete superstructure was weightless. The ceiling was also designed in V-shaped folds of concrete and roofed with a flat slab of concrete sloping to the narrow end of the trapezoid, the south end of the church.

The interior of the 1953 design reveals how space and ornament would be fashioned. Breuer placed a large balcony across the north end of the building to accommodate the large number of worshipers the church would have on feast days and during the school year. He positioned the high altar and its circular baldachin (or canopy) between the laity and the semicircular choir. The abbot's throne, surmounted by the apse screen, terminated the design at the building's southernmost end. Color was the key to the building's decorative quality. In addition to color provided by materials such as red brick for the floors, wood for the choir stalls, and white and black marble for the altar and abbot's throne, Breuer envisioned a gilded ceiling, white side walls, a gilt and blue baldachin, and a blue background for the abbot's throne. The most important figural element of the decorative scheme was the apse screen mosaic featuring the imagery of Christ *Pantocrator,* or Christ the Almighty and Ruler of all.[14]

THE SPIRITUAL AND LITURGICAL AXIS OF THE ABBEY CHURCH

In addition to reflecting a contemporary architectural style, the church design had to have some novelty in its design in order to facilitate liturgical reforms promoted by the Benedictines. These reforms sought not only to unify the clergy and laity as mutual participants celebrating the mystery of the Mass, but they also placed a special emphasis on the importance of the sacraments. With the help of the church committee, Breuer expressed these notions in his design for the sacred axis of the main floor.

The axis begins with the bell banner, described by the Benedictines as the threshold of the sacred axis and a transition from the profane to the sacred realm. Breuer's understanding of it was more architectural, finding it akin to "the archaic column, gothic arch, and renaissance dome" [sic].[15]

Moving under the banner into the baptistery symbolized entering the living church and being born again of water and the Spirit. Breuer's domestic sensibility is revealed in the one-story scale of the space as well as in its top-lit courtyard-like feeling. The gray granite baptismal font (designed by Breuer) is placed three steps below the main-floor level of the baptistery, symbolizing baptism by immersion, as was done in the early church. Plants in the corner of the space symbolize life, as does the simple agitation in the water running through the font.

The worshiper moves forward along the axis through a tripartite doorway into the rear of the nave, passing between the confessionals and under the balcony. The altar is the focal point of the journey, followed by the monastic choir and the abbot's throne. Breuer's original design did not provide for a lantern over the altar, but discussions with the building committee led to its introduction. The light places a palpable focus on the altar, as does the placement of the altar between the monastic choir and the congregation. Breuer also designed the interior furnishings, including the altar, lectern, communion tables, and choir stalls, showcasing his understanding of sculptural form in a variety of materials.

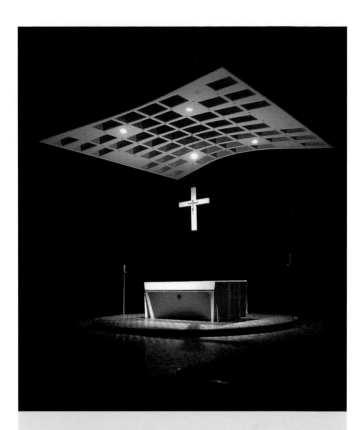

The Baldachin

Architect Marcel Breuer was perhaps the first to point out that the massive concrete abbey church is a tribute to carpentry, not to buckets of concrete. Whether you look at the imposing bell banner, the massive "folded concrete" beams high above the nave, or the gentle curves of the cantilevered balcony, every inch of the concrete surface reveals the delicate pattern of wood grain. Breuer explained that all the church's many shapes were "constructed in reverse" by skilled carpenters, who built the forms into which the concrete was poured, and this concrete structure speaks to the skills of carpentry.

Abbot Baldwin Dworschak told the story of the building committee's frustrating search for artisans to construct the large wooden baldachin that hangs suspended over the main altar. When the carpenters who had built all of the forms for the concrete learned of the search, a representative stepped forward and made a persuasive case that the carpenters already on the job had demonstrated that they had the skills required to fabricate the baldachin, one of the few wooden details in the concrete structure. They got the job.

Construction underway on the footings and crypt

Church under construction with steel framework inside to support the wooden framework

Construction—aerial view of finished roof and banner almost done

Building the Abbey Church 1958–1961: Making the Liturgical a Concrete Reality

With the design and funds in place, construction of the abbey church began on May 19, 1958. Breuer sent architect Valerius L. Michelson to manage the site.[16] Michelson worked closely with the local associated architect Ray Hermanson from Saint Cloud, Minnesota, and the construction crew of McGough and Associates of Saint Paul, Minnesota, led by field superintendent Ted Hoffmeyer.[17]

Building the church was not an easy feat. Creation of the concrete shell alone required more than 250 pages of shop drawings and more than 60 carloads of lumber from the western United States for the formwork.[18] Twenty-seven different trades worked on the project; most dominant in numbers and importance were the carpenters who laid up the formwork for the large-scale concrete pours. From the onset of construction there were some Benedictines on the job, including Brothers Julius Terfehr and Stephen Thell, who put in over 6,500 hours of work on the church, inserting the steel reinforcing rods and bush-hammering the concrete. The clerics also joined in, working over 3,200 hours, mostly during the first summer of digging the foundations of the church and unloading the railroad carloads of lumber needed for the formwork.[19]

McGough Construction spent the summer of 1958 pouring the foundations of the church, enclosing the basement or crypt of the church by November 1 of that same year. The final designs for the basement included, from north to south, a mechanical room under the baptistery; a reliquary chapel with the remains of the sixth-century boy-saint Peregrin; a parish chapel; thirty-four private chapels; a sacristy; and a brothers' chapel dedicated to Saint Benedict.

The reliquary chapel of Saint Peregrin shows Breuer's love of solids and voids, as well as his understanding of current architectural trends. In 1956 Breuer visited Le Corbusier's recently completed pilgrimage chapel Notre Dame du Haut in Ronchamp, France. The south wall of Notre Dame du Haut consists of irregularly sized windows punched out of the thick concrete and stone wall and filled with clear, colored, and painted glass. Breuer used the voids in Saint Peregrin's chapel as niches or alcoves, filling them with additional relics. But on the crypt level of the north wall of the church, he filled his irregularly sized windows with clear glass, a creative yet practical solution that brought in light to the lower level.

With the crypt in place, construction could move forward on the banner and upper church. Abbot Baldwin laid the cornerstone on November 19, 1958. During the cold winter months of 1958 and 1959, McGough Construction fabricated the wooden framework for the 112-foot-high banner. Its cantilevered slab of reinforced concrete rests on parabolic supports that are only 4 feet square at the base but extend 15 feet below ground for strength. It weighs 2,500 tons and was poured in place from April to December 1959.

The construction of the church during this same time frame required a temporary steel support system for the wooden formwork, which upon first glance appears like a steel frame skeleton for a small office building. Breuer employed twelve deep, pleated folds of poured-in-place, reinforced concrete, each six to eight inches thick, for the side walls of the building. The modified folded roof structure is comprised of nine-inch-thick V-shaped walls forming tents ranging in height from eight to fourteen feet, all covered by a roof plate.[20] The roof folds were created using gunite, a concrete mixture that is sprayed from a special gun over steel reinforcements in a bottom wooden formwork only.[21] The gunite was shot onto the oiled wooden formwork with a zero slump, a process that uses minimal water in the mixture. Breuer did not want to use gunite, but Michelson and Hoffmeyer convinced him to do so because it was quicker to set and dried harder and stronger than a conventional concrete pour.

Considering the scale of the building, the mistakes made during construction were minimal, with the most serious one occurring in the roof. In the spring of 1960 several of the folded plate roof trusses developed active sheer cracks. Although the roof was not in danger of collapsing, the engineers and construction crew decided that repairs were needed.[22] McGough Construction workers spent the next six months drilling into the V-folds and adding more steel and concrete.[23] Steel had to be added because once concrete cracks, the steel bears all the tensile weight and weakens. An independent professional inspector analyzed the situation in September 1960 and concluded that changes made to the original design, a delay in some of the placement of concrete, and a variance between the gunite and poured concrete mixtures were to blame for the cracks.[24]

In January 1960 McGough poured the concrete for the cantilevered balcony, the foundation posts for the pews and choir stalls, the walls surrounding the choir, and the hexagons of the north window wall. Breuer originally intended to cast individual and complete concrete hexagons. An experimental hexagon pour indicated two major problems with this method. First, although oiled, the wooden formwork damaged the edges of the concrete when removed, and second, a wall of these individual units required continuous reinforcing in order to be secure. Breuer decided that in order to strengthen the wall, the shape poured should be that of a half hexagon, so he devised a formwork that could shape seven half sections. Michelson and Hoffmeyer made the formwork of steel because its reuse "might prove to be more economical in the long run."[25] Fabricating the hexagons in this way provided the stability the wall needed.

The completion of the north window wall in the fall of 1960 signified the end of the exterior construction of the abbey church. Finishing touches could then be added. On the exterior this included the hanging of the bells and cross in the banner and the placement of granite veneer from local quarries on the walls of the baptistery and church. On the interior the concrete was left raw and unadorned. Breuer's original plan to cover the concrete with gold leaf on the ceiling and white paint on the walls was scrapped when he saw the wonderful shades of gray in the concrete and the formwork marks. Furthermore, the simplicity of concrete roughed up only by the wooden framework highlights not only the engineered character of this building but also its wonderful materiality.

Workers on roof shooting gunite

Workers facing the exterior with granite

Monastic choir and organ gallery under construction.

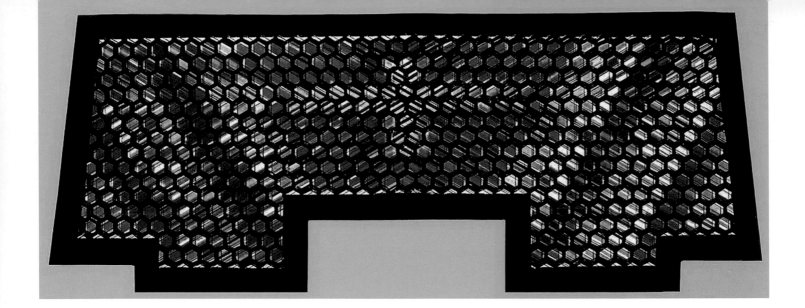

Josef Albers' design for the north window

Medieval Benedictines were great builders precisely because they looked to the future, refusing to be bound by the accomplishments of the past.

Waxed red brick covers the floor in continuity with the warm homemade brick of the nineteenth-century Quadrangle visible through the west-side windows of the church. The design also includes darkly stained wood, brass, stained glass, gold leaf, terracotta tile walls framing the cloister gardens outside the church, and blue tesserae for a mosaic wall in the Lady Chapel. An understanding of materials and interest in the building's smallest details, including door handles and floor tiles, came from Breuer's seven years at the Bauhaus in Germany, where all elements of design were as important as the building in which they were housed. With the help of liturgical coordinator Frank Kacmarcik, contemporary art made its way into the building, most noticeably in the north wall of stained glass. Breuer intended to have his friend and former Bauhaus colleague Josef Albers complete the window, but in the end he yielded to the committee's choice of Bronislaw Bak, then an instructor in the university's art department.

CONSECRATION AND COMPLETION: A MONUMENT TO THE LORD

In August 1961 the bishop of Saint Cloud, Peter Bartholome, consecrated the abbey church. At a time when so many designers and religious leaders supported the use of traditional building methods, materials, imagery, and plans, the completion of Saint John's Abbey and University Church proved that a material like concrete could create a new language of form, function, and meaning, with the ability to transcend centuries and styles. The publication of the church and other designs for Saint John's in more than twenty religious, popular, and architectural journals upheld the Benedictines' desire to make their complex a visible paradigm of modern religious space. Yet, being modern was nothing new for the Benedictine Order, as Father Cloud Meinberg told the community early on in the project:

> We are Benedictines and Benedictines historically have a tradition of inventive architecture. William of Volpiano, Lanfranc, and Suger of Saint Denis at one time led Europe in architectural development. They were great builders precisely because they looked to the future, refusing to be bound by the accomplishments of the past. Nothing could be more uncharacteristic of our Order than to fall back upon limitations of the past, no matter how successful.[26]

With Marcel Breuer's assistance, Saint John's had created an architectural monument to the Lord by boldly casting Catholic ideals in concrete forms that would be valid and functional for centuries to come.

[1] Abbot Baldwin Dworschak to various architects, Office of the Abbot. New Church and Monastery Building Records, 1952–1981 (bulk 1953–1962). Saint John's Abbey (Collegeville, Minnesota), Box 2 Folder 13. Further references to this archive will be referred to as SJA.

[2] Ibid.

[3] Other members of the committee included subprior Father John Eidenschink, Fathers Fintan Bromenshenkel, Matthew Kiess, Cloud Meinberg, Adelard Thuente, Joachim Watrin, and Brother Hubert Schneider.

[4] Ronald Roloff, O.S.B., "Building Committee Minutes," 20 April 1953, SJA Box 5 Folder 4. Saarinen and Belluschi were the only two who declined the invitation, citing both their current professional and academic commitments as too great to take on the project.

[5] "Notes and Observations on the Visits of Mr. Neutra and Mr. Gropius," 30 March 1953, SJA Box 2 Folder 8.

[6] Ronald Roloff, "Minutes of the Building Committee," 20 April 1953, SJA Box 5 Folder 4.

[7] "Notes and Observations on the Visit of Mr. Breuer to Saint John's," 20 April 1953, SJA Box 2 Folder 14.

[8] They compiled a notebook of information during this visit, which included: a history of the many parishes run by the Benedictines in the Upper Midwest; maps of the Watab Valley; ten aerial photographs; plans and descriptions of the abbey buildings; space and occupancy study drawings of the nineteenth-century church and Quadrangle, and the brothers' and fathers' daily schedules. This binder is now in Breuer office archives at Syracuse University Library, Box 70 File 6. (Further citations for this source will be listed as SUL.)

[9] Breuer's copy of the Rule of Saint Benedict can be found in the office archives at SUL in Box 70 Folder 6. Liturgical notations and their architectural statements came from reading Peter F. Anson, *Churches: Their Plan and Furnishing* (Milwaukee: The Bruce Publishing Company, 1948); H. A. Reinhold, *Speaking of Liturgical Architecture* (Notre Dame: Liturgical Programs, 1952); and John B. O'Connell, *Church Building and Furnishing: The Church's Way. A Study In Liturgical Law* (London: Burns & Oates, 1955), copies of which the Benedictines provided for the architects.

[10] Traditionally, Catholic churches were laid out on an east-west line, with the east end containing the sanctuary and altar so that the clergy and laity would face the direction of the rising sun, as Christ was often referred to in the liturgy. Saint John's understood that there were exceptions to this practice and that no ecclesiastical law mandated an east-west orientation. The first abbey church, although placed on an east-west line, had the altar on the west end. Site conditions usually dictated a building's orientation. For more see Father Cloud Meinberg, "Orientation of Church," SUL Box 114 Folder 4.

[11] Marcel Breuer, *Marcel Breuer: Sun and Shadow* (New York: Dodd, Mead & Co., 1955) 70–71.

[12] Whitney Stoddard, *Adventure in Architecture* (New York, London and Toronto: Longmans, Green and Company, 1958) 98, notes Breuer's travels through the Greek Islands in 1931 and 1932, and Isabelle Hyman mentions on page 222 of her work *Marcel Breuer, Architect* (New York: Abrams, 2001) a photograph in the Breuer archives of San José, Laguna Pueblo, New Mexico, on which Breuer had labeled "adobe wall with bells reminiscent to concrete banner of Saint John's church."

[13] Hyman, *Marcel Breuer, Architect,* 222.

[14] Breuer's iconography in the *Pantocrator* recalled the apse of the first abbey church, which had been painted with this theme by Beuronese artist Clement Frischauf in 1939.

[15] Marcel Breuer, *Marcel Breuer: Sun and Shadow,* 71.

[16] Michelson was Russian born and trained, studying architecture at the National Academy of Fine Arts in Leningrad from 1935 to 1941. After surviving World War II, he attended the Technische Hochschule in Karlsruhe, Germany, before immigrating to the United States with his wife in 1949. In 1952 he completed an architecture degree at Columbia University while working in Percival Goodman's office. For more on Michelson, see the Val Michelson papers at the Northwest Architectural Archives, University of Minnesota, and Linda Mack "From Russia, with Visions of Modernism," *Minneapolis Star Tribune* (October 22, 2000) F5.

[17] For more on McGough, see Brian Johnson, "McGough Construction—Still Prospering after Five Generations," *Finance and Commerce* (17 April 2001). Hoffmeyer went to Siberia with Albert Kahn from 1929 to 1932 to build cities for the Soviets, and during World War II he built airports for the military. Upon seeing the design proposal for the abbey church in an advertisement for Universal Atlas Cement Company, Hoffmeyer convinced Pete McGough to hire him as the field superintendent. Hoffmeyer took hundreds of photos during the construction of the abbey church, leaving behind a wonderful chronicle of the building's history. These photos are now in the archives at Saint John's Abbey.

All the concrete for the project was provided by the Universal Atlas Cement Company of New York City, who paid for the fabrication of the 1957 model of the church, which they used in their own publicity. Greg Schweitz, "Saint John's Abbey Church: A Modern, Lasting Expression of Concrete Faith and Form," *L&M Concrete News* 3, 1 (Spring 2002) 8–9.

[18] McGough Construction Co. of Saint Paul, Brochure ca. 1973, SJA Box 3 Folder 3. Over 416,000 feet of lumber were used during the construction of the church.

[19] Information on the monastic workforce is taken from Brian Millette, O.S.B., "Saint John's New Abbey Church: A Chronicle of Construction," *The Scriptorium* 20, 1 (1961) 79–80.

[20] This structure is technically modified because it has a roof plate. The walls are true folded construction.

[21] Gunite is also known as shotcrete. See T. A. Hoffmeyer, "Wet-Mix Shotcrete Practice," *Shotcreting,* SP-14, 59–74. American Concrete Institute, Detroit, MI. Hoffmeyer worked with the Gun-All Corporation of Tulsa, Oklahoma, perfecting the mixture for Saint John's.

[22] The engineers included the New York City firm working with Breuer on this commission, Weisenfeld, Hayward & Leon, as well as Nervi.

[23] Larry McGough in a roundtable discussion at Saint John's Abbey, 24 October 2001.

[24] J. Henry Schipke, "Report on the Structural Safety of Roof Trusses at Saint John's Abbey Church, Collegeville, Minnesota," 27 September 1960, SUL Box 70 Folder 11.

[25] Val Michelson memorandum, Collegeville, to Marcel Breuer, New York City, 6 October 1958, typescript, SUL Box 102 Folder 1.

[26] "The Monastic Church," delivered by Father Cloud Meinberg before the community on 29 September 1953. SJA Box 5 Folder 19.

Mary, Throne of Wisdom, was carved from a single piece of oak somewhere in Burgundy in the twelfth century. The donor preferred that this Romanesque sculpture be in a place of prayer. It stands in the Blessed Virgin shrine at the west entrance to the church.

CHAPTER 12

For Beauty as Well as Bread: Saint John's and the Land

Derek R. Larson

THE GREAT NINETEENTH-CENTURY NATURALIST JOHN MUIR once wrote: "Everybody needs beauty as well as bread, places to play in and pray in, where nature may heal and give strength to body and soul alike." Some of us travel great distances to fill this need, on pilgrimage to places like Yosemite or Yellowstone. Others may seek their beauty in a weekend at a northwoods cabin or even a quiet afternoon in the garden. Remarkable for today's world, Saint John's offers an encounter with nature to anyone who cares to exit the freeway, be it for a few minutes or a lifetime. When I first visited in 1998, I was astounded by the relative wildness of the land surrounding the inner campus. What was it about this place that originally drew the monks here, I wondered. Then, over time, the environmental historian in me raised other questions: Why wasn't the forest cleared, as it obviously had been in the surrounding area? How was the land used in the past, and how had those uses changed? Did the community view its land as a spiritual resource, as Muir might have? As it turns out, the story of the land at Saint John's is as interesting as that of the institution itself—and an inseparable part of it as well.

TAMING THE INDIANBUSH

When the final decision was made to relocate the Saint Cloud Benedictine priory some thirteen miles west onto unsettled land in 1865, the monks still called the new site "the Indianbush," as its prior use was most likely as a hunting ground for Sioux and Ojibwe Indians. The first Benedictines to visit the area had been delighted by "the excellent timber and beautiful meadow of wild hay which grew higher than their heads," and not long after, signs reading "Application for this land is made to Congress for Saint John's College" were erected to discourage other claimants. Over the ensuing decades an occasionally haphazard series of initiatives drove the conversion of the Indianbush from wild land into a prosperous mix of pasture, woodlot, lakes, and buildings that set the monastery apart from its neighboring family farms and, eventually, from most other monasteries in North America.

In less than a decade Saint John's took shape on the hill overlooking Lake Sagatagan (originally

◀ Arboretum education coordinator Sarah Gainey introduces a pair of students to snowshoe hare and beaver pelts.

129

The church was less than a year old when Peter Engel took this front view of the buildings and the brickyard from the water reservoir hill on June 18, 1883. The frame house and the old stone house still stand. The main building has a graceful open cupola. The towers have no clocks. There is no Quad, but there is a good-sized barn behind the church. Presumably the white picket fence encloses a tidy lawn with its row of planted trees. In the foreground is the brickyard.

called Saint Louis Lake), the centerpiece of the monastery lands. A half-dozen other lakes and several dozen seasonal ponds were scattered around the property, but the dominant feature away from the lake was the mixed-hardwood forest that covered the rolling hills east of the monastery. In 1868 the Watab River was dammed for a sawmill, providing a cheap way to process logs from the property into lumber. Around the same time work began on a brickyard, and from 1869 onward brick produced on site from native clay would be the building material of choice.

Before long the structures included a stone house, a brick building for the college, a brick blacksmith shop, a slaughterhouse, a laundry on the shore of the lake, and assorted frame buildings used as quarters for lay workers, for stables, or for the storage of farm implements. A chapel was constructed on the lakeshore opposite the monastery in 1872, and in 1875 a small reservoir was created on a hill adjacent to the buildings, insurance against fire as well as a convenient source of water. Much of this construction was guided by Abbot Alexius Edelbrock, who, in keeping with Benedictine tradition, insisted that the monastery be self-supporting and saw to it that food, fuel, and building supplies were produced from monastic lands whenever possible.

While some documentation of these construction projects remains in the archives, there is little record of land management practices for the first half-century of Saint John's history. Limited photographic evidence and a few surviving memoirs suggest that a substantial amount of land was cleared for pasture and that large areas of the forest were logged for fuel, lumber, roads, or building sites. The composition of the original forest is uncertain today, but most early accounts suggest a dominant mixed-hardwood composition of red and white oak, maples, basswood, and birch, with smaller stands of tamarack, aspen, black ash, and various conifers dispersed according to soil, slope, and drainage patterns. In addition to the production of fuel and building supplies from the forest, two to three hundred acres of the land at any one time were

given over to agriculture, typically to grow rye, barley, and oats, which were ground into animal feed at the abbey's grist mill. Cattle, sheep, chickens, and hogs were raised for milk, meat, and eggs, with the combined dairy/beef herd exceeding three hundred head at its peak.

Not surprisingly, the cattle operation impacted the land only slightly less than the logging as hundreds of acres of maple-basswood forest were cleared for pasture, while the practice of grazing sheep within the forest itself impacted regeneration, favoring red oak by eliminating its competitor species. In the mid-1880s the demand for food production prompted the monastery to purchase approximately one thousand acres of additional land forty miles northwest of the monastery; this prairie land was considered superior for farming and within a few years was producing over 5,000 bushels of grain and 250 tons of hay annually. This off-site farm production reduced the pressure to convert more of the monastic lands surrounding Lake Sagatagan to agriculture, leaving development of the original holdings to proceed at a slower pace than it would have otherwise. Thus, in contrast to many of their neighbors, the men of Saint John's were able to provide for most of their needs from the land without converting it entirely to pasture or woodlot, allowing for significant acreage to remain relatively wild while the surrounding township fell increasingly under the yoke of production.

As was typical of frontier settlers of the latter nineteenth century, the Benedictines of Saint John's spent little time reflecting on the changes they imposed on nature. They invested in land as their secular neighbors did, perhaps even more aggressively, as they knew from their European predecessors the benefits of extensive land ownership and the stability it afforded (indeed, stability is a central tenet of the Rule of Benedict). Aesthetic appreciation for the land was typically limited to the pastoral, reflecting the utilitarian bent of the agriculturalist, but the Germanic culture of the monks taught them to appreciate the forest as well as the field. Memories of Bavarian forests may have played a role

With this distant shot from chapel island the photographer shows how the 1894 tornado cleared the ground and how quickly the community repaired, indeed improved the damaged south wing by adding a third floor with mansard roof to match the rest of the Quad, completed in 1886. The year is 1897, and the clock and the bells are brand new. The graceful cupola has been replaced with a square turret in making over the top floor of the main building as a student dormitory.

A view of the monastery farm near West Union, known locally as the Brotherhood Farm.

What we know about this photo is that the Robert Morley look-alike holding a scroll of papers is John Katzner. The bearded monk with hat in hand is Adrian Schmitt, whose father sent pine seeds from Bavaria. To Katzner's left is Severin Gertken, future abbot of Saint Peter's Abbey in Saskatchewan. The monk seated on the railing is David Yuenger, English teacher in the prep school and college. The monk seated on the steps is Alcuin Deutsch, to become abbot of Saint John's in December 1921. They are gathered at the entrance to the school. What we do not know is what the happy occasion is, who the four well-dressed laymen are, and why one of them holds a tennis racket.

Excerpts from Father John Katzner

I was still pursuing my studies at Saint John's College and had all the opportunities to observe what different varieties of fruits were grown at this institution in 1875. . . . I always had a predilection for horticulture as far as I can think back. Even as a boy of eight years I had already transplanted a small pear tree from the woods to my grandfather's garden in July. Of course, three days later the tree was dead. In our school the teacher spoke interestingly on horticulture and one time showed us boys how to graft trees.

Later as a student and professor I had no time to do any horticultural work. It was only when our old orchard at Saint John's had been removed and no one ever thought of planting a new one, that I felt a desire to do something in this line.

On June 27, 1894, a cyclone passed over Saint John's leaving only ruin and destruction in its track. I was told my orchard was all ruined. After two days I went out to see the extent of the damage. No trees in the orchard were broken off, but the side of the trees facing the cyclone was full of sand driven into the bark. All the trees recovered.

In July of that year I joined the Minnesota State Horticultural Society, of which I am still [1914] a member. . . . Every beginner in fruit-growing should become a member of this society and be guided by the practical instructions of the old horticulturists who blazed the way to success.

John Katzner, in *History of Stearns County* (1915), 740, 744.

here, but certainly the monks were also aware of the careful timber management practices that had kept some European monasteries supplied with timber for centuries, leading them to adopt a fairly conservative attitude toward their forests as compared with other settlers in the region.

EXPERIMENTS IN SELF-SUFFICIENCY

The overriding characteristic of the first century of land management at Saint John's was a willingness to experiment with new techniques as priorities changed. Directions in land management were driven by economics, by the influence of innovative ideas from outside, and even by the personal interests of the abbots and various religious in charge of the resources. Nowhere are these changing practices so evident as with the forests of Saint John's. Though the lack of records prior to the 1930s leaves the details of early forest management unclear, we do know that extensive logging was followed by sporadic efforts at reforestation as early as the 1880s. Reflecting back in 1926, Father Alexius Hoffmann recalled the original trees somewhat wistfully: "The tallest trees found hereabout were pines—they are all gone, I think. The tallest ones, in the hollow behind the reservoir, may have measured 60 feet. They have disappeared."

The original trees may have been gone, but their replacements were already in the ground. In 1884 a recently cleared 3.5- acre stand was planted with Scotch pine, Norway spruce, and white pine intended for lumber production. By the turn of the century a substantial reforestation effort was underway, suggesting that the lessons learned by European Benedictines were being taken well in hand. Father Adrian Schmitt, in fact, went directly to the source by sending soil samples to foresters in Germany (his father and brothers) for analysis and advice on evergreen planting, an important step in an era when the United States had no foresters of its own.

This replanting stands in sharp contrast to common practice in the rest of Minnesota at the time, when the great pine forests were being decimated by industrial logging practices that demonstrated no concern for future growth. In the worst cases this cut-and-run logging left behind denuded landscapes strewn with waste and sparked such conflagrations as the infamous Hinckley fire, which burned over 400 square miles of forest and killed 418 people in 1894. By limiting harvests and actively replanting for long-term growth, Saint John's was at the cutting edge (pun intended) of the emerging field of "scientific forestry" in the 1890s, though it is uncertain whether anyone in the monastery was directly influenced by the pioneers of silviculture, or tree farming.

While some were managing timber as a crop to be harvested and planted again for the future, other community members experimented with orchards. In 1915 Father John Katzner recalled his years as a student at Saint John's forty

In the summer of 1892, notes Alexius Hoffmann, "the road around the 'beat' was extended . . . to the chapel island. Two rustic bridges . . . made the chapel accessible afoot." Here Abbot Bernard inaugurates the bridge across the narrow channel that still makes chapel island an island in years when the lake is high.

years earlier, noting the variety of trees and vines already under cultivation in his youth:

> I remember well the Tetofsky, Duchess, and Transparent apples, and also the Transcendent and Hyslop crabs. One year the Transcendent bore so well that 100 bushels of them were picked. I remember, too, that there were about 50 grapevines in the garden and the trouble the gardener had to get them all. There were also rows of Red Dutch currants bearing lots of fruit and a few plum trees.

Between 1894 and 1930, under Katzner's direction, Saint John's produced large crops of apples (yielding as high as eight hundred bushels in 1913), plums, cherries, grapes, and even winter-hardy pears developed on site. Of his work with the pears, Katzner noted, "Some of my pear trees are quite a combination. The root is German, the stem Chinese and the graft a hybrid of a large standard sort and a Siberian wild pear."

Turning logs into lumber that will furnish the campus with hardwood tables, chairs, bookshelves, and desks from the 1860s to the present. The figures in the picture above are not identified. Brother Julius Terfehr, farm manager and work boss, runs the saw in the 1940s shot below.

The monks' approach to agriculture reflected the fact that few of them had much depth of experience living off the land in Minnesota. But the experimental tradition was also part of their European monastic heritage, and the size and relative prosperity of the monastery made indulgence in the occasional risky endeavor possible. In the early twentieth century those responsible for managing the community's resources would no doubt have also been aware of the growing national emphasis on conservation, a trend spread from Theodore Roosevelt's White House through new federal agencies such as the U.S. Forest Service and popularized by research programs in the land grant universities and through quasi-scientific articles in the popular press. The common emphasis of the conservationists was on the long-term benefits of

scientific management of natural resources, which was said to guarantee "the greatest good, to the greatest number, over the longest period of time," as opposed to the short-sighted and wasteful practices of industry, whereby benefits accrued only to the few. Since roughly the same philosophical orientation had guided the Benedictines for centuries, it should not be surprising that Saint John's tried applying conservation techniques on its land as well.

This interest in conservation was probably most evident in 1901, when the monastery requested exclusive fishing rights to Lake Sagatagan from the state in an attempt to forestall the overfishing plaguing nearby lakes. They hoped to limit public access to the lake and retain the fish as a source of food for the community, but scientific management meant more than simply reducing the harvest. In 1906 construction of a fish hatchery was begun "in order to keep the lake well stocked for the local fishermen," evidence of a desire to maintain congenial relations with their neighbors, but also suggesting their willingness to adopt modern methods to help secure the supply of fish and to introduce more desirable species than those native to the lake.

The fish hatchery on the east shore of the Watab in 1910. In 2004 the grounds crew removed the last traces of the shed once labeled the "Ding an sich" by a philosophically inclined generation of monks; it stands at water's edge behind the skaters in the lower picture.

The hatchery, supplied by springs and an artesian well that provided water at a steady fifty-four degrees throughout the year, produced rainbow trout in large numbers. At its peak output in 1909, some fifty thousand fry were planted in Lake Sagatagan, while the area surrounding the hatchery developed a reputation as "the main beauty spot of campus." Within a few years, however, drought and the recurrent theft of fish from the tanks led to the hatchery's demise and the eventual decay of the site itself. The abandonment of the hatchery underscores the degree to which the whims of the abbot could impact land-use practices at Saint John's, for many of the experiments begun in the early twentieth century were discontinued after the election in 1921 of a new abbot who was less interested in such ventures than his predecessors.

New Land-use Practices

As Saint John's expanded into the 1930s and 1940s, the changing needs of the community prompted the end of some long-held land-use practices and the adoption of a few new ones. Large-scale clear-cutting was employed as a timber harvest technique in these years, as Brother Julius Terfehr recalled in 1977: ". . . that year [1930] we cut one tract of 57 acres, and several other smaller tracts. We cut, that winter, a total of 2,600 cords of wood and 2,200 saw logs. The cordwood was for fuel and the logs were all sawed into lumber. It was for our use here."

The Depression decade saw a dramatic expansion in tree-*planting* activity as well, with more than twenty-five acres planted in pines in 1934 alone. At the same time crews from the federal Works Progress Administration helped with the removal of trees stricken by white pine blister rust, a project that continued with monastic labor for some time thereafter. A series of consultants were also brought in during this period to evaluate the health and management of the forest, the first of these proclaiming that the pine plantations of Saint John's were the "oldest forest tree plantations in the state for which authentic data as to date of planting and spacing are available." He found that the pines planted in 1894 had reached a height of fifty feet or more and an average diameter of fifteen inches by 1931.

A second forester, working for the state Department of Conservation, conducted a more complete inventory in 1937 and described Saint John's' forest practices in some detail. His report shows that replanting favored conifers, while also noting the beginning of the transition from burning wood to coal as an energy source for the campus:

> [The current] . . . method of forest management is clear-cutting of the original stand of hardwoods and planting with coniferous trees—white pine, Scotch, and Norway pine being the favored species. The hardwoods when cut are used largely for fuel; the power plant at the university requiring eight to nine hundred cords of wood per year. In the past a large share of this wood was bought from nearby farmers. Now the wood supply shortage results in the use of a certain amount of coal. Material suitable for lumber is sawed and finished at the University by members of the community.

The maple sap collector is Abbot Jerome Theisen.

A decade later a detailed forest inventory found 1,075 acres of "good hardwoods," 117 acres of coniferous plantations, and 156 acres of scenic forest reserved around the shore of Lake Sagatagan and along the entrance road. Not long after that inventory was completed, clear-cutting was abandoned in favor of selective cutting as the primary harvest method. As coal was increasingly substituted for wood, the timber production became focused on hardwoods to supply the woodworking shop rather than cordwood for fuel.

Tom Kroll followed Father Paul Schwietz as land manager and director of the arboretum. His familiarity with German forestry has been a boon in addressing the long-term sustainability of the Saint John's environment and establishing a cordial relationship with other landholders in the Avon Hills region.

During the early years of World War II, another use for the forest was discovered: maple syrup production. Wartime rationing of sugar increased both the price and demand for syrup, and with a good stock of sugar maples on the property, an attempt at sugar production made perfect sense. In the spring of 1942 a test was made by tapping 150 trees and boiling the sap in the candle shop. The resulting syrup passed muster, so a dedicated evaporation house was constructed that fall to support a sap collection effort that eventually peaked at 3,700 taps. This "sugar shack" served the roughly biennial syrup production project until it burned down in 1970; its replacement has seen even heavier use since the late 1990s as the Saint John's Arboretum has turned syruping into an annual community event. In recent years hundreds of people from the surrounding area, including many families, have learned about the syrup-making process and about Saint John's

135

Shortly before his death in 2000, Father Paul Schwietz surveyed the oak savanna that he had cleared of other growth on the south side of the entrance wetlands.

Paul Schwietz, O.S.B. (1947–2000)

Father Paul Schwietz earned his master's degree in silviculture from the University of Minnesota in 1985 and that year was named land manager of Saint John's 2,400 acres. His tenure was marked by his philosophy that "spiritual and aesthetic concerns are the primary values of the land."

Although he was dubbed "Padre of the Pines" after his death, those non-indigenous pines were not Father Paul's first love. Instead, during the last fifteen years of his abbreviated life, he partnered with nature and encouraged native vegetation and wildlife to flourish. Wetlands drained in the cause of the abbey's dairy herd were dammed and became wet once again, and a variety of wildlife, including forty-five species of waterfowl, songbirds, and fur-bearing animals, took up residence in the restored habitat.

Beginning in 1991, Father Paul helped to reintroduce native grasses to the surrounding acres. All in all, he directed the restoration of a 150-acre wildlife habitat, with 60 acres of wetland, 40 acres of prairie, and 40 acres of oak savanna.

Father Paul's vision and dedication attracted funding from a variety of sources for the Saint John's Arboretum and resulted in the Minnesota Horticultural Society awarding him its bronze medal in 1996. His work is being continued by Saint John's to assure that Father Paul's dream will be realized. The Arboretum will continue to provide splendid accommodations for a growing variety of wildlife; a beautiful ecological welcome for campus visitors; an exceptional outdoor classroom/laboratory for research and learning; and it probably continues to put a smile on Mother Nature's face!

Lee A. Hanley '58

tradition of self-sufficiency through these events. In 2002 Brother Walter Kieffer, who has led the syrup-making for decades, summed up his reasons for continuing the tradition quite simply: "It is done for the love and exercise, not to mention the good eating of pure syrup which was made here, by us, for us."

Despite continued efforts at self-sufficiency, the monks of Saint John's eventually found themselves unable to continue meeting all their needs from the land. Rising labor costs (outside labor, rather than monastic, was widely used by the 1940s) made it hard to compete with larger, more efficient commercial producers, and by the mid-1950s most farming activity was discontinued in the wake of a critical examination of the abbey's agricultural and industrial enterprises.

The hog operation was among the first to go, because the cost of feed exceeded revenues from the sale of surplus pork; in the words of the report, "We are buying in a rigged market and selling in a free market." Not long after that, new federal regulations made the continued production of milk unprofitable, putting an end to the dairy herd; the beef herd was sold off as well when maintaining slaughtering and butchering operations no longer made financial sense. Without the cattle, sheep, hogs, and chickens, the need to produce feed was gone, and with it went the harvest of grains, alfalfa, and hay. Even the sawmill was closed when it became cheaper to send raw logs off-site for milling.

By mid-century expansion of the order's pastoral and mission work, as well as the growth of the college, had corresponded with a decline in the number of monks interested in forestry or tending herds, gardens, orchards, and the other agricultural enterprises of the abbey. When economic factors suggested it was time to shut these operations down, the decisions were not terribly controversial. In less than a century the Benedictine tradition of self-sufficiency at Saint John's had been outstripped by a changing world, but the land itself remained largely intact, thanks to decades of careful management, long-term planning, and a values system that could recognize something more than dollar signs in a stand of timber or an open field.

The Environmental Era

In the 1960s, popular books like Rachel Carson's *Silent Spring* and high-profile events like the Santa Barbara oil spill drove public concern over pollution and other quality-of-life issues to a frenzy. Culminating with the first Earth Day celebration in 1970, the resulting environmental movement popularized once-esoteric pursuits like backpacking and organic farming on its way to becoming an important political force. For the Benedictines of Saint John's, this growing secular interest in the environment offered an opportunity to celebrate their relative success in preserving the character of their original estate, especially when compared with other landowners around the region. Students and visitors were attracted to the campus by pictures of the lakes and woods, and new ideas began to creep into land management discussions, including the possibility of establishing a "biological reserve" on the property and encouraging recreational use of the land now that farming operations had ceased.

By the 1980s such ideas began to steer Saint John's' land-management policy, leading to ambitious ecological projects, including the restoration of a sixty-acre wetland, the planting of fifty acres of native prairie grasses and wild flowers, and the gradual development of a forty-acre parcel of oak savanna, one of the rarest habitats in Minnesota due to past agricultural practices. The culmination of this process came in 1997, when the entire 2,400-acre land base beyond the developed inner campus was officially designated the Saint John's Arboretum. Of these changing priorities, Father John Kulas, who was raised in the area and educated at Saint John's from prep school through seminary, explained that

> [o]ur land-management policy of recent years reflects a keen sense of stewardship and a concern for the preservation of resources that can rightly be considered a local patrimony. It represents the preservation of place, not only for Saint John's but for the locality as well.

As the land itself became an element of the sense of place surrounding Saint John's, people spoke more directly of its spiritual value as well. For example, one monk of recent profession found the physical setting of the monastery central to his religious life:

> Saint John's, the Indianbush, has a spiritual power in its setting and purpose. The northern forest meets the prairie at Lake Sagatagan, which has no creeks feeding or exiting the lake. This meeting of natural forces provides a spiritual place from which the monastic community can carry on its original purpose of serving . . . the church.

Thus, for many people the identity of Saint John's is deeply linked to the land and the idea of nature as a place for retreat, a physical setting for solitude and reflection, and a source of spiritual inspiration. So as American tastes turned from a nineteenth-century pastoral aesthetic to a more wilderness-oriented one in the second half of the twentieth century, the monks of Saint John's came to understand that their remaining natural landscapes evoked a deep appreciation from even casual visitors, leading them to favor a preservation program over developing resources which were in truth no longer needed to sustain the monastery and which could instead be dedicated to higher purposes.

Today the lands of Saint John's are more than just a home to the monastic community. Thousands of alumni carry with

From Thomas Merton's journals at Saint John's

August 2, 1956

The loons on the lake. To begin with they are two. They allow no others. They need plenty of room for themselves. They are seldom together. Once I saw them fly. They seemed to be chasing other loons away from the lake. They were filling the grey windy sky with their weird call.

The other day I tried to sneak up on one in a rowboat. He dived and stayed down I do not know [how] long because I did not see him when he came up in a totally different part of the lake. There he sat calmly while I rowed away. Yesterday afternoon, walking under the pines of the point, I would see his white breast as he sat on the waters of the wave and sometimes laughed.

The loon, I think, is a very serious bird and I take him very seriously. To me it is not crazy but even, in a way, beautiful. It means distances, wind, water, forests, the loneliness of the North.

Thomas Merton, *A Search for Solitude,* ed. Lawrence S. Cunningham (HarperSanFrancisco, 1996) 61.
Used by permission.

them memories of afternoons spent by the lakes, quiet walks in the forest, or early morning hours enjoying the transient beauty of migrating cranes. Current students and faculty conduct a wide range of ecological research projects in the arboretum, which serves as a living laboratory few colleges can equal. Ever-growing numbers of school children find themselves enchanted by tadpoles, spitbugs, and gall wasps as their environmental education field trips visit the campus each fall. Retreatants find peace in the sound of crickets on summer nights, and local fishermen still huddle over the winter ice as their great-great-grandfathers did. Perhaps most important, the land provides temporary shelter or permanent homes for innumerable species of plants, mammals, birds, and insects that need a refuge from the crush of development that is fragmenting their habitats throughout the region.

A thoughtful, evolving relationship with the land has become a vital element of the Saint John's identity. Most people who have spent even an afternoon on campus leave with a sense that the natural setting is as important as the buildings in how the place works. In recent years a core set of ideas, often labeled "Benedictine stewardship," has come to explain not only the basis of the land-management philosophy but increasingly to underscore the values behind the day-to-day operation of the entire enterprise. In the twenty-first century the concept that everyone needs beauty as well as bread is mainstream enough to print on a T-shirt, even as opportunities to fulfill that need become more scarce. While John Muir may have been most inspired by the grandeur of Yosemite, he was raised on a Wisconsin dirt farm, and I have no doubt that he would take great pleasure in walking the trails of Saint John's and finding out how quickly the pressures of modern life dissolve just a few steps down the path.

The natural setting is as important as the buildings in how the place works.

The Saint John's Arboretum

Interview with Sarah Gainey,
Arboretum Education Coordinator, October 2005

Your field is environmental education. How did you get into it?
I always have been interested in working with kids and loved being outdoors but wasn't always sure how to combine the two. At the University of Minnesota I majored in biology and then had job opportunities at various environmental centers that made it possible for me to pursue my interest in the environment and working with young people.

How long have you been at the Saint John's Arboretum?
I started here in August 2004.

What's the advantage of having an arboretum? Isn't it enough just to welcome people to experience the woods the way they always have?
I see two big advantages to having an arboretum; the first is being able to be thoughtful about land conservation and sustainability and the second is being able to educate people about the land. I'm involved in helping people as early as pre-kindergarten discover what there is to experience in the woods, and to appreciate the land and the outdoors. Educating people early in life helps them to make good decisions about the environment later in life— although it is never too late to start!

Do a lot of people come?
We currently have over 4,000 school children a year from pre-kindergarten to twelfth grade involved in our education program. For some of them it's the first time they have been in a natural setting like this and they're excited about everything they see.

How about your relationship to the colleges?
Lots of students, faculty, and staff take advantage of the arboretum. It's a good place to connect what is being studied in class with what happens in the environment. Oftentimes I take classes on a tour of part of the arboretum or I am a guest lecturer in their classroom.

Do you see any exciting developments in the future—a monorail to the chapel, for example, or a petting zoo for toddlers?
It's hard for me to imagine a monorail traveling to the chapel! But that is our heaviest-used trail and we are planning some work on the trail and the chapel. Most of our future plans center around broadening the reach of our education programs. We want to ensure that this place is around for the next 150 years.

What's the risk that it won't be preserved?
There will always be pressure for development—we just want to make sure it is done in a thoughtful way. The Avon Hills Initiative is one group of many we work with to help maintain the rural landscape of this area. There's bound to be development, but it can be thought out and planned so the natural and rural setting isn't sacrificed in the process.

What's the most fun in this job for you?
Seeing the connections kids draw between nature and their own lives and helping them understand they are a part of the environment. It's also great when they discover something for the first time, like a new insect they've never seen. Their enthusiasm is contagious!

Where can I learn more about the arboretum?
Visit our website at www.csbsju.edu/arboretum, read our quarterly newsletter, *Sagatagan Seasons*, attend an event, become a member, or stop by our offices in the new science building. We would love to have you!

John Elton, master gardener   School children on a field day at the arboretum

Afterword

Dietrich Reinhart, O.S.B.

WHEN I CAME TO SAINT JOHN'S as a freshman in 1967, the campus was filled with brand new buildings by Marcel Breuer, the Ecumenical Institute and Minnesota Public Radio were in their first year, the Hill Museum & Manuscript Library in its second, and alumnus Eugene McCarthy was running for president. Saint John's was the most exciting place I had ever been. It opened up to a large world and invited a deep reckoning with human needs. I discovered a group of monks who read books and listened to classical music, who loved conversation, and who befriended me. I got to know Prof Heininger, who straight off drafted me into the Mike Shop; Father Tom Thole (then Titus), whose room was the heart of Ground Benet; my boss, Father Vincent Tegeder, who drew me into all manner of projects to support the teaching of history; Bill and Pat VanCleve, who opened their house to a small group of students for a Lenten series of discussions; and Brother Willie, who wandered the buildings at night making sure all was in order. (None of us were sure what he could see, but he came to know us inside out!)

In 1971, when I joined the monastery, the last novice received by Abbot Baldwin, I came to know the heart of Saint John's, monks of great individuality, each with a different take on the Saint John's story; lay colleagues, each with a passion for a particular part of Saint John's; alumni from all generations making journeys, often solitary, back to campus as part of life stories I could only imagine; and friends from all parts of the compass coming to experience the life we can so easily take for granted.

I never dreamt I would one day serve as president. I simply showed up. I wanted to help consolidate what had gone before, to be part of Saint John's stretching to meet the needs of a new age. I focused on whatever task was at hand, discovering generous collaboration at every turn. To the extent I have led, it has been within community, not above it. This is the story of lots of people touched by Saint John's. We don't think the world owes us anything. We are in awe of what has been given to us. We just show up. We pull together. And we make a difference.

Saint John's has always been a "work in progress" created by people who show up. The signature characteristics of Saint John's—monastic life in a new culture, college preparatory, residential liberal arts and graduate theological education, liturgical renewal, ecumenism, an unabashed reckoning with gender, collaborative ministry, cultural preservation, art and architecture, the Bible as inclusive tool for renewal and common purpose—were not present, full-blown, at the start of things. They were created because courageous people saw new needs in the broader world, most often anticipated them, endured opposition, and pulled together to make new things happen. It is this tradition of transformation to meet the deepest needs of others that drives the story of Saint John's. And that story is not over.

Roster of Abbots and Academic Officers

Saint John's was chartered as Saint John's Seminary in 1857 but was called Saint John's College until the name was changed to Saint John's University in 1883. Before 1866 the priors of the community served as ex-officio presidents of the school without the title. Rupert Seidenbusch, the first abbot, appointed Wolfgang Northman president of Saint John's College in 1867. In 1872 Alexius Edelbrock was appointed president, and he kept the title for himself and his successors when he was elected abbot three years later. Abbot Baldwin Dworschak separated the offices of abbot and president in 1958, taking the title of chancellor of the university.

Between 1870 and 1922 an academic administrator called the vice president, sometimes with the additional title of director of the college or rector, was responsible for operation of the school at all levels, elementary through seminary, although the seminary gained its own rector or prefect beginning in 1898. In 1922 the university was restructured as the college preparatory school, the college of arts and sciences, and the seminary, each with its own dean, and the office of vice president was phased out.

Confusing nomenclature has sometimes led to the impression that the prep school had its own director or headmaster before 1922. This is not the case. Beginning with the first cata-

logue in 1870, the first three years of the classical course—an Americanized version of the German *gymnasium*—were designated as the "academic" or junior course. This was followed by three more years designated as the "collegiate" or senior course, expanded to four years in 1891. The vice president was responsible for all six years plus the ecclesiastical course (the seminary), the commercial course, and the elementary course. The last was renamed the preparatory department in 1884 with no change in the catalogue description. It was a flexible program offering religion, penmanship, spelling, arithmetic, rudiments of grammar, geography, and history for farm boys and others whose schooling had been irregular but who wanted to qualify for enrollment in the classical course or the commercial course. In 1909 the "academic or high school" course was expanded to four years. In 1916 the preparatory department, described by then as serving "young men who are behind in their studies," was listed in the catalogue for the last time.

All the men listed in this roster were or are monks of Saint John's Abbey except William Renner, Harold Dimmerling, and Mark Willenbring, priests of the Diocese of Saint Cloud. Deans of the college from 1922 to 1958 are listed because many of the functions of the presidency fell to them until the appointment of a full-time president.

Abbots

Rupert Seidenbusch
    December 12, 1866–February 12, 1875
Alexius Edelbrock
        June 2, 1875–November 27, 1889
Bernard Locnikar
        May 7, 1890–November 7, 1894
Peter Engel
    November 28, 1894–November 27, 1921
Alcuin Deutsch
    December 29, 1921–October 19, 1950
Baldwin Dworschak
        December 28, 1950–July 23, 1971
John Eidenschink
        August 24, 1971–August 20, 1979
Jerome Theisen
        August 22, 1979–September 19, 1992
Timothy Kelly
    November 27, 1992–November 23, 2000
John Klassen   November 24, 2000–

Presidents

Cornelius Wittmann	1857–1858
Benedict Haindl	1858–1862
Othmar Wirtz	1862–1865
Benedict Haindl	1865–1867
Wolfgang Northman	1867–1872
Alexius Edelbrock	1872–1889
Bernard Locnikar	1890–1894
Peter Engel	1894–1921
Alcuin Deutsch	1921–1950
Baldwin Dworschak	1951–1958
Arno Gustin	1958–1964
Colman Barry	1964–1971
Michael Blecker	1971–1982
Alberic Culhane	
	1980–1981 (Acting President)

Gunther Rolfson	
	1981 (Summer, Acting President)
Hilary Thimmesh	1982–1991
Dietrich Reinhart	1991–

Vice Presidents of Saint John's College, after 1883 Saint John's University

Alexius Edelbrock	1870–1872
Bernard Locnikar	1872–1873
Ulric Northman	1873–1884
Chrysostom Schreiner	1884–1890
Alexius Hoffmann	1890–1899
Bruno Doerfler	1899–1902
Leonard Kapsner	1902–1905
Albert Erkens	1905–1909
Alcuin Deutsch	1909–1913
Kilian Heid	1913–1920
Charles Cannon	1920–1921
Alphonse Sausen	1921–1924

Rectors of Saint John's Seminary

Athanasius Meyer	1898–1899
Bernard Kevenhoerster	1899–1907
Alcuin Deutsch	1907–1909
Severin Gertken	1909–1922
Odilo Kohler	1922–1928
Basil Stegmann	1928–1929
Ulric Beste	1929–1939
Gregory Roettger	1939–1950
Msgr. William A. Renner	1950–1963
Fr. Harold Dimmerling	1963–1969
John Eidenschink	1969–1971
Alfred Deutsch	1971–1977
Kieran Nolan	1977–1978
William Skudlarek	1980–1984
Fr. Mark Willenbring	1984–1988
Kevin Seasoltz	1988–1992

Timothy Kelly	
	July 1992–November 1992
Dale Launderville	1992–1997
Robert Pierson	1997–1999
Luke Steiner	1999–2001
Abbot John Klassen	2002–

Heads of the Preparatory School

Virgil Michel	1922–1923
Lambert Weckwerth	1923–1924
Walter Reger	1924–1927
Mark Braun	1927–1928
Theodore Krebsbach	1928–1936
Arno Gustin	1936–1940
Vincent Tegeder	1940–1942
Philibert Harrer	1942–1946
Alfred Deutsch	1946–1952
Stanley Roche	1952–1958
Gregory Soukup	1958–1972
James Tingerthal	1972–1974
Alan Steichen	1974–1979
Linus Ascheman	1980–1988
Thomas Andert	1988–1994
Mark Thamert	1994–1998
Gordon Tavis	1998–

Deans of the College to 1958

Severin Gertken	1922–1923
Virgil Michel	1923 (Fall)
Gilbert Winkelman	1924 (Spring)
Mark Braun	1924–1933
Virgil Michel	1933–1938
Walter Reger	
	1938–1939 (Acting Dean)
Ernest Kilzer	1939–1943
Martin Schirber	1943–1952
Arno Gustin	1952–1958

Acknowledgments

Hilary Thimmesh, O.S.B.

This book is the work of many hands. Besides the contributors noted separately, I particularly want to thank our archivists, David Klingeman, O.S.B., and Brennan Maiers, O.S.B., who were patient, professional, and upbeat with dozens of research items; photo consultants, Greg Becker and Placid Stuckenschneider, O.S.B.; Elizabeth Doyle and Arleen Hynes, O.S.B., for family photos; Allen Tarlton, O.S.B., for background on the Oblates of Saint Benedict; Tom Andert, O.S.B., Mike Mullin, and Mark Thamert, O.S.B., for the recent history of the prep school; Dale Launderville, O.S.B., for the recent history of the School of Theology; Sisters Angelo Haspert, O.S.B., and Emmanuel Renner, O.S.B., for details of the history of the Benedictine Institute of Sacred Theology (BIST); Dave Bennetts, Aubrey Immelman, and Michael Livingston for their memorials of three faculty colleagues; Ted Shide for his help with a 1914 Buick; Jean Stottlemyer for weighing "The Athlete"; Patrick Henry, Sister Katherine Howard, O.S.B., Abbot Timothy Kelly, O.S.B., and Vincent Tegeder, O.S.B., for reading and commenting on drafts of the text. Not least I want to thank the members of the "non-committee" that metamorphosed into the editorial board as we went from thinking what this book could be to making it what it is: Annette Atkins, Peter Dwyer, Lee Hanley, David Klingeman, O.S.B., and William Skudlarek, O.S.B.

Contributors

Annette Atkins teaches history and makes history exciting to read in two books and numerous articles for the Minnesota Historical Society. She has a history of Minnesota in progress. She and her husband, Tom Joyce, also a contributor to this book, have an 1890s stone house on the back road to Saint John's. Annette was on the editorial board for this book.

Brenda Child is an associate professor of american studies at the University of Minnesota and the author of a highly praised book entitled *Boarding Schools and American Indian Families*. She is a member of the Red Lake band of the Ojibwe.

Senator David Durenberger '55, served in the U. S. Senate from 1978 to 1994. He is an expert on health care policies and chairs the National Institute of Health Policy at a Catholic university in Saint Paul with which Saint John's has an athletic rivalry that was already historic when Dave grew up in Flynntown a couple of blocks from the football field.

Bernard Evans works in the areas of Catholic social teaching, environmental theology, and rural ministry. He teaches courses at Saint John's and works with other schools and churches to engage people of faith in the effort to build a more just society.

Joseph Farry is professor emeritus in political science. He was dean of the college from 1991 to 1996. He and his wife Jill live on the Old Collegeville Road in the section the pioneers called Indianbush.

R. William Franklin is a distinguished voice in the Anglican communion who went from lay to clerical with his ordination in 2005. He was on the history faculty at Saint John's from 1974 to 1992 and directed the Christian humanism program. He co-authored *Virgil Michel: American Catholic* with Robert Spaeth '59, then dean of the college, in 1988.

Larry Haeg is an alumnus of the prep school, '63, and the college, '67. A former editor of *The Record,* he is now vice president for corporate communications with Wells Fargo & Company, San Francisco, and a trustee of the College of Saint Benedict. His first book, *In the Shadow of Gatsby,* a life of Charles Flandrau, was published in 2004.

Colleen Haggerty, O.S.B., made her monastic profession at Saint Benedict's Monastery in 1953 and was coordinator of the renovation of Sacred Heart Chapel, 1981–1983. She served as president of the Federation of Saint Benedict from 1991 to 2003.

Lee Hanley '58, founding editor of the *Saint John's* magazine, retired in 1997 after more than thirty years in institutional advancement at Saint John's. After five years of retirement he returned to Saint John's as the abbey's director of communications. He was on the editorial board for this book. His photographic contributions to this book span a period of 50 years.

Jon Hassler '55, perhaps Minnesota's most beloved contemporary author, taught high school and college English for many years be-fore coming to Saint John's as writer-in-residence in 1980. He is noted for his watercolors as well as his dozen novels, books of short stories, journals, and plays. He has retired from teaching but not from writing. He and his wife Gretchen live in Minneapolis.

Patrick Henry was executive director of the Collegeville Institute for Ecumenical and Cultural Research from 1984 until his retirement in 2004 and previously professor of religion at Swarthmore College. His recent books are *Benedict's Dharma: Buddhists Reflect on the Rule of Saint Benedict* (editor) and *The Ironic Christian's Companion: Finding the Marks of God's Grace in the World*.

Eva Hooker, C.S.C., regents professor of poetry, is a Sister of the Holy Cross whose poetry appears in the *Harvard Review* and other literary journals. Her chapbook *The Winter Keeper* was a finalist for the 2001 Minnesota Book Award in poetry. She served as academic vice president from 1983 to 1992 and continued on the faculty in English through the 2005–2006 school year.

Arleen Hynes, O.S.B., was Emerson's wife for thirty years. Later, in 1981, as biblio/poetry therapist and writer, she became a member of Saint Benedict's Monastery, Saint Joseph.

Thomas Joyce '61, possibly the most-traveled Saint John's graduate thanks to his international career in securities and corporate finance with Wall Street and London firms, remarked after a vacation in Antarctica that penguins are less interesting after a week. He was the perfect conversational partner for Father Godfrey, who had been everywhere else. Tom chaired the board of regents from 1982 to 1985.

John Klassen, O.S.B., '71, a native of Elrosa in western Stearns County, made his monastic profession in 1972 and was ordained in 1977. He was a member of the faculty in chemistry when elected tenth abbot of Saint John's on November 24, 2000. He had previously served as formation director for novices and junior monks and was active in the American Benedictine Academy.

In college **William Kling** '64, demonstrated his technological bent by running an unobtrusive wire from a fuse box in the corridor to power his Benet Hall room after lights out at 11 p.m. From there to KSJR to MPR to national leadership in public radio was only a matter of time and entrepreneurial genius.

Norma Loso Koetter comes from one of the founding families of Saint Joseph. She is office assistant for the history department and the chair in critical thinking and works for the directors of Asian, environmental, and Latin American studies programs. She has co-chaired the Support Staff Guild Association. She won the extraordinary performance award in 2001.

Derek Larson is an environmental historian and assistant professor of history. He directs the environmental studies program. A native of Oregon, his research interests center on the Pacific Northwest and the role of environment in American culture and politics.

Zach Lewis '05, grew up on a farm just outside Jackson, Minnesota. While an undergraduate he worked in the history department and conducted many of the interviews with the lay and monastic workers. He majored in biology and is now attending medical school.

Senator Eugene McCarthy '35, philosopher, author, poet, sardonic pundit, lived in retirement in Georgetown. Al Eisele '58, Vice President Mondale's press secretary and founding editor of *The Hill*, transcribed Gene's recollections of Father Hildebrand Eickhoff '07, pastor of Saint Joseph's in Mandan. Senator McCarthy died on December 10, 2005.

Kilian McDonnell, O.S.B., '49, entered the novitiate in 1945, became a priest in 1951, and only began to enjoy robust health when sent abroad to study Protestant theology. Professor of theology, author of major works in theology and spirituality, member of ecumenical commissions on Catholic relations with Lutherans, Presbyterians, Disciples of Christ, Pentecostals—his achievements beggar description. When he reached seventy-five, he turned his mind to higher things and started writing poetry—good poetry like all his other works.

Larry Millett '69, became an authority on the historic buildings of Minneapolis and Saint Paul as architecture critic for the *Saint Paul Pioneer Press* and editor of two definitive and prize-winning books on the subject for the Minnesota Historical Society. Then he branched out into detective fiction with five annotated volumes on Sherlock Holmes in Minnesota. Lately he has come back to news writing with *Strange Days, Dangerous Nights: Photos from the Speed Graphic Era,* a collection of photos, some staid, some grisly, presented with characteristically informed and wry commentary.

Carl Phillips is associate professor of English and afro-american studies at Washington University in Saint Louis. He has published several books of poetry to wide critical acclaim. He visited Saint John's and the College of Saint Benedict during the fall term in 2000 and offered to let us use his poem about the crew whenever we wished. This seemed the right time.

Robin Pierzina, O.S.B., '75, professed vows as a Benedictine monk in 1977. He edited *The Bible Today* for twenty-six years and has chaired the design committee since 1984, consistently writing minutes that are worth reading. He was appointed secretary of the corporation, one of the three corporate officers according to the 1857 charter, by Abbot John Klassen in 2001.

Julian Plante '61, established high scholarly standards during his twenty-seven years as founding director of the Hill Museum & Manuscript Library. He also exercised consummate diplomacy in dealing with cautious monastic librarians, dignitaries like Abuna Theophilus, patriarch of the Ethiopian Orthodox Church, and the National Endowment for the Humanities, from which HMML got thirteen grants during his tenure.

Katherine A. Powers is the eldest of J. F. and Betty Wahl Powers' five children. She writes about books and lives in Massachusetts.

Jana and Charles Preble are Benedictine Oblates who live near Saint John's Abbey and Saint Benedict's Monastery. They enjoy friendships with Benedictines in both communities and have each served as spiritual directors and retreat guides for monastic men and women for over forty years.

Dietrich Reinhart, O.S.B., '71, made his monastic profession in 1972. He taught history and served as dean of the college before being appointed president of Saint John's University in 1991.

Hamilton Smith became an associate of Marcel Breuer shortly before the Saint John's project commenced. He accompanied Breuer on virtually all the architect's visits to Saint John's and sometimes came in his place. He excelled in quiet mastery of every detail and became a familiar and welcome presence on campus in his own right.

Columba Stewart, O.S.B., was professed a monk of Saint John's Abbey in 1982 and ordained a priest in 1990. He teaches monastic history and spirituality and currently serves as the executive director of the Hill Museum & Manuscript Library. Formerly formation director at the abbey, he is author of *Prayer and Community* and *Cassian the Monk.*

Vincent Tegeder, O.S.B., '33, professor emeritus, is a walking database of Saint John's history and a standing-room-only speaker on the subject. He made vows in 1931, was ordained in 1937, taught history for a long career in the college classroom, and then served as abbey and university archivist.

Hilary Thimmesh, O.S.B., '50, professed in 1948 and ordained in 1954, subsequently divided his time between teaching English and holding various administrative positions at Saint John's and at Saint Martin's Abbey in Lacey, Washington. He was president of Saint John's University from 1982 to 1991.

Mark Twomey '59, retired as editorial director of the Liturgical Press in 2005 while this book was in progress. For thirty-five years his wife Judy and he were able to keep an eye on his workplace from their hilltop home on Fruit Farm Road due west of the campus, where they moved in 1970.

Victoria Young is assistant professor of modern architectural history at the University of Saint Thomas, Saint Paul. Marcel Breuer's design and his response to liturgical reforms were the subject of her dissertation at the University of Virginia. A member of the Minnesota chapter of the Society of Architectural Historians and vice president of the Recent Past Preservation Network, she is currently at work on a book to document all Breuer's buildings at Saint John's.

Index

Aarriola, Ned, 27
Abadia de San Antonio Abad, 67
Abbey church, comprehensive plan and design, 120–23; consecration of, 126
Abbey Guest House, 16
Abbots of Saint John's, 142
Academic merger of Saint John's University and College of Saint Benedict, 39–40
Academic officers of Saint John's, 142
Administrative Assembly, 107
Albers, Josef, 126
Anderl, John, O.S.B., 15, 103
Anderson, Robert, 79
Arboretum, Saint John's, 138
Arca Artium, 98
Architect, selection of for new abbey church, 117–120
Architecture at Saint John's, 93–94
Arnott, David, 90
Ascheman, Linus, O.S.B., 104
Assumption Abbey, Richardton, North Dakota, 66
Assumption Catholic Church, Saint Paul, 61
Atkins, Annette, 107, 108
Axtman, Boniface, O.S.B., 66

Backes, Bryan, 18
Bahamas mission, history of, commitment to, 65
Bak, Bronislaw, 126
Baldachin in abbey church, 123
Baran, Oswald, O.S.B., 66
Barry, Colman, O.S.B., 12, 13, 17, 36, 38, 43, 50, 64, 81
Bartemeier, Leo, 24
Bartholome, Peter, 35, 81, 126
Bavarian immigrants, early, 2
Becker, Johanna, O.S.B., 105, 115
Benda, Joe, 8
Benedicta Art Center, College of Saint Benedict, 94
Benedictine foundations closed, 68
Benedictine Institute of Sacred Theology, 36
Benedictine outreach, 61–68
Benedictine parish communities, 112–13
Benedictine stewardship of the earth, 137–38
Benedictine Volunteer Program, 15
Bennetts, Dave, 39
Berger, Mary Jane, O.S.B., 115
Bertocchi, Luigi, O.S.B., 27
Beste, Ulric, O.S.B., 114
Bilheimer, Robert, 81
Blake, Eugene Carson, 81
Blecker, Michael, O.S.B., 38, 81, 98, 105
Blekum, Joel, O.S.B., 67
Blenkner, Louis, O.S.B., 103
Bohan, Jay, 15
Bonnette, Gerald, 93
Borgerding, Christopher, 31
Borgerding, Henry, O.S.B., 114
Borgerding, Thomas, O.S.B., 63, 113
Borgerding, William, O.S.B., 102, 141
Botz, Julian, 106
Botz, Paschal, O.S.B., 113
Botz, Roger, O.S.B., 68

Bouley, Allan, O.S.B., 23
Braceland, Francis, 24
Braun, Lioba, O.S.B., 112
Braun, Mark, O.S.B., 66
Bresnahan, Richard, 91, 96, 97
Breuer, Marcel, 35, 38, 77, 81, 92, 94, 97, 117, 118, 119, 123, 126, 141
Broker, Henry, 10
Bromenshenkel, Fintan, O.S.B., 17, 65
Bronx, New York, Benedictine parishes in, 65
Bucher, Vitus, O.S.B., 23
Buildings, early Saint John's, 11
Buildings, history of, 94–98
Bularzik, Rembert, O.S.B., 74
Burke, Herbert, 52
Butler, Aimee Mott, 81
Butler Charitable Trust, 83
Butler Foundation in Saint Paul, 81
Butler, Patrick, 81
Butler, Peter, 81
Byrne, Barry, 119–20

Cadena, Aldo, O.S.B., 66
Campos, Manuel, 30
Carroll, Terence, O.S.B., 59, 67
Child, Brenda, 42
China, Benedictines in, 67
Chittister, Joan, O.S.B., 49
Choir monks, 20–21
Chonzin, Ngawang, 115
Chu, Philip, 30
Cichy, Elmer, O.S.B., 59
Cicognani, Amleto, 13
Clemens, Bill, 53
Cody, Nick, 55
Coen, Rena, 101
Cofell, Bill, 52
Colegio del Tepeyac, 66, 67
Collaboration of Saint John's and Saint Benedict's Monastic Communities, 112–15
College of Saint Benedict, cooperation with, 34, 36, 38, 39–40
Collegeville Institute for Ecumenical and Cultural Research, 14, 36, 79, 141
Coller, Jerome, O.S.B., 91
Collins, Corwin, O.S.B., 50
Comeau, Harry, 48
Connors, Cletus, O.S.B., 69
Corrigan, Michael, 64
Cotter, Joseph, 31
Coval, Andrew, O.S.B., 37
Cozzens, Donald, 74
Creed, Tom, 39
Cretin, Joseph, 61
Culhane, Alberic, O.S.B., 50, 77, 111
Curriculum expansion in 1950s, 35

Damertz, Victor, O.S.B., 14
Day, Dorothy, 84, 87
de Hamel, Christopher, 99
de Marogna, Demetrius, O.S.B., 61
Design Committee, Saint John's, 96
Deutsch, Alcuin, O.S.B., 7, 8, 9, 12, 27, 49, 51–52, 65, 67, 73, 85, 87, 94, 95, 114, 132
Deutsch, Alfred, O.S.B., 23, 33, 50, 51, 54

Diamond jubilee, 1931, schedules, tuition, demographics, 9
Diederichs, Sabina, 8, 9
Diekmann, Conrad, O.S.B., 50, 54
Diekmann, Godfrey, O.S.B., 12, 13, 23, 50, 76, 77, 78, 81, 105, 111
Dillenburg, Theodore, 92
Dimmick, William, 79
Dirkes, Cindy, 106
Diversity of Saint John's workforce, 106
Dockendorf, John, 14
Douvier, Joe, 107
Douvier, Marilyn, 109
Doyle, Betty and Leonard, 84, 86
Doyle, Leonard, 83
Drexel, Katherine, 112
Drought and pestilence in 1930s, 4
Duerr, Joseph, 45
Duluth, Benedictine parishes in, 62
Durenberger, David, 49
Durenberger, George, 8, 49, 51, 105
Durenberger, Isabelle, 49
Durken, Daniel, O.S.B., 50, 53, 74
Dworschak, Baldwin, O.S.B., 12, 13, 17, 34, 35, 43, 50, 66, 68, 76, 93, 94, 117, 124, 141
Dworschak, Leo, 76
Dwyer, John, 74
Dwyer, Peter, 74

Edelbrock, Alexius, O.S.B., 4, 7, 11, 13, 42, 45, 60, 61, 62, 63, 64, 95, 104, 114, 130
Edin, Colt, 56
Eibensteiner, Gregory, O.S.B., 59, 92, 112
Eibensteiner, Lavonne, O.S.B., 112
Eich, Amalia, O.S.B., 113
Eich, Marlin, 101
Eich, Peter, 92, 105
Eich, Peter and family, 101
Eichhorst, Jack, 81
Eickhoff, Hildebrand, O.S.B., 62
Eidenschink, John, O.S.B., 8, 66, 68, 76
Emmanuel Renner, O.S.B., 114
Emmel, Henry, 45
Engel, Peter, O.S.B., 7, 11, 32, 45, 64, 66, 91, 95, 130
Episcopal House of Prayer, 79–80
Escher, Firmin, O.S.B., 90
Evans, Bernard, 76, 83
Eversmann, William, O.S.B., 66
Experimentation, early agricultural, 3

Fair, Christopher, O.S.B., 92
Farming at Saint John's, early, 131–37
Farnsworth, Dana, 24
Farrell, Gerard, O.S.B., 91
Farry, Joseph, 14, 31, 52
Feely, Tom, 53
Fine arts, 89–92
Fish hatchery, 134
Flynn, Edward J., 51, 105
Forbes, Donald, 106
Franklin, R. William, 23, 71
Frischauf, Clement, O.S.B., 72, 92

Froehle, Peter, 37
Fulton, Robert, 68
Furfey, Paul Hanley, 85

Gable, Mariella, O.S.B., 85
Gagliardi, John, 52, 53, 54
Gagliardi, John and Peggy, 105
Gainey, Sarah, 138
Galovich, Jennifer, 40
Gatje, Bob, 119, 120
Germain, Aidan, O.S.B., 67
Gertken, Luke and Margaret family, 112
Gertken, Severin, O.S.B., 66, 132
Goeb, Cuthbert, O.S.B., 66
Goeb, Egbert, O.S.B., 59
Goeteman, Gordon, 91
Graves, Clarus, O.S.B., 62, 67
Gregorian chant, 73
Greil, Patrick, O.S.B., 10
Grimm, Wendelin, 3
Gropius, Walter, 119
Gross, Francis A., 31
Gustin, Arno, O.S.B., 35, 36, 40, 54

Haeg, Larry, 45, 54
Haeg, Sr., Larry, 17
Haggarty, Paul Leonard, O.S.B., 65
Haggerty, Colleen, O.S.B., 94
Hall, Jeremy, O.S.B., 111, 114
Hamm, William, 46
Hanna, Adam, 54
Hansen, Bonaventure, O.S.B., 59
Harrington, John, 54
Haspert, Angelo, O.S.B., 113
Hassler, Jon, 38
Hauser, Nathanael, O.S.B., 55
Hays, Henry Bryan Beaumont, O.S.B., 91
Heckman, A. A., 43
Heidt, William, O.S.B., 74
Heininger, Joe, 51, 52, 54
Hendershot, Jim, 91
Hendley, Clark, 40
Hennen, Betty, 106
Hennepin, Louis, 2
Henry, Ed, 52
Henry, Patrick, 81, 115
Hermanson, Ray, 92, 124
Hermanutz, Aloysius, O.S.B., 63, 112
Hesse, Robert, 56
Hill, Jerome, 43
Hill Monastic Manuscript Library, 13, 36, 43, 99
Hill Museum & Manuscript Library, 98, 141
Himsl, Clarus, O.S.B., 90
Himsl, Louis, 101
Hoermann, Thaddeus, O.S.B., 102
Hoeschen, John, 31
Hoffmann, Alexius, O.S.B., 9, 10, 31, 32, 33, 41, 47, 60, 64, 68, 89, 132, 133
Hoffmeyer, Ted, 124
Hohmann, Othmar, O.S.B., 62
Hooker, Eva, C.S.C., 39, 40
Horning, Ross, 52
Houle, Bill, 8
Howard, Katherine, O.S.B., 115
Hughes, Fred, 8
Human Life Center, 14
Hume, Basil, O.S.B., 14, 15
Humphrey, Don and Mary, 84
Humphrey, Hubert, 69

Humphrey, Stephen B., 38, 41, 53, 55, 107
Hundred-year plan, 35, 38
Huschle, Catherine and Marie, 105
Hyman, Isabelle, 122
Hynes, Arleen, O.S.B., 84
Hynes, Emerson, 52, 83, 84, 85, 86, 106

Ice, Richard, 56
Immelman, Aubrey, 39
Independent status of abbey 1866, 10
International outreach, 113
IOGD, 6, 7, 45
Ireland, John, 2, 11

Jackson, Donald, 16
Jacobsen, Hugh Newell, 91, 97
James, Vincent, 16
Jay Phillips Chair in Jewish Studies, 14
Jean-Noel, Herard, O.S.B., 37
Joint Faculty Assembly, 107
Jonas, Ann, 106
Joyce, Thomas, 77

Kacmarcik, Frank, Obl.S.B., 93, 94, 96, 118, 119, 126
Kapsner, Oliver, O.S.B., 37, 43
Katzner, John, O.S.B., 3, 64, 132, 133
Kaufman, Philip, O.S.B., 81
Kaus, Jon, 54
Keating, Ryan, 53
Keillor, Garrison, 17, 61, 85
Keller, Dominic, O.S.B., 90
Kelly, James, O.S.B., 90
Kelly, Timothy, O.S.B., 16, 25, 68, 114, 115
Keogh, Casper, O.S.B., 17
Kerst, Scholastica, O.S.B., 114
Ketten, Philomena, O.S.B., 112
Kevenhoerster, Bernard, O.S.B., 65
Kiefer, Rupert, O.S.B., 65
Kieffer, Walter, O.S.B., 136
Kiley, Daniel, 97
Kinnick, Bernie, 51
Klassen, John, O.S.B., viii, ix, 16
Klein, George, 104, 105
Kling, William, 17
Klostermann, Henry, 45
Knapp, Raphael, O.S.B., 91, 92, 95, 109
Knuttila, Kari, 23
Koetter, Norma Loso, 107, 108
Koopmann, Robert, O.S.B., 23, 91
Korte, Alexander, O.S.B., 67
Kritzeck, James, 76
Kroll, Tom, 135
Krych, Aaron, 53
KSJR radio station, 17
Kulas, John, O.S.B., 137
Küng, Hans, 77

Lake Sagatagan, 129
Lake Wobegon trail, 11
Lampe, Simon, O.S.B., 63, 113
Land conservation at Saint John's, 134
Lange, Jack, 38, 52
Laux, Michael, O.S.B., 59
Lawrence, Emeric, O.S.B., 53, 84
Lay brothers, 21
Lay faculty, 52
Lectio divina, 25, 27

LeMay, Don, O.S.B., 50, 90
Leuthner, Benedict, O.S.B., 104
Lewis, Sinclair, 61
Lewis, Zach, 107
Licari, Jonathan, O.S.B., 16
Lickteig, Samuel, O.S.B., 103
Lind, John, 3
Lindblad, Owen, O.S.B., 63
Liturgical movement, beginnings of, 71–75; and Benedictine monasticism, 73; centrality of Eucharist, 72; Saint John's Abbey as home of, 73; contributions of Godfrey Diekmann, O.S.B., and Michael Marx, O.S.B., to, 77–79
Liturgical music, 75
Liturgical Press, 74–75, 93
"Livery-horsing," 11–12
Livingston, Michael, 39
Locnikar, Bernard, O.S.B., 11, 65, 73, 78, 133
Locnikar, Claudina, O.S.B., 112
Locnikar, Florian, O.S.B., 112
Luetmer, Wendelin, O.S.B., 23
Luft, Matthew, O.S.B., 19, 69
Luger, Bille, 54
Lust, Jeanne Marie, O.S.B., 30

Mailloux, Noel, O.P., 24
Manahan, David, O.S.B., 93
Manderfeld, Christine, O.S.B., 111
Maple syrup production, 135–36
Marrin, K. C., 92
Martin, Leo, O.S.B., 92
Marty, Martin, O.S.B., 62
Marx, Michael, O.S.B., 78–79, 111
Marx, Paul, O.S.B., 14, 81
Matt, Alphonse Sr., 86
Matt, Joseph, 86
Maurin, Peter, 84, 87
May Bowle, 49
Mayer, Jordana, O.S.B., 108
Mayhew, Louis, 39
McCall, Aidan, O.S.B., 50
McCarthy, Eugene, 62, 141
McDonnell, Kilian, O.S.B., 14, 29, 36, 81
McHugh, Antonia, 76
McMahon, Victor, O.S.B., 102
McNally, John Vincent, 50–51
McNulty, Evangelista, O.S.B., 113
Mealey, Linda, 39
Meinberg, Cloud, O.S.B., 7, 93, 118, 126
Meinz, Pius, O.S.B., 48
Mental Health Institute for clergy, 24
Merton, Thomas, 20, 21, 137
Metten Abbey, 1
Mexico, Benedictines in, 67
Meyer, Ralph, 107
Michel, Virgil (George), O.S.B., 34, 49, 50, 63, 71, 73, 78, 83, 84, 85, 86 ; contribution to liturgical movement, 74–76; on capitalism, 86; as founder of Institute for Social Study, 86–87; and National Catholic Rural Life Conference, 87; and Catholic Worker Movement, 87
Michels, Aloysius, O.S.B., 67
Michelson, Val, 37, 124
Miller, Gregory, O.S.B., 59
Millett, Larry, 61

Ministry of Saint Benedict's and Saint John's, 115
Minneapolis/Saint Paul area, Benedictine parishes in, 62
Minnesota Public Radio, 13, 17, 36, 141
Mitra, Madhu, 56
Monastic culture, shifts in, 26–28
Monastic Experience Program, 15
Monastic foundations, involvement of Saint John's, 12, 13
Monastic identity, shaping, 21–22
Monastic Interreligious Dialogue, 115
Monastic observance, 19–20
Monastic spirituality, 25–26
Muckenthaler, Benno, O.S.B., 10
Muggli, Florian, O.S.B., 81
Muir, John, 129
Murphy, Jim, 39
Murphy, Joseph Denis, 119
Murray, John Courtney, 77

National Catholic Rural Life Conference, 84
National Catholic Youth Choir, 91
Naughton, Michael, O.S.B., 74
Nelson, Josh, 53
Nelson, Knute, 4, 11, 42
Nervi, Pier Luigi, 122
Neutra, Richard, 118–19
Niebauer, Paul-Vincent, O.S.B., 37, 90
Niess, Ansgar, O.S.B., 102
Norris, Kathleen, 26
North Central accreditation, 34
Northman, Bede, O.S.B., 62, 68
Northman, Wolfgang, O.S.B., 32, 46
Notch, Larry, 92

Oblates of Saint John's Abbey, 27
O'Connell, Joe, 52
O'Connell, Joe and Jodie, 84, 85
Office of the Hours, 22, 23
Ojibwe education at Saint John's, 42
Ojibwe reservations, 1, 63
O'Meara, Shaun, O.S.B., 115
O'Neill, Virgil, O.S.B., 43
Orate Fratres (Worship), 74, 75, 76, 78
Ortmann, Anselm, O.S.B., 59
O'Shaughnessy, Ignatius, 48
Ottenhoff, Don, 81

Parish ministry, early, 11–12
Paul, Cyril, 90
Payne, Herbert, 105
Pedrizetti, Raymond, O.S.B., 69
Peking Catholic University, 113
Peter, Francis, O.S.B., 25
Petheo, Bela, 23, 91
Pflueger, Herb, 105
Pflueger, Robert and Louise, 105
Phan, Simon-Hoa, 91
Phillips, Carl, 57
Pierzina, Robin, O.S.B., 89
Pinder, Patrick, 65
Plante, Julian, 43
Pond, Frances, 105
Power, Eugene B., 43
Powers, Betty, 84
Powers, Betty Wahl and J. F., 105
Powers, J. F., 61, 83, 84, 85
Powers, Katherine, 85
Pratschner, Rosamond, O.S.B., 114

Prayer, changes in community, 23–24
Preble, Charles and Jana, 111
Preparatory School, headmasters of, 142
Primitive conditions in early years, 45–47
Primus, George, O.S.B., 103
Priories founded by Saint John's, 12
Pueringer, John, 104
Puerto Rico, Benedictines in, 67

Quadrangle, story of the, 95
Quinn, Roger, 55

Rafferty, George, 97
Ramler, Agnes, 59, 109
Rat pack, 53
Raverty, Aaron, O.S.B., 23, 115
Record, The, birth of, 7, 47, 49
Red Lake reservation, 63, 112, 113
Reed, Alan, O.S.B., 96
Reforestation at Saint John's, 132
Reger, Walter, O.S.B., 34, 49, 50, 54, 81, 84
Reinhart, Dietrich, O.S.B., 41, 77, 104
Reitmeier, Placid, O.S.B., 67
Reliquary chapel of Saint Peregrin, 124
Retirement Center (Saint Raphael's Hall), 14
Rettenmaier, Paul, O.S.B., 62, 65
Rhoades, Joachim, O.S.B., 93
Richard, Paul, O.S.B., 15, 90, 91
Ricker, Berthold, O.S.B., 67
Riss, Bruno, O.S.B., 10, 16, 59, 60, 61
Roach, John, 15
Rodell, Charles, 30
Roettger, Gregory, O.S.B., 74
Roetzer, Alexius, O.S.B., 60
Roloff, Ronald, O.S.B., 74
Roske, Joe, 107
Roske, Michael, 92
Roske, Sr., Michael and Veronica family, 104
Ruff, Anthony, O.S.B., 91
Ruprecht, Rich, 108
Ryan, John A., 84, 85
Ryan, Kelly, O.S.B., 104

Sagatagan Lake, 5, 6, 47
Saint Anselm's Monastery, Tokyo, 113
Saint Anselm's Parish, Tokyo, 67
Saint Augustine's College, Nassau, Bahamas, 65
Saint Augustine's Monastery, Bahamas, 65, 113
Saint Benedict and Saint Scholastica woodcarvings, 27
Saint Benedict's Academy Industrial School, 42
Saint Benedict's Academy, 37
Saint Gregory's Abbey, Shawnee, Oklahoma, 66
Saint John's Alumni Association, creation of, 49
Saint John's Bible, The, 16, 98, 99
Saint John's Boys' Choir, 15, 91
Saint John's classes, 55–56
Saint John's foundations, 66
Saint John's Indian Industrial School, 42
Saint John's Preparatory school, 36–37
Saint John's Seminary, 33

Saint John's University, early developments of, 32–34
Saint Joseph Catholic Church, Saint Joseph, Minnesota, 58
Saint Mark's Priory, Kentucky, 68
Saint Martin's Abbey, Lacey, Washington, 66
Saint Maur's monastery, Kentucky, 67
Saint Peter's Abbey, Saskatchewan, 66
Saint Thomas, College of, 3
Saint Vincent Archabbey, 7
Santiago, José M. Rodriguez, O.S.B., 67
Sayles, Bartholomew, O.S.B., 90
Schirber, Martin, O.S.B., 8, 23, 34, 50, 54, 84, 85
Schlick, Frank, 46
Schmerbach, Joseph, O.S.B., 67
Schmitt, Adrian, O.S.B., 132
Schmitt, Martin, O.S.B., 62
Schneider, Hubert, O.S.B., 92, 93, 102
Schoenberg, David, 108
Schoffman, Francis, 8
School of Theology, 40
Schreiner, Chrysostom, O.S.B., 64, 65
Schreiner, Ted, 107
Schwietz, Paul, O.S.B., 135, 136
Schwinghammer, Aloysius, 49
Schmitt, Adrian, O.S.B., 88
Seasoltz, Kevin, O.S.B., 78
Seidenbusch, Rupert, O.S.B., 10, 60, 62, 63
Self-sufficiency, experiments in, 132–36
Senta, Louis, 55
Service, Benedict's teaching on, 27
Sexton, Bill, 98
Sexual abuse by Catholic clergy, 16, 28
Shanley, John, 31
Simon, Jane Pflueger, 105
Simon, Julian, O.S.B., 67
Sivertsen, Sarah-Maud and Bob, 17
Smith, Hamilton, 118, 120
Smith, Jim, 52, 54
Smoleroff, Darryl, 54
Social justice movements at Saint John's, 83–87
Soukup, Gervase, O.S.B., 15, 50, 81
Soukup, Gregory, O.S.B., 37, 50
Stahlberger, Andrew, 45
Staub, Clement, O.S.B., 61
Stearns County parishes staffed by Saint John's, 61
Stegmann, Basil, O.S.B., 67
Steil, Gregory, O.S.B., 95
Steiner, Luke, O.S.B., 40
Steinkogler, Wolfgang, O.S.B., 66
Stewart, Columba, O.S.B., 25, 27
Stottlemyer, Jean, 106
Stuckenschneider, Placid, O.S.B., 59, 74, 93
Sullivan, Patrick, O.S.B., 102
Swisshelm, Jane Grey, 1

Talafous, Don, O.S.B., 50, 111
Tarlton, Allen, O.S.B., 12
Tavis, Gordon, O.S.B., 17, 37, 90
Taylor, Mel, O.S.B., 65
Tegeder, Vincent, O.S.B., 31, 50, 141
Tegels, Aelred, O.S.B., 78
Tekippe, Owen, O.S.B., 66

Terfehr, Julius, O.S.B., 124, 134–35
Terhaar, Herman J., 31
Thamert, Mark, O.S.B., 37
Theimer, Axel, 90
Theisen, Jerome, O.S.B., 25, 68, 79, 135
Theisen, Sylvester, 52, 85
Thelen, Valerian, O.S.B., 62
Thell, Stephen, O.S.B., 124
Thell, Steven, O.S.B., 15
Thimmesh, Hilary, O.S.B., 39, 50, 59
Thole, Tom, O.S.B., 141
Thuente, Adelard, O.S.B., 50, 54, 55
Tollefson, Lee, 97, 98
Tornado of 1894, 131
Track, Gerhard, 90
Traditional hours of prayer, 20
Traufler, Louis, O.S.B., 48, 59
Trinity Benedictine Monastery, Fujimi, 67
Tucker, Dunstan, O.S.B., 50, 54
Tupa, Jerome, O.S.B., 18, 91, 94
Twomey, Mark, 74

United States Conference of Catholic Bishops, 97
Unterberger, Andrew, O.S.B., 92

VanCleve, Bill and Pat, 141
Vatican Council II, effects of on Saint John's, 13, 21–22
Vebelun, Edward, O.S.B., 67
Veteran enrollment, World War II, 52
Vietnam War, 5
Vogel, Dan, 106
Vogel, Elaine, 106

Wagner, Mary Anthony, O.S.B., 111, 113, 114
Wahl, Thomas, O.S.B., 40, 77, 105
Watrin, Joseph, O.S.B., 93
Weber, Arnold, O.S.B., 50, 62
Weber, Bernard and Louise family, 112
Wee, Morris, 81
Wegleitner, Fabian, O.S.B., 50
Weigel, Gustave, 77
Wenner, Waldemar, 17
Wenninger, Magnus, O.S.B., 25
White Earth reservation, 63, 112
Willebrands, Jan, 81
Wimmer, Boniface, O.S.B., 10, 19, 62, 89, 93, 98
Winkelman, Gilbert, O.S.B., 92, 111
Wittmann, Cornelius, O.S.B., 10, 27, 31, 46, 50, 56, 59, 91
Witzmann, Hugh, O.S.B., 28, 91
Wolf, George, O.S.B., 65
Woodworking, 92–93
Workers' Guild, 106–07
World War I, and anti-German sentiment, 4
World War II veterans, 34
Worship and Work, 12
Wurdak, Elizabeth, 30

Yaiser, Hildebrand, O.S.B., 67
Yuenger, David, O.S.B., 132
Yzermans, Vincent, 17

Zankl, Angelo, O.S.B., 8, 19, 50, 91
Zapp, Edward, 31
Zapp, John, 31
Zardetti, Otto, 64
Zilboorg, Gregory, 24
Zimmerman, Odo, O.S.B., 66
Zwack, Edward, O.S.B., 102

Production Credits

Editor: Hilary Thimmesh, O.S.B.
Photo editors: David Manahan, O.S.B., and Lee Hanley
Copy editor: John Schneider
Production manager: Colleen Stiller
Desktop publisher: Julie Surma
Proofreaders: Stephanie Lancour and Jan Brown
Index: Dolores Schuh, C.H.M.
Printer: Regent Publishing Services, Ltd.
Art direction and design: Ann Blattner

Illustrations and Photos

Arca Artium Collection, Saint John's University: pages 75 (bottom), 95 (bottom); Michael Bauer: page 53 (bottom); Greg Becker: pages iv, viii, x, 6, 36 (top left), 41, 44, 56 (bottom), 70, 140; John Biasi: page 54 (both); Michael Crouser: pages 19, 128, 129, 138; Doyle Family: page 86 (top); Durenberger Family: page 49; Joseph Federer, '04: page 72 (bottom); Joseph Feders, O.S.B.: page 29; Luke Fischer, '07: page 100; Daniel Goede, '80: page 22; John Howard Griffin, Saint John's Abbey Archives: page 77; Lee Hanley: pages i, vi, 7, 11 (bottom), 20, 25 (middle), 30, 35 (top), 37 (all), 51, 52, 56 (top), 58, 68, 69 (right top and bottom), 74 (bottom), 80 (both), 81 (bottom), 82, 90 (top), 91 (bottom), 95 (top), 97, 98 (all), 103 (top), 108 (top), 110, 118, 122 (bottom), 125 (bottom), 139 (bottom left), 143, endsheets; Hill Museum & Manuscript Library (HMML Bean MS 4, Book of Revelation): page 43 (bottom right); Fran Hoefgen, O.S.B.: page 137; Hynes Family: page 84; Liturgical Press Archives: pages 75 (both), 87; David Manahan, O.S.B.: pages 65 (bottom), 69 (left), 123 (right); Minnesota Historical Society: page 1; Minnesota Public Radio: page 17 (top and bottom); Kieran Nolan, O.S.B.: page 67 (both); Mackert, Cass: pages 146, 147; New Horizons Aerial and Architectural Photography: ii, iii; Bela Petheo, 23 (bottom left); Simon-Hoa Phan, O.S.B.: page 16; Powers Family: pages 85, 105 (top); Alan Reed, O.S.B., Saint John's Abbey Curator: pages 27 (both), 126, 127 (bottom); Saint Benedict's Monastery Archives: pages 113, 114 (both), 115; Saint John's Abbey Archives: pages 4 (bottom), 9, 10, 11 (top), 12, 13, 14, 15 (top), 21, 23 (top right), 32 (all), 33, 34, 35 (bottom), 36 (bottom right), 42, 43 (middle right), 45, 46, 47, 48 (both), 59, 60, 61, 62, 63 (both), 64, 65 (top), 66 (both), 71, 72 (top), 73, 74 (top), 76, 78, 81 (top), 86 (bottom), 88, 89, 90 (middle), 91 (top), 92 (both), 93 (top), 94 (both), 96, 101, 102 (bottom), 103 (bottom), 104, 107, 108 (bottom), 109, 111, 112 (top), 116, 117, 121 (bottom), 122 (top), 124 (all), 125 (top and middle), 130, 131 (both), 132, 133 (all), 134 (both), 150; Saint John's Abbey Vocation Office: pages 23 (middle and bottom right), 24, 25 (top and bottom); Saint John's Arboretum: pages 135 (bottom), 136, 139 (top and bottom right); Saint John's Bible Project: page 99 (all); Saint John's University Archives: pages 36 (bottom left), 38, 39 (all), 40, 43 (top left), 50, 79, 90 (bottom), 102 (top); Michael Sipe: page 57; Stearns County Historical Society: pages 2, 3, 5; Placid Stuckenschneider, O.S.B.: pages 93 (bottom), 135 (top); Syracuse University Library: pages 119, 120 (all), 121 (top); Hilary Thimmesh, O.S.B.: pages 15 (bottom), 55, 83, 106; Elaine Vogel: page 105 (bottom); Steven Voit: pages 18, 31, 53 (top); Arnold Weber, O.S.B., family photo: page 112 (bottom); Hugh Witzmann, O.S.B.: page 28; Angelo Zankl, O.S.B., Saint John's Abbey Archives: page 8.

12 11 10 09 08 07 06   1 2 3 4 5

Library of Congress Cataloging-in-Publication Data

Saint John's at 150 : a portrait of this place called Collegeville, 1856–2006 / edited by Hilary Thimmesh.

     p.   cm.
   Includes index.
   ISBN-13: 978-0-9740992-1-7 (hard cover : alk. paper)
   ISBN-10: 0-9740992-1-X (hard cover : alk. paper)
   1. St. John's Abbey (Collegeville, Minn.)—History. 2. St. John's University (Collegeville, Minn.)—History. 3. Benedictines—Minnesota—Collegeville—History. 4. Collegeville (Minn.)—Church history. 5. Collegeville (Minn.)—History. I. Thimmesh, Hilary.

BX2525.C65S25 2006
271'.1077647—dc22   2005030665